266.09

TONGUES OF FIRE

Books by Frances Parkinson Keyes

FICTION

I, THE KING

THE EXPLORER

MADAME CASTEL'S LODGER

THE RESTLESS LADY AND OTHER STORIES

STATION WAGON IN SPAIN

THE CHESS PLAYERS

VICTORINE

BLUE CAMELLIA

THE ROYAL BOX

STEAMBOAT GOTHIC

JOY STREET

DINNER AT ANTOINE'S

CAME A CAVALIER

THE RIVER ROAD

ALSO THE HILLS

CRESCENT CARNIVAL

ALL THAT GLITTERS

FIELDING'S FOLLY

THE GREAT TRADITION

PARTS UNKNOWN

HONOR BRIGHT

SENATOR MARLOWE'S DAUGHTER

THE SAFE BRIDGE

LADY BLANCHE FARM

QUEEN ANNE'S LACE

THE CAREER OF DAVID NOBLE

THE OLD GRAY HOMESTEAD

NONFICTION

ROSES IN DECEMBER

THE THIRD MYSTIC OF AVILA

FRANCES PARKINSON KEYES' CHRISTMAS
  GIFT

LAND OF STONES AND SAINTS

THREE WAYS OF LOVE

ST. ANNE: GRANDMOTHER OF OUR
  SAVIOUR

THE FRANCES PARKINSON KEYES
  COOKBOOK

THE COST OF A BEST SELLER

THERESE: SAINT OF A LITTLE WAY

ALL THIS IS LOUISIANA

THE GRACE OF GUADALUPE

BERNADETTE OF LOURDES

THE ROSE AND THE LILY

ALONG A LITTLE WAY

CAPITAL KALEIDOSCOPE

SILVER SEAS AND GOLDEN CITIES

LETTERS FROM A SENATOR'S WIFE

JUVENILE

MOTHER CABRINI, MISSIONARY TO THE WORLD

ONCE ON ESPLANADE

POETRY

THE HAPPY WANDERER

A TREASURY OF FAVORITE POEMS

FRANCES PARKINSON KEYES

Tongues of Fire

Coward-McCann, Inc.

New York

COPYRIGHT © 1966 BY FRANCES PARKINSON KEYES

Library of Congress Catalog Card Number: 66-20153

PRINTED IN THE UNITED STATES OF AMERICA

ACKNOWLEDGMENTS

The publisher wishes to thank those listed below for permission to include the following excerpts in our book:

Abingdon Press for *Men of the Outposts* by Herbert Welch, copyright © 1937 by Abingdon Press; The Bruce Publishing Company for *The Glory of Christ* by Mark L. Kent; Robert L. Crager & Company for *Fabulous New Orleans* by Lyle Saxon, copyright 1928, 1950 by Robert L. Crager; Doubleday & Company, Inc., for *The Steadfast Man* by Paul Gallico, copyright © 1958 by Paul Gallico, used by permission of Doubleday & Company, Inc.; Farrar, Straus & Giroux, Inc., for "St. Francis Xavier—Letter to the Society at Goa" from *A Treasury of Catholic Reading* by John Chapin; Harper & Row, Publishers, for *The Twentieth Century Outside Europe*, Volume V, *Christianity in a Revolutionary Age* by Kenneth Scott Latourette, copyright © 1962 by Kenneth Scott Latourette, for *St. Francis of Assisi* by Leo Sherley-Price, copyright © 1959 by A. R. Mowbray & Co., Ltd., and for *The White Nile* by Alan Moorehead, copyright © 1960 by Alan Moorehead, reprinted by permission of Harper & Row, Publishers; Hawthorn Books, Inc., for *The Saints, A Concise Biographical Dictionary* by John Coulson and for *The Fishers of Men* by Michele Saponaro; Alfred A. Knopf, Inc., for *Warriors of God* by Walter Nigg, edited and translated from the German by Mary Ilford; *Life* Magazine for its December 4, 1964, article on Dr. Paul Carlson, copyright © 1964 by Time Inc., reprinted by courtesy of *Life* Magazine; Methuen & Co., Ltd., for *Franciscan Italy* by Harold Goad; Thomas Nelson & Sons for *Ten Torchbearers* by Dorothy Heiderstadt, copyright © 1961 by Dorothy Heiderstadt; *Time* Magazine for "Prescription for Travel" (June 14, 1963), for "Albert Schweitzer—An Anachronism" (June 21, 1963), and for its cover story on Dr. Paul Carlson (December 4, 1964), copyright © 1963, 1964 by Time Inc., reprinted by courtesy of *Time* Magazine; St. Anthony's Guild for *Franciscans Came First* by Fanchón Royer, copyright © 1951 by St. Anthony's Guild, Paterson, N.J., and for *St. Francis Solanus, Apostle to America* by Fanchón Royer, copyright © 1955 by Fanchón Royer.

Introduction

MY earliest memory of churchgoing centers in that bulwark of Congregationalism, the New Old South—yes, that is what it was called seventy-five years ago and what it is still called in Boston. I have sometimes said, half in jest and half in earnest, it was then and there that I took my first steps toward Catholicism, guided by the Reverend George Gordon. This statement is largely based on the fact that his sermons lasted at least an hour and, as I wiggled restlessly around on the hard seat of the family pew while he went on and on, talking about things which I did not understand, I began to wonder if there were not some form of divine service which would be less of an endurance test and more of a joyous experience to a little girl.

Years afterward, I found that for me there was an affirmative answer to this. But I also became aware that I had absorbed more of Dr. Gordon's sermons than I realized when I was only five years old and, indeed, that one point he made, over and over again, *had* been comprehensible and convincing to me from the beginning: at the end of an eloquent discourse, with a gesture so forceful as to be almost menacing, he would thunder from the pulpit, "If you do not believe in foreign missions, your religion is a lie!" After this broadside, he would announce a missionary hymn and while it was being sung, the collection was taken up. It was always a substantial one. No proper Bostonian was willing to be branded as a liar.

I have thought of Dr. Gordon's challenge every time I have heard presumably devout Christians say, "Of course I believe in doing good in my own community, in my own country. But I do not believe in *foreign* missions. Other peoples have other ways of life and of obedience We should not try to interfere with these. They are much better off if they are left to work out their salvation by themselves." And I have never been able to understand how such presumably devout Christians reconciled their viewpoint with the last command of Our Lord and Saviour to His disciples before He was "gathered up into Heaven," when He "appeared unto the Eleven" that sat at meat and said, "Go ye into all the world and preach the gospel to every creature." [1]

They were, He further told them, to go to Jerusalem and wait for the coming of the Holy Ghost which would give them power to be witnesses to Him. They obeyed Him and they did not have long to wait. The story of what happened next has been wonderfully told many times but nowhere as glowingly as in the Acts of the Apostles.

"And when the day of Pentecost was fully come, they were all with one accord in one place.

"And suddenly there came a sound from heaven as of a rushing mighty wind, and it filled all the house where they were sitting.

"And there appeared unto them eleven tongues like as of fire, and it sat upon each of them.

"And they were all filled with the Holy Ghost, and began to speak with other tongues, as the Spirit gave them utterance." [2]

The tongues of fire became living flame. Immediately after this first Pentecost, which we sometimes also call the first Whitsunday and which is still commemorated on twenty Sundays of the calendar of the Catholic Church, "they went forth, and preached every where, the Lord working with them, and confirming the word with signs following." [3] According to St. Luke, there had also been a previous command given first to Peter and James and John and to seventy-two others who were sent "two by two before His face into every city and place whither He Himself was to come." [4] Their instructions were explicit.

"Go: Behold I send you as lambs among wolves.

"Carry neither purse, nor scrip, nor shoes; and salute no man by the way.

"Into whatsoever house you enter, first say: Peace be to this house.

"And if the son of peace be there, your peace shall rest upon him; but if not, it shall return to you.

"And in the same house, remain, eating and drinking such things as they have: for the laborer is worthy of his hire Remove not from house to house.

"And into what city soever you enter, and they receive you, eat such things as are set before you.

"And heal the sick that are therein, and say to them: The kingdom of God is come nigh unto you." [5]

Such was the beginning of the missionary movement which spread from what we now call the Holy Land to every part of the then known world in obedience to Christ's command, and which the disciples and followers of the Chosen Few have been faithfully spreading ever since, to a world which, by slow degrees, has grown larger and larger.

This book represents an endeavor to tell how it was done, as far as possible in the words of the men and women who have done it and which have been preserved in their letters and prayers. Where none of these have been available, contemporary writers have been quoted, if these were adequate and available, and if not, the best modern sources. The present editor has confined her personal contributions largely to brief explanations of her own impressions and convictions and to short biographical sketches in which she has made a special effort to emphasize the contributions to the missionary movement by certain saints who are better known for different activities and to correct false impressions about other holy persons.

She is deeply grateful for the generous cooperation of Paul Gallico, author of *The Steadfast Man*, and Gordon Langley Hall, author of *Golden Boats From Burma*, who have graciously permitted her to use condensations of these two remarkable books as part of her text. She is also deeply grateful to Alan Moorehead, author of *The White Nile*; Fanchón Royer, author of *St. Francis Solanus, Apostle to America* and *The Franciscans Came First*; Father Maynard J. Geiger, author of *The Life and Times of Junipero Serra*; Father Antonine Tibesar, editor of *The Writings of Junipero Serra*—both published by the Academy of American Franciscan History—for permission to quote at length from their books; and to Hawthorn Books, Inc. for permission to quote at length from any works they have published. On the other hand, she understands the basic reasons why some authors and publishers have felt they could not cooperate to this extent or, indeed, to any extent which would make inclusion of their works possible. The same problem arose with the author's *A Treasury of Favorite Poems* and though she deeply regrets certain omissions, she hopes the biographies of saints omitted for this reason will be read as originally presented.

Quite aside from this difficulty, the problem of selection as to both subject and treatment became more and more serious as we approached the present. There could be no question that the disciples and their first followers should occupy a primary place in a book of this type or that such outstanding saints as Patrick, Francis of Assisi, Anthony of Padua, Dominic, Ignatius, Francis Xavier—who has been called "the greatest missionary after St. Paul" [6]—and Francis Solano—the Wonder Worker of the New World—should next appear. Then the choice became more difficult. Junípero Serra was, of course, a must; but his fellow Majorcan, Ramón Lull, who is far less famous, was responsible for no small share of Serra's inspiration and education and Lull's field of endeavor among the Moslems forms a challenging contrast to his disciple's work in America. With these two considerations in mind, it seemed impossible to pass Lull by, even at the risk of being reminded that the number of Spaniards included in the volume is out of proportion to those of other nationalities. Of course, there is an answer to that also: during the great period of Spanish colonization, its clerics kept pace with its explorers; no other country furnished as many notable examples of both.

Many outstanding examples of missionary endeavor and success have been omitted because so much has been written about them already that it seems impossible to add anything further to such thorough documentation. Among these is the story of the missions to Hawaii initiated by Hiram Bingham and his twelve associates, the story of Wilfred Grenfell in Labrador and the story of Tom Dooley in Laos. On the other hand, a few besides have been included for the very reason that they had been overlooked or underestimated and this seemed a fitting occasion to bring them to public attention.

It may seem to the critical reader that the number of Catholic missionaries whose biographies are included is out of proportion to the number of Protestant missionaries. The answer to this—not as obvious as perhaps it might be—is that, of course, there could be no Protestant missionaries until after the Reformation, the great religious movement of the sixteenth century which had for its objective the reformation of the Western Catholic Church and which led to the establishment of the Protestant churches. It was not until this movement, in which Luther and Calvin were among the leaders, had become an "establishment" that Protestant missionaries began their great work. Officially, there are no saints in their rosters. Nevertheless, the names of many must be recorded in the golden books of the angels. And in this age, when the example and precepts of Pope John have given fresh impetus to the movement and glory in the name of ecumenism, a Catholic editor, who has long felt we needed to stress the bonds that unite us rather than the details that divide us, welcomes the opportunity of paying them her tribute. All Trinitarians subscribe to the same Creed and recite the prayer taught us by Jesus Christ. With these as the basis for harmony, it should not be too difficult for us to go forward together.

Illustrations follow page 164

CONTENTS

CONTENTS

Part I

OUT FROM THE HOLY LAND

1

The Earliest Christian Envoys

IT is usual to speak of St. Paul as "the first Christian missionary"; indeed, St. Luke, who was his earliest biographer and his companion in many of his journeys, refers to him as such and this designation is regarded as authentic by many official sources. Paul was, to be sure, the first to achieve fame as a missionary, but he did not become a Christian until he was vouchsafed Christian vision on the road to Damascus after the martyrdom of Stephen, when he held the coats of those who did the stoning; and this was probably in 34 or 35 A.D. Immediately after his baptism, he retired for two years in the desert, for prayer and meditation, before returning to Damascus, going to Jerusalem to confer with the Apostles and—still later—going back to Tarsus, his birthplace. It was not until the early forties that St. Barnabas, commissioned by the Apostles to develop a program of systematic preaching to non-Jews, bethought him of St. Paul, living forgotten at Tarsus, and he went there to seek him out. Paul returned with him to Antioch and from that time onward, devoted himself wholly to missionary work and propaganda.

Long before this, many of Christ's followers were already active in the missionary field. We are told that only four of the first twelve Apostles remained in Jerusalem: Peter; James, the son of Zebedee and John his brother; and James, the son of Cleophas Alphaeus, known as James the Less. "The others took up the pack and mantle of the pilgrim; they placed the few relics of the Gospel in their pack and went on their way. Perhaps young Lazarus went too, and also perhaps his sisters, Mary and Martha, along with other nameless ones." [1]

The research which I myself did when writing *St. Anne: Grandmother of Our Saviour* leads me to believe that Lazarus, Mary and Martha did indeed set out as missionaries soon after the coming of the Holy Ghost—that is to say, after that first wonderful Pentecost. They had the private means which would permit them to undertake an extended journey without being a burden to anyone, and it is unthinkable that there could have been any other purpose to which they would so eagerly have put their wealth. Moreover, they may well have had humanly selfish reasons for being glad to leave Palestine: Lazarus was the object of especial suspicion and hostility on the part of the Sanhedrin, who had no belief in immortality, and to whom the very thought of a miracle whereby a dead man had been resurrected was anathema. They were almost equally skeptical and scathing on the subject of Mary Magdalene's repentance; certainly they could have made life very unpleasant, if not actually dangerous, for this brother and sister. The second sister, Martha, would have been more troubled than ever over many things if she had thought the others were in peril. It was natural that Maximin, a cousin of this trio, should be glad to accompany them; it is a little less clear why Mary Jacobe and Mary Salome should have been selected to form a part of this particular company, as evidently they had; but it is probably because, as cousins of Jesus, they had become acquainted with His personal friends and fond of them. Their inclusion in the group of missionaries certainly had a very marked effect upon its character, for, besides being the cousins of Jesus, they were nieces[2] of Anne; in leaving their native land, they evidently felt that they could not bear to be eternally separated from all tangible contact with their blood relations, especially since this contact was also their closest link with their acknowledged Saviour. Jesus' mother, who kept so many things in her heart, must have understood this; certainly it was with her willing consent that, when Mary Jacobe and Mary Salome left Nazareth for good, they took with them a coffer, fashioned from cedar wood, containing the relics they so ardently desired to possess and to transport to their new home.

"Evidently the boat on which these missionaries traveled carried many others as well, and stopped at numerous ports along the way, to permit disembarkation of passengers for several other points, before it finally reached Massilia, which we know as Marseilles. Then, as now, it was a great commercial city, superbly located; its harbor and its surrounding country-side must have looked very beautiful to the weary pilgrims; and evidently the group in which we are especially interested was warmly welcomed by those Jews who themselves had made a Pentecostal pilgrimage to Jerusalem, who had there been converted to Christianity, and who already knew the voluntary exiles, either personally or by reputation; indeed, we may assume that they had been partially responsible for the destination of the others. The mechanics of the new apostolate were promptly put into operation: Lazarus became the first Bishop of Marseilles; Mary Magdalene, who later withdrew into strict seclusion at Sainte Baume, remained with her brother long enough to help him in the organization of his mission, thus following the custom, general among early converts, whereby men and women who were blood relations complemented each other's work. Maximin pushed further inland to the little city of Apt, which nestles among the mountains, and Martha, in accordance with the same custom, accompanied him. The two Marys transshipped to a smaller vessel, and took up their abode in a wild, marshy region, where their work would be largely among humble fisherfolk. It was the way of life which they deliberately chose, well aware of the primitive conditions under which they must labor and the hardships they must endure. But they did not feel it could provide a suitable shrine for their precious relic. They, therefore, entrusted this to the safe-keeping of Lazarus, hoping only to visit it from time to time, as needed intervals of rest permitted.

"The apostolate of Lazarus was long and fruitful; when he died, the mission he had founded was prosperous and seemed secure. But eventually Massilia, like Jerusalem before it, became the scene of repeated invasion and siege. In time, a successor to Lazarus decided that the relic of St. Anne was no longer safe in his keeping; he took counsel with other churchmen, and it was decided that the Bishopric of Apt, founded by Maximin, should have the honor of protecting it." [3]

Part of this admittedly is legend, but it is still legend interwoven with history and, as Michele Saponaro reminds us in his inspired work, *The Fishers of Men*, we do not have to depend on legend for the record of most of the missionary apostles. "Andrew, Peter's younger brother, took the road north. He crossed Samaria, Galilee, Syria, and Cappadocia, and reached the shore of the Black Sea. He travelled around it and penetrated into Scythia. These were unexplored barbarian lands, known as 'lands of the countries of cannibals.' Then he went down into the civilized countries of Macedonia and the Peloponnesian peninsula.

"The fisherman of Bethsaida was a man as calm and grave as his older brother was restless and impetuous. He had never called attention to himself in the group around Jesus because he never felt it necessary; the strength of his common sense called attention to him anyway. At difficult moments, the comrades asked his advice, as when they had been faced with the problem of appeasing the hunger of a multitude of followers and had only a few loaves of bread and a few fishes in their packs.

"He had been the first to discover Jesus at the ford of Betharabah and he may have been the first to die for Him. How many young men were to follow him: what travail did he suffer? At Patras it was said that he was seen nailed to a cross. Aegeas, the governor of the city, had condemned him to death, and the prayers of the people, led by the governor's own brother, were not enough to liberate him. The cross to which he was nailed was said to be X-shaped, and was called Saint Andrew's cross thereafter in his memory. A merciful Samaritan woman asked for the remains of the Apostle, and she buried him.

"Philip, the third fisherman from Bethsaida, shy, timid, solitary Philip, also crossed Asia Minor and the Black Sea. After the Master's death, he displayed an unsuspected combative

spirit, and he dedicated his ingenuity above all else to smooth-
ing the way for those who were to follow, battling against the
bestial pagan cults which were obstacles in the path of the
advance of the new faith. He demolished old structures so that
others could rebuild on their ruins. He preached against the
cult of Mars in Scythia, and against the snake cult in Hier-
apolis. . . .

"The man who had asked the Master to let him see God
went in search of God himself in the godless lands, where God
always is. No one was found who said he had seen his death.
Perhaps he died in bed in a natural way. Perhaps he, too, was
crucified at an advanced age in Emperor Domitian's time. In
his pilgrimages, he was often accompanied by his sister, Marian.

"John's older brother, James, the great apostle, strong, proud,
and audacious, the 'Son of Thunder,' who one day wanted
to set fire to an unfriendly village, stayed in Jerusalem with his
brother, Peter, and James the Less. Golden-winged legend took
him one day and flew him across the Mediterranean as far as
the columns of Hercules. He sowed the seed in Spain, and in
Galicia there germinated a special cult in his name from that
seed. But history then reclaims James for its own, leads him
back to Jerusalem, where he was beheaded about the year 42
A.D." [4]

The "golden-winged legend" which Saponaro thus dismisses
in a couple of sentences is treated at great length by many
authors, among them Anna Jameson in Sacred and Legendary
Art; and her version of the saint's story corresponds closely
with that which I have heard in Spain. There is no question
whatsoever that devout Spanish Catholics, supported by their
clergy, believe that St. James the Great actually came to Spain;
if they did not, he would never have become Spain's patron
saint, which he is. What is more, aside from the belief in Spain,
vast numbers of pilgrims would not have been visiting his
shrine from the earliest Christian era to the present day. So let
us accept the golden-winged legend, even if we must do so with
reservations, and go back to the place where Michele Saponaro
continues his apostolic narrative with Nathanael Bartholomew,
Thomas, Matthew, Jude and Simon.

"Nathanael Bartholomew was the handsome, prosperous, young man among the group of hard-working laborers—Bartholomew, the son of the plow; Nathanael, the gift of God. The son of the plough had inherited goods and land from his father; the gift of God dispensed to his companions the gay and pleasing nature bestowed on him by God. Jesus, seeing him beneath the fig tree from afar, had recognized him as an Israelite without guile, and the young enthusiast became a guileless Nazarene, open-hearted and incisive in the fervor of his preaching.

"He traveled the world over. Like Andrew and Philip, he too started out on the roads to the north, which must have been the traditional roads. Then he turned toward the Orient, went back south, and reached the Red Sea at Aden. He penetrated into the land of the Parthians, into Armenia, and into India. The legend which saw the young man grow old dictated as follows for history: 'In greater Armenia, Bartholomew led King Polimius and his wife and all the population of the twelve cities into the faith of Christ; but so many and such illustrious conversions aroused the envy of the priests of other religions, and they incited the King's brother, Astiage, against Polimius. Astiage ordered Bartholomew captured and flayed alive, then beheaded after removing his skin.' Legend ventures into the horrible and the macabre; it is tinged with the bloodiest of colors. But history is not less so.

"When Thomas, the doubter for love, found the certainty he was seeking, he went forward without ever looking back. A naturally melancholy soul, he made his melancholy a most subtle and penetrating method of communication.

"Who was Thomas, what was his life before he was received into the company of the Apostles? The doubter for love wanders in a half-light of poetic twilight. Some say that he was a man of art and craftsmanship, an architect who built stately synagogues and houses. Others say that he was a poor lad, who was perhaps an orphan, and that this was the cause of his melancholy, which made him a fervent and persuasive evangelist. 'Lord, we know not whither Thou goeth?' he had once said to the Master: now he knew that the Master traveled all roads, and on every road Thomaṣ followed Him, invisible and omnipresent as our own conscience. One has to have once doubted to achieve such perfect certainty.

"Thomas crossed all the lands of the Levant. He preached in the lands of the Medes and Persians, of the Ircanians and the Bactrians. He may have reached Tibet and breached her mountains. Perhaps he even saw the shores of the boundless Pacific.[5]

"The tax collector, Matthew, may have stayed with the four major apostles longer than the others. He had left the customs-house at Capharnaum on the first day he felt the call to follow Jesus, but he kept money in reserve and, if he was not the treasurer (an office assigned at the time to others), he may have been the financier of the community for some time.

"He spent the first years in the environs of Jerusalem; he retraced the itinerary of the Good News in reverse, from Calvary to Gennesaret. He wanted to revisit the scenes of his happiest days. He went in search of those who had known Jesus before him. He climbed the mountain of Capharnaum to ask the echoes of the night to bring back that divine voice he had heard there. 'Blessed are they that have suffered persecution for the sake of justice . . . Blessed are the poor in spirit . . . Blessed are the merciful . . . Blessed are the peacemakers . . . But woe unto the rich . . . Woe to you, ye that laugh now. . . .'

"He had recorded those wondrous words, now he went back over his notes and rearranged them in accordance with his own memories and those of the others. In the still evident traces of the steps of Jesus, he found the pronouncements and images of Him divine. Being a wealthy man, he had been struck above all by the exhortations to poverty by Jesus. These words had shaped his life and he put them into the account he had been writing for others. It was the duty of the disciples to live in poverty as the Master had taught them: 'Ask and it shall be given unto you,' 'Carry neither gold nor silver nor copper money in your belt,' 'Lay not up for yourselves the treasures on earth, where moth and rust consume. . . .' Freely they must give, as they freely received.

"Then Matthew, too, left the land of Israel. He journeyed into Arabia and Persia. He was said to have been devoured by man-eaters. Or beheaded. Or burned alive. He crossed the desert and the Red Sea, and sojourned in Ethiopia beyond the boundaries of the lions. There is a legend which makes him perform the miracle of resuscitating the maiden daughter of the king of Ethiopia, with the result that the king, the royal family, and the entire populace were converted to the new faith. But when the apostle opposed the brother of the converted king in his plan to wed Iphigenia, the resurrected virgin who was dedicated to God, the brother, Atarco, had the apostle spitted on a sword while he knelt at prayer. Legend then takes the Gospel from the hands of the dead Matthew and transfers it to Nathanael, who bore it to the faraway lands of India.

"Jude, or Judas Thaddeus, and Simon the Zealot were also cousins of Jesus and perhaps were also the brothers of James the Less. As pale shadows, they hover in the dim unknown.

"Was Jude the young husband of the wedding at Cana? Did Jesus perform his first and happiest miracle, that of changing the springs of water into wine, to enliven the wedding banquet? Jude was a courageous man, but the outlines of his deeds are obscured by a gray twilight. A farmer in the company of fishermen and artisans, the things that stayed in his stubborn peasant brain were the invective and admonitions of his great Cousin, and he shouted them from the rooftops in his harsh voice. He, too, journeyed over all the roads the brethren traveled, in Samaria, Idumea, Syria, Mesopotamia, and Persia, but the winds of the desert cover his footsteps with sand. He met his brother Simon in Persia; together they joined in battles against the sorcerers Zaroes and Arfatax, and together they were martyred in Beirut.

"But legends are like winds that never rest, changing direction at every moment. Another light wind rises to take Jude from that martyrdom and bring him back to Jerusalem where he is granted a long life. But there is no wind which isolates Jesus' younger cousin and shapes him into an attractive and expressive figure. Simon the unknown, was still almost a child among the twelve. The intransigence of his youth made him a zealot, and his preaching regarding the Kingdom of Heaven was said to be the most earthly and expedient of all.

"His immovable character gave him the right to succeed his older brother James as head of the church in Jerusalem, and he is borne to that high office by the wind which takes him away from the martyrdom of Beirut. According to legend, he will die a centegenarian in the early part of the second century, in the reign of Trajan. He will die on the cross, like his Master, says one legend; while another one, more gloomy, predicts that he will be quartered.

"And the winds scatter the pollen over the expectant earth as the lethargy of winter awaits the blessing of spring. All the weeds of superstition and idolatry are heaped upon the earth; and the rising waters of love sweep away the cesspools of corruption and vice. No one knows the source of these winds, because the sky over the Roman Empire is heavy with clouds and mist, and is shot with blinding bolts of lightning. The horizons are closed but one can note a nearly invisible movement in the air. No one sees or touches the invisible pollen, but a new warmth, a new tremor, a secret and unrestrainable need to open up and receive these words of pollen can be felt. The community of men feels an indistinct anxiety in the deepest viscera for fertilization: a new life stirs in its very lap." [6]

2

The First Letter-Writing Missionaries

The earliest Christian envoys left no writings, at least none which have been widely distributed or accepted as authentic; probably that is why the extent of their travels and their valiant and often highly effective missionary work has been so largely overlooked or forgotten. But though Peter and James the Less (so-called to distinguish him from James the Great, patron saint of Spain) did not leave Jerusalem with the same dispatch as their respective brothers, Andrew and Simon, they both did notable missionary work and wrote, briefly but with great eloquence and spirituality, to their charges, either before St. Paul did so or about the same time.

We think of Peter primarily—and correctly—as the first pope, the one to whom Our Lord entrusted the keys to the kingdom of heaven; we are apt to overlook the fact that he fulfilled this trust in more ways than one. "After the Ascension Peter's leadership of the Twelve seems to have been unquestioned.[1] It is he who, before Pentecost, tells the assembled brethren that the place left vacant by Judas's fall should be filled. He is the spokesman to the crowd gathered at Pentecost. He 'visits the saints (i.e., the Christians) everywhere' and takes the crucial step of admitting the Gentile Cornelius to baptism. When Herod found the Jews pleased by the execution of James, the brother of John, 'he went further and laid hands on Peter also.' The author of the Acts relates Peter's escape from prison, and promptly tells the story of Herod's fatal illness. At the Council of Jerusalem Peter takes Paul's side in the discussion on circumcision, as also does James, who by now appears to be the head of the local church of Jerusalem and therefore the leader of Jewish Christianity. In the Acts no further mention is made of Peter. But we know from Galatians that Peter visited Antioch (possibly before the Council of Jerusalem), and from I Peter we may infer that he visited many churches in Asia Minor. It is just possible that when Paul (Romans 15:22) explains his own delay in visiting Rome by his reluctance to 'build on the foundation another man had laid' he is thinking of Peter, who may have visited Corinth (cf. I Corinthians 1:12) *en route* for Rome."[2]

None of this is legend. It all has the ring of authenticity. We also know that Peter, or, as he was then called, Simon the Fisherman, was one of the very earliest disciples and was one of the first to believe in the divinity of Christ and to acknowledge it. His apostolate is beatified by innumerable miracles, fulfilling the prophecy of our Lord that His chosen followers would inherit those supernatural gifts of His: "Verily, verily, I say unto you, He that believeth on me, the works that I do shall he do also; and greater works than these shall he do; because I go unto my Father." [3] Peter's writings are permeated with the rare beauty which might logically be expected of a man imbued with great faith which revealed itself in great deeds.[4] Therefore, I have chosen, I believe advisedly, to use an extract from his first epistle as an introduction to those that have come down to us from the earliest Christian envoys.

"Peter, an apostle of Jesus Christ, to the sojourners of the Dispersion in Pontus, Galatia, Cappadocia, Asia and Bithynia, chosen

"unto the sanctification of the Spirit according to the foreknowledge of God the Father, unto obedience to Jesus Christ and the sprinkling of his blood: grace and peace be given you in abundance.

"Blessed be the God and Father of our Lord Jesus Christ, who according to his great mercy has begotten us again, through the resurrection of Jesus Christ from the dead, unto a living hope,

"unto an incorruptible inheritance—undefiled and unfading, reserved for you in heaven.

"By the power of God you are guarded through faith for salvation, which is ready to be revealed in the last time.

"Over this you rejoice; though now for a little while, if need be, you are made sorrowful by various trials,

"that the temper of your faith—more precious by far than gold which is tried by fire—may be found unto praise and glory and honor at the revelation of Jesus Christ.

"Him, though you have not seen, you love. In him, though you do not see him, yet believing, you exult with a joy unspeakable and triumphant;

"receiving, as the final issue of your faith, the salvation of your souls." [5]

Apparently James the Less did little or no actual traveling; but, if we accept him as the author of the epistle bearing his name, he is unmistakably stamped as a missionary through the scope and character of the written word; and, despite the skepticism of some authorities, I have no hesitancy in so accepting him.[6]

Even if there were grounds for doubting that the Epistle of James was actually written by the Lord's brother, these do not seem to me to outweigh two other important considerations: first, that its authenticity is unquestioned by at least two recognized authorities, even if they do not agree as to dates, and second, that it is sheer poetry and, as literature, should be given a place in missionary annals. With these considerations in mind, I have chosen to use extracts from it in the same chapter as extracts from the Epistle of Peter as an introduction to the writings of the earliest Christian envoys.

"James, a servant of God and of the Lord Jesus Christ, to the twelve tribes which are scattered abroad, greeting.

"My brethren, count it all joy when ye fall into divers temptations;

"Knowing *this,* that the trying of your faith worketh patience.

"But let patience have *her* perfect work, that ye may be perfect and entire, wanting nothing.

"If any of you lack wisdom, let him ask of God, that giveth to all *men* liberally, and upbraideth not; and it shall be given him.

"But let him ask in faith, nothing wavering. For he that wavereth is like a wave of the sea driven with the wind and tossed.

"For let not that man think that he shall receive any thing of the Lord.

"A double minded man *is* unstable in all his ways.

"Let the brother of low degree rejoice in that he is exalted:

"But the rich, in that he is made low: because as the flower of the grass he shall pass away.

"For the sun is no sooner risen with a burning heat, but it withereth the grass, and the flower thereof falleth, and the grace of the fashion of it perisheth; so also shall the rich man fade away in his ways.

"Blessed *is* the man that endureth temptation: for when

he is tried, he shall receive the crown of life, which the Lord hath promised to them that love him. . . .

"Every good gift and every perfect gift is from above, and cometh down from the Father of lights, with whom is no variableness, neither shadow of turning.

"Of his own will begat he us with the word of truth, that we should be of a kind of firstfruits of his creatures.

"Wherefore, my beloved brethren, let every man be swift to hear, slow to speak, slow to wrath:

"For the wrath of man worketh not the righteousness of God.

"Wherefore lay apart all filthiness and superfluity of naughtiness, and receive with meekness the engrafted word, which is able to save your souls.

"But be ye doers of the word, and not hearers only, deceiving your own selves.

"For if any be a hearer of the word, and not a doer, he is like unto a man beholding his natural face in a glass:

"For he beholdeth himself, and goeth his way, and straightway forgetteth what manner of man he was.

"But whoso looketh into the perfect law of liberty, and continueth *therein*, he being not a forgetful hearer, but a doer of the work, this man shall be blessed in his deed.

"If any man among you seem to be religious, and bridleth not his tongue, but deceiveth his own heart, this man's religion *is* vain.

"Pure religion and undefiled before God and the Father is this, To visit the fatherless and widows in their affliction, *and* to keep himself unspotted from the world." [7]

3

St. Paul, the First Famous Missionary

Together, the two epistles of Peter contain only eight chapters; the one epistle of James contains only five. Paul, on the other hand, wrote fourteen epistles containing a total of one hundred chapters, which, in volume, occupy more space in the New Testament than the work of any other one person. No wonder that Paul Horgan, in his excellent work, *Rome Eternal*, asks: "What letters ever written have had such power in the world?" And no wonder that Paul overshadowed all his fellow workers in early missionary history!

St. Luke, Paul's first biographer, left us, in the Acts of the Apostles, an inimitable record of the journeys that the two took together. But these journeys did not begin until Paul was over forty and his life, before that, was by no means uneventful. This part of it, as well as his background, was to have an important bearing on his writings.

"Paul, or Saul, was born of Jewish parents of the tribe of Benjamin about the same time that Christ was born. He was a native of Tarsus, the chief city of the Roman province of Cilicia in Asia Minor and a center of Greek culture and learning. Saul was brought up a Pharisee. The Pharisees were the leading and most strict of Jewish sects. He was educated in Jerusalem in the school of Gamaliel, the most renowned of Jewish scholars at that time. Saul's vernacular language was Greek, but he learned Hebrew in Jerusalem. Either at his home or in Jerusalem, he was taught tent-making, as it was customary for every Jewish youth to learn a trade. Saul became a bigoted persecutor of the early Christians, persecuting many of them even unto death." [1]

As we have already noted, he held the coats of those who did the stoning at the martyrdom of Stephen, and after that he brought about the imprisonment of many Christians in and around Jerusalem. In fact, with authority from the chief priests, he was on his way to continue such anti-Christian activities in Damascus when he was suddenly overwhelmed and blinded by a great light from heaven and confronted with the question, "Saul, Saul, why persecutest thou Me?" His conversion was followed by several years of retirement for meditation, prayer and unconscious preparation for his lifework. Therefore, he was ready when Barnabas sought him out and put him to work.

"There is no need to follow in his unresting footsteps as, in journey after journey, he evangelized Cyprus, Asia Minor, Macedonia and Greece. Wherever he went there was a storm— of enthusiasm on one side and of execration on the other. He was imprisoned, stoned, beaten, shipwrecked, attacked by illness and even by fits of despondency; but on he went. And wherever he went he talked—in synagogues, quoting Scripture, or in public places, quoting classical poets—and wherever he talked there sprang up a little center of Christianity. It was like an acolyte going swiftly to and fro lighting candles. And in a dozen years or less (45-57 A.D.) he had changed what had been (humanly speaking) little more than a Jewish sect into the embryo of a world-religion.

"Then, in 57, he returned to Jerusalem. His friends implored him not to. They knew how bitterly he was hated by the Sanhedrin and how little the church could do to protect him. But he pressed on, undaunted, and for a week or so all seemed well. Then came the inevitable riot, and only the intervention of the Roman garrison saved Paul from being lynched. Two years of imprisonment followed (quite unjust, but the Roman governor was hoping for a bribe) during which St. Paul took, or made, every possible opportunity to preach his doctrines to any and every audience—greatly alarming the governor, Antonius Felix, with the prospects of a future life for the unjust and incontinent, and 'almost persuading' Herod Agrippa 'to turn Christian.'

"On Felix's supersession by Festus, however, Paul's appeal

to the Emperor was attended to and he was sent with Julius, a centurion of the Augustan cohort, to Rome. Everyone knows how the ship was caught in a storm and wrecked on the coast of Malta, but the way in which St. Paul took charge of things in the emergency shows his inborn qualities of leadership. It was not until the spring of the next year (60 or 61) that the party at length reached the capital, where St. Peter was already established, and thereafter St. Paul once again fades into the shadows. About his further travels, probably to Spain and certainly back to the Near East, we have scant information. Even the date and manner of his martyrdom are uncertain. Tradition, supported by some internal evidence, speaks of a second and more rigorous imprisonment under Nero (the first emperor to make Christianity a crime) and tells us he was beheaded at Tre Fontane about 66 A.D. But the New Testament itself is silent.

"Yet the historical instinct of his companion St. Luke, who ends the story with their arrival at Rome, was sound. St. Paul had been injected, like a vaccine, into the bloodstream of the civilized world at Damascus. He had traveled along its veins and arteries, bearing the healing medicine of Christ to one organ and ganglion after another. But at Rome he had reached its heart. Thenceforward the quickening grace could be left, pumped along the arteries of commerce and administration, to find its own way to the empire's remotest corners and beyond.

"What exactly, though, was the serum that he carried? The church of Rome was already founded, as St. Paul's own epistle to it proves. The chief of the Apostles was established there. The sacraments were being administered, the gospel preached —perhaps already put into writing by St. Mark. What was St. Paul's particular contribution?

"First, his fiery zeal and the example which it set. To see and hear St. Paul in action made others feel that they themselves were woefully timid and tepid. But mainly he brought intellectual stiffening to the church—oaken ribs of closely reasoned thought to strengthen the Fisherman's barque against the storms ahead. For he was a man who detested all vagueness and who worried out every logical consequence and implication. To speak of 'Pauline doctrines' is not strictly accurate. St. Paul did not originate doctrines. But he unraveled them— wrung them out, as it were, from the gospel which he had received. Thus, from the bare statement that 'Jesus is the Christ' he squeezed out a completely new interpretation of the Old Testament, with the church as a new Israel, Grace taking the place of the Mosaic Law, and with Christ as a new Adam, the perfect 'Image' of God (a doctrine closely akin to St. John's 'Logos-doctrine,' but using a visual instead of an aural metaphor). From the words 'Saul, Saul, why persecutest thou me?' he developed the doctrine of the Mystical Body: 'There is nothing but Christ in any of us' (Colossians 3:11), and from the parable of the laborers in the vineyard, or of the king whose invited guests were replaced by chance-met strangers from the highways and hedges, he deduced the end of the old Israel and the old Jerusalem to be replaced by a new Jerusalem, where there is 'no more gentile and Jew, barbarian or Scythian, slave or free.'

"And perhaps it was this last doctrine, this bold and uncompromising acceptance of the church's *Catholicity*, which was the most typically Pauline contribution of him who called himself the Apostle to the Gentiles. St. Peter had been timid on this issue, but St. Paul would have no compromise, and it was he more than any other man who showed how and why the church must be Catholic, universal, and what that Catholicity implies." [2]

In making my selections for quotations, I have chosen my own favorite passages which have meant a great deal to me during the course of my entire life. I hope they will mean as much to my readers. I will begin with the first thirteen verses of the thirteenth chapter of I Corinthians.

"Though I speak with the tongues of men and of angels, and have not charity, I am become *as* sounding brass, or a tinkling cymbal.

"And though I have *the gift of* prophecy, and understand all mysteries, and all knowledge; and though I have all faith, so that I could remove mountains, and have not charity, I am nothing.

"And though I bestow all my goods to feed *the poor,* and though I give my body to be burned, and have not charity, it profiteth me nothing.

"Charity suffereth long, *and* is kind; charity envieth not; charity vaunteth not itself, is not puffed up,

"Doth not behave itself unseemly; seeketh not her own, is not easily provoked, thinketh no evil;

"Rejoiceth not in iniquity, but rejoiceth in the truth;

"Beareth all things, believeth all things, hopeth all things, endureth all things.

"Charity never faileth: but whether *there be* prophecies, they shall fail; whether *there be* tongues, they shall cease; whether *there be* knowledge, it shall vanish away.

"For we know in part, and we prophesy in part.

"But when that which is perfect is come, then that which is in part shall be done away.

"When I was a child, I spake as a child, I understood as a child, I thought as a child: but when I became a man, I put away childish things.

"For now we see through a glass, darkly; but then face to face: now I know in part; but then shall I know even as also I am known.

"And now abideth faith, hope, charity, these three; but the greatest of these *is* charity."

Another favorite is found in the sixth chapter of the Epistle to the Ephesians, tenth through the eighteenth verses.

"Finally, my brethren, be strong in the Lord, and in the power of his might.

"Put on the whole armour of God, that ye may be able to stand against the wiles of the devil.

"For we wrestle not against flesh and blood, but against principalities, against powers, against the rulers of the darkness of this world, against spiritual wickedness in high *places.*

"Wherefore take unto you the whole armour of God, that ye may be able to withstand in the evil day, and having done all, to stand.

"Stand therefore, having your loins girt about with truth, and having on the breastplate of righteousness;

"And your feet shod with the preparation of the gospel of peace;

"Above all, taking the shield of faith, wherewith ye shall be able to quench all the fiery darts of the wicked.

"And take the helmet of salvation, and the sword of the Spirit, which is the word of God:

"Praying always with all prayer and supplication in the Spirit, and watching thereunto with all perseverance and supplication for all saints."

And next, for my great favorite, verses one through forty, eleventh chapter, of the Epistle to the Hebrews.

"Now faith is the substance of things hoped for, the evidence of things not seen.

"For by it the elders obtained a good report.

"Through faith we understand that the worlds were framed by the word of God, so that things which are seen were not made of things which do appear.

"By faith Abel offered unto God a more excellent sacrifice than Cain, by which he obtained witness that he was righteous, God testifying of his gifts: and by it he being dead yet speaketh.

"By faith Enoch was translated that he should not see death; and was not found, because God had translated him: for before his translation he had this testimony, that he pleased God.

"But without faith *it is* impossible to please *him:* for he that cometh to God must believe that he is, and *that* he is a rewarder of them that diligently seek him.

"By faith Noah, being warned of God of things not seen as yet, moved with fear, prepared an ark to the saving of his house; by the which he condemned the world, and became heir of the righteousness which is by faith.

"By faith Abraham, when he was called to go out into a place which he should after receive for an inheritance, obeyed; and he went out, not knowing whither he went.

"By faith he sojourned in the land of promise, as *in* a strange country, dwelling in tabernacles with Isaac and Jacob, the heirs with him of the same promise:

"For he looked for a city which hath foundations, whose builder and maker *is* God.

"Through faith also Sara herself received strength to conceive seed, and was delivered of a child when she was past age, because she judged him faithful who had promised.

"Therefore sprang there even of one, and him as good as dead, *so many* as the stars of the sky in multitude, and as the sand which is by the sea shore innumerable.

"These all died in faith, not having received the promises, but having seen them afar off, and were persuaded of *them,* and embraced *them,* and confessed that they were strangers and pilgrims on the earth.

"For they that say such things declare plainly that they seek a country.

"And truly, if they had been mindful of that *country* from whence they came out, they might have had opportunity to have returned.

"But now they desire a better *country,* that is, an heavenly: wherefore God is not ashamed to be called their God: for he hath prepared for them a city.

"By faith Abraham, when he was tried, offered up Isaac; and he that had received the promises offered up his only begotten *son,*

"Of whom it was said, That in Isaac shall thy seed be called:

"Accounting that God *was* able to raise *him* up, even from the dead; from whence also he received him in a figure.

"By faith Isaac blessed Jacob and Esau concerning things to come.

"By faith Jacob, when he was a dying, blessed both the sons of Joseph; and worshipped, *leaning* upon the top of his staff.

"By faith Joseph, when he died, made mention of the departing of the children of Israel; and gave commandment concerning his bones.

"By faith Moses, when he was born, was hid three months of his parents, because they saw *he was* a proper child; and they were not afraid of the king's commandment.

"By faith Moses, when he was come to years, refused to be called the son of Pharaoh's daughter;

"Choosing rather to suffer affliction with the people of God, than to enjoy the pleasures of sin for a season;

"Esteeming the reproach of Christ greater riches than the treasures in Egypt: for he had respect unto the recompence of the reward.

"By faith he forsook Egypt, not fearing the wrath of the king: for he endured, as seeing him who is invisible.

"Through faith he kept the passover, and the sprinkling of blood, lest he that destroyed the firstborn should touch them.

"By faith they passed through the Red sea as by dry *land:* which the Egyptians assaying to do were drowned.

"By faith the walls of Jericho fell down, after they were compassed about seven days.

"By faith the harlot Rahab perished not with them that believed not, when she had received the spies with peace.

"And what shall I more say? For the time would fail me to tell of Gideon, and of Barak, and of Samson, and of Jephthae; of David also, and Samuel, and of the prophets:

"Who through faith subdued kingdoms, wrought righteousness, obtaining promises, stopped the mouths of lions,

"Quenched the violence of fire, escaped the edge of the sword, out of weakness were made strong, waxed valiant in fight, turned to flight the armies of the aliens.

"Women received their dead raised to life again: and others were tortured, not accepting deliverance; that they might obtain a better resurrection:

"And others had trial of cruel mockings and scourgings, yes, moreover of bonds and imprisonment:

"They were stoned, they were sawn asunder, were tempted, were slain with the sword: they wandered about in sheepskins and goatskins; being destitute, afflicted, tormented;

"(Of whom the world was not worthy:) they wandered in deserts, and in mountains, and in dens and caves of the earth.

"And these all, having obtained a good report through faith, received not the promise:

"God having provided some better thing for us, that they without us should not be made perfect."

And finally, the brief, powerful statement of his own design for living—third chapter of the Epistle to the Philippians, verses thirteen and fourteen.

"Brethren, I count not myself to have apprehended: but *this* one thing *I do,* forgetting those things which are behind, and reaching forth unto those things which are before,

"I press toward the mark for the prize of the high calling of God in Christ Jesus."

Part II

CONQUERORS FOR CHRIST

4

St. Patrick in Ireland—A Golden Page in Missionary History

"DISCIPLES came from all over to follow the supporters of Jesus, and though they had been only a hundred and twenty at the Master's death, in a few months, they had already risen to five hundred. . . . After a year or two the five hundred had become three thousand. . . . Before the century was over the three thousand of the first Pentecost were hundreds of thousands. The soldiers' legions had conquered an empire for Rome; the martyrs' legions will [would] conquer the world for Christ." [1]

During the next three centuries, there were fewer and fewer conquests by the legions, more and more by the martyrs. In most cases, we do not even know who these early Christians were. "History has lost all trace of them. The known world was confined: a few lands around the Mediterranean, along the Nile and the Euphrates. There were still regions partly unexplored in Gaul, Germany, and Britain, and some islands at the edge of the ocean. But in that small world, the roads had no limits, the deserts were boundless, the mountains almost impassable, and the seas stormy." [2]

From Britain, a country which was still part of the dying empire, but in which the state religion was now Christianity, a freeborn Roman belonging to a well-to-do landed family went to Ireland, first as a captive and later as a bishop. He became one of the great missionary saints of all time. His name we do know. It was Patrick.

As I said in my Introduction there are several saints who are best remembered—or rather, most generally remembered—for attributes or episodes which, though authentic enough, do not actually reveal to us the most remarkable aspects of their lives. For instance, we think of Francis of Assisi as the preacher to the birds; of Anthony of Padua as Saint of the Lost; of Dominic de Guzmán as the chief proponent of the rosary. And, by so doing, we lose sight in each case of the missionary and the mystic. As far as St. Patrick is concerned, our error is apt to be even greater, for it is not a question of stressing the less important episode or attribute, but in first making a mistake about his nationality, and then going on to make a great many others. For St. Patrick was not an Irishman; he was a Roman, and quite as proud of this as St. Paul, who so strongly stressed the fact that he was "born free." Patrick's first connection with Ireland was that of a kidnapped slave, abducted from his home; and escaping, after years of bondage, to rejoin his parents in Britain and later to work and study in Gaul before his voluntary return to Ireland as a missionary.

The date of his birth is open to dispute; it was probably around 385 A.D. He does not disclose this in his so-called *Confession,* written near the end of his life, which is so clear and vivid in many other respects. But he does tell us that his father, Calpurnius, was a Roman *ducurion,* that is to say, a collector of imperial taxes, and a member of a council governing a Roman settlement. Whatever the exact date of Patrick's birth, it occurred during the days of Rome's decline as an empire, but not after it had finally relinquished its hold on Britain. Calpurnius had a "country seat" near the village of Benaven Taberniae, which was close to the mouth of the Severns in Wales, a district not infrequently raided by pirates, and it was there the boy Patrick was captured.

"I was then about sixteen years of age," Patrick tells us in the famous *Confession.* "I did not know the true God. I was taken into captivity to Ireland with many thousands of people —and deservedly so, because we turned away from God, and did not keep His commandments, and did not obey our priests, who used to remind us of our salvation. And the Lord brought over us the wrath of His anger and scattered us among many nations, even unto the utmost part of the earth, where now my littleness is placed among strangers.

"And there the Lord opened the sense of my unbelief that I might at last remember my sins and be converted with all my heart to the Lord my God, who had regard for my abjection, and mercy on my youth and ignorance, and watched over me before I knew Him, and before I was able to distinguish between good and evil, and guarded me, and comforted me as would a father his son." [3]

Patrick's captivity was marked by many hardships, but it was not without its ultimate benefits; for—and this also he tells us himself—every day he had to tend sheep and, as has happened over and over again since the days of David, this seemingly humble occupation led the way to sainthood. "Many times a day I prayed," he wrote, "the love of God and His fear came to me more and more, and my faith was strengthened. And my spirit was moved so that in a single day I would say as many as a hundred prayers, and almost as many in the night, and this even when I was staying in the woods and on the mountain; and I used to get up for prayer before daylight, through snow, through frost, through rain, and I felt no harm, and there was no sloth in me—as I now see, because the spirit within me was then fervent.

"And there one night I heard in my sleep a voice saying to me: 'It is well that you fast, soon you will go to your own country.' And again, after a short while, I heard a voice saying to me: 'See, your ship is ready.' And it was not near, but at a distance of perhaps two hundred miles, and I had never been there, nor did I know a living soul there; and then I took to flight, and I left the man with whom I had stayed for six years. And I went in the strength of God who directed my way to my good, and I feared nothing until I came to that ship.

"And the day that I arrived the ship was set afloat, and I said that I was able to pay for my passage with them. But the captain was not pleased, and with indignation he answered harshly: 'It is of no use for you to ask us to go along with us.' And when I heard this, I left them in order to return to the hut where I was staying. And as I went, I began to pray; and before I had ended my prayer, I heard one of them shouting behind me, 'Come, hurry, we shall take you on in good faith; make friends with us in whatever way you like.' . . . And thus I had my way with them, and we set sail at once.

"And after three days we reached land, and for twenty-eight days we traveled through deserted country. And they lacked food, and hunger overcame them; and the next day the captain said to me: 'Tell me, Christian: you say that your God is great and all-powerful; why, then, do you not pray for us? As you can see, we are suffering from hunger; it is unlikely indeed that we shall ever see a human being again.'

"I said to them full of confidence: 'Be truly converted with all your heart to the Lord my God, because nothing is impossible for Him, and this day He may send you food on your way until you be satisfied; for He has abundance everywhere.' And, with the help of God, so it came to pass: suddenly a herd of pigs appeared on the road before our eyes, and they killed many of them; and there they stopped for two nights and fully recovered their strength, and their hounds received their fill, for many of them had grown weak and were half-dead along the way. And from that day they had plenty of food." [4]

Where they landed and just what happened next is a matter of conjecture. Patrick does not tell us himself, and no one else has done so conclusively. "Yet one faint light beams to us through the darkness of Patrick's whereabouts between the time he took leave of the Irish captain and his comrades and his own report of his return to Britain," Paul Gallico reminds us in his wonderful biography of St. Patrick, entitled *The Steadfast Man*. "In the prefix of the work of the Irish monk, Tirechán, seventh-century compiler of a memoir on some of the travels and work of St. Patrick, and his church foundations in Ireland, and appearing in the great *Book of Armagh*, are three disconnected 'Sayings of St. Patrick' which the chronicler had either from some now lost written source, or from his master, Bishop Ultan, who commissioned Tirechán's work.

"And one of them places the twenty-two-year-old escaped

slave, the British-born Patrick, in France, Italy, and that area now known as the Côte d'Azur. The saying:

" 'The fear of God I had as my guide through Gaul and Italy and the islands of the Tyrrhene Sea.' [The Mediterranean.]

"It is this saying or fragment that is the basis, along with a further report of Tirechán's on Bishop Ultan's authority for placing Patrick on the monastery island of Lérins, founded by Honoratus, a monk and scholar.

"There appears to be no document or evidence of record that Patrick ever studied or was present at the monastery of Lérins beyond Tirechán's report of something Bishop Ultan knew or had read more than two hundred years following the death of Patrick, who himself never referred to this island refuge.

"Yet there is an odd link that has persisted down through the centuries, one that seems to be bound up in the apocryphal legend that St. Patrick drove the snakes out of Ireland. He did not, but Honoratus DID drive the snakes out of Lérins."

I had been waiting, as I think everyone must do, who is reading the details of St. Patrick's life for the first time, to hear about the snakes; for of course I believed—as again, doesn't almost everyone?—that he had driven them out of Ireland! Now it seems I have made a mistake about that, too, not as serious as the one about his nationality, but still a mistake. And somehow I cannot feel sorry, for that has led me to a fascinating story, told in Paul Gallico's inimitable way:

"Bede, writing at the beginning of the eighth century, is one of the first to refer in literature to the non-existence of snakes in Ireland. [He says] 'There are no reptiles and no snake can exist there; for although often brought over from Britain, as soon as the ship nears land, they breathe its scented air and die. In fact almost everything in this isle enjoys immunity to poison, and I have heard that folk suffering from snake-bite have drunk water in which scrapings from the leaves of books from Ireland have been steeped, and that this remedy checked the spreading poison and reduced the swelling. The island abounds in milk and honey, and there is no lack of vines, fish and birds, while deer and goats are widely hunted.'

"If Bede's pharmacopoeia and natural history reflect the age during which he wrote and flourished, the fact that Ireland, for whatever reason, did not support snakes was known to him and sources long before him, such as Orosius and Tacitus.

"At the same time it seems to have been known before and ever since the time and after, as well, of Honoratus—a Gallic prelate who had spent much time in the East—that the little island of Lérins, lying beyond that of Lero, off the cape of Cannes, in the Provence area of the South of France, was uninhabitable because it was a mass of tangled undergrowth infested with snakes.

"Honoratus, or St. Honoratus, as he became, selected this island to build a monastic retreat, cleaned out the underbrush, cleared the island of snakes, lizards, and scorpions, dug wells, planted vines, built cells and refectory and founded there a monastery which became famous for the saints, bishops, and scholars who spent time there. It became distinguished in the region almost immediately.

"The date of its foundation cannot be ascertained, the first years of the fifth century being suggested. Since we are aware of the two chronologies for Patrick, one of which places his birth circa A.D. 385 and the other thirty years later, it is fruitless to speculate that Patrick might even have been a laborer during the clearing of the island and the foundation of the famous monastery.

"But the mere fact of there being no snakes in Ireland and the possible historical placing of Patrick upon *another* island from which snakes were driven in the course of its clearing could be sufficient for legend shaping about his figure to confuse the two islands, and even the two men, and transfer the episode of the banishing of the snakes from Honoratus to Patrick and from Lérins to Ireland.

"Speculation upon various periods in the life of St. Patrick may be endless—and often fruitless—when it comes to shedding light upon the personality and character of the man. Yet there remains a fascination about that isolated sentence, remembered or somewhere written down, that has survived the centuries: 'The fear of God I had as my guide through Gaul and Italy and the islands of the Tyrrhene Sea,' since it refers obviously to his first journey in France, the one undertaken with the Irish traders who facilitated his escape.

"For this journey, instead of returning him to the home in Britain for which he had so longed and toward which his escape was directed, took him ever further away from it, as far east as Italy and the *islands* (there were also monastic cells and establishments upon Lero, the sister island of Lérins) in the Tyrrhene Sea.

"The fear of God was the boy's guide during the wanderings of several years, friendless and penniless among strangers who spoke a strange language and where the only universal speech was the Latin of the scholars, of which Patrick had no more than a smattering. But there was more than merely the fear of God to be his guide; there was the recent discovery of and yielding himself up to God. . . .

"It may be imagined that Patrick greatly needed someone to talk to about these events, to help him resolve and evaluate them. . . . If then he found himself on that sun-drenched shelf between Saint-Tropez and Genova, the fame of Lérins and the brilliant and saintly men gathered there would have reached his ears. He beat his way back along the coastal road in an attempt to reach Marseilles and a passage on a ship to Britain. It requires no stretch of the imagination to picture him stopping off at Lérins to seek a sympathetic ear, instruction and comfort, and finding the peace and the company such that he remained for several years before the call of home again set his youthful feet upon the road.

"But, upon this episode in his life—if it ever took place—Patrick remains completely silent.

"The next words that we have from him at the conclusion of the great adventure of escape, when at last the party encountered people and habitations once more and were saved, are brief and stark: 'And again after a few years, I was in Britain with my kin who received me as a son, and sincerely besought me that at all events now, after the great tribulations which I had undergone, I should not leave them and go elsewhere.' . . .

"But shortly after his return, as he was beginning to settle down in the bosom of his family, Patrick had a dream, which reminded him in no uncertain fashion that it was not for nothing God had led him out of captivity and the wilderness of Hibernia. The Lord had work for him to do."

Although Patrick recorded nothing about his wanderings, and the theory concerning the Isle of Lérins and its snakes is ours to reject or accept as we choose, he does tell us about his dream—or rather, about three dreams. And this account we must take as factual.

"I saw in the night the vision of a man, whose name was Victoricus, coming as it were from Ireland, with countless letters. And he gave me one of them, and I read the opening words of the letter, which were, 'The voice of the Irish'; and as I read the beginning of the letter I thought that at the same moment I heard their voices—they were those beside the Wood of Voclut, which is near the Western Sea—and thus did they cry as with one mouth: 'We ask thee, boy, come and walk among us once more.' . . .

"And another night—whether within me, or beside me, I know not, God knoweth—they called me most unmistakably with words which I heard but could not understand, except that at the end of the prayer He spoke thus: 'He that has laid down His life for thee, it is He that speaketh in thee'; and so I awoke full of joy. . . .

"And again I saw Him praying in me, and I was as it were within my body, and I heard Him above me, that is, over the inward man, and there He prayed mightily with groanings. And all the time I was astonished, and wondered and thought with myself who it could be that prayed in me. But at the end of the prayer He spoke, saying that He was the Spirit; and so I woke up, and remembered the Apostle [Paul] saying: 'The Spirit helpeth the infirmities of our prayer. For we know not what we should pray for as we ought; but the Spirit Himself asketh for us with unspeakable groanings, which cannot be expressed in words'; and again: 'The Lord our advocate asketh for us.' " [5]

The three dreams, visions, or inner revelations fixed Patrick with an unwavering determination to carry the Gospel to the Irish. From that moment on he became the steadfast man who could not be turned from his purpose.

"And then once more—when most we would like to accompany him along the thorny road he trod, to see how he overcame the obstacles piled in his path, to learn from example how an indomitable will to achieve is not to be turned aside—he vanishes from our ken. No more than faint echoes of his struggles come through to us out of the past and the welter of confused and confusing legends, surmises and miracle tales. He himself is silent as to the years and the manner of his preparation for his task." [6]

So there is, as Paul Gallico carefully points out, very little material, if any, which can be considered as basically authentic; what is even more baffling, and what he does not point out— probably for fear of making confusion worse confounded—is that the story of a bishop of Ireland named Palladius and the story of Patrick are so interwoven at one stage that it is hard to distinguish between the two. Some chroniclers have practically come to blows because of their divergent views on the subject, and some have given up trying to unravel the various mysteries. We are variously told that Palladius had a second name, which was Patrick, and, according to the careful analysis made by Thomas F. O'Rahilly, the author of *The Two Patricks*, Palladius was the first and our hero the second one; other authors insist that a St. Patrick, now called the Elder, of whom we know almost nothing, was *not* the same person as Palladius, but a forerunner, in a different sense, of our hero, who is properly called St. Patrick the Younger; and still others maintain that Palladius and Patrick—our Patrick—or Patrick the Elder, and Patrick the Younger were one and the same person, that there was no forerunner to our Patrick, no failure and no martyrdom!

Whole tomes have been written on this subject, and I respect the eagerness and veneration for truth which have inspired learned scholars to spend years of their lives in trying to discover the truth connected with this particular mystery. But I do not think it should be allowed, in the case of the average person, to obscure the greater truth—the most basic one—that a freeborn Roman named Patrick, who rose from the ecclesiastical rank of deacon to the ecclesiastical rank of bishop at some period of his career, did go to Ireland as a missionary toward the end of the fifth century and that he consecrated the rest of his life to the conversion of that country, thereby writing what has been justly called "a golden page in Christian history." [7]

To be sure, none of the little church buildings, which he constructed with such care, have survived the centuries, though the sites where they stood, like the sites of his wells—many of which are still fountainheads—may still be traced. The church buildings were made of perishable materials—wood, wattles and clay—and were indeed "little more than huts," [8] unlike the great stone cathedrals which soon began to arise on the continent and were suited to become and remain shrines of popular pilgrimage. But no such monuments are needed to perpetuate Patrick's memory and stimulate devotion to it; the whole country is his shrine.

"When he died almost the whole of Ireland had been Christianized and the Catholic Church established. Christian ethics and church law had been made a part of Irish law. The Latin alphabet had been introduced. Schools and monasteries had been established and there was already a flourishing native Irish priesthood, and a church hierarchy and organization along Gallo-Roman monastic lines. There was no breath of heresy. Patrick himself had converted and baptized thousands upon thousands of the pagans, captured their kings and princes in his net, and won young men and women to the celibate servitude of Christ.

"So strong was the Catholicism, the faith and doctrine he implanted on this emerald isle that when a century or so after his death the final splitting asunder of the [Roman] empire, and the descent of the barbarian hordes, brought such confusion and darkness to the continent of Europe that it threatened to engulf Christianity as well, it was the monks of Ireland who dipped their torches in the flame kindled by Patrick and brought the light back to western Europe.

"And, finally, he left upon Ireland a personal impression that has endured for fifteen centuries. True, it is a distorted confused picture that has emerged from the memory consciousness of the descendants of those who originally fell beneath the spell of the missionary, and by now has lost almost all traces of resemblance to the man whose personality and tongue they were unable to resist. His real imprint lies rather in the steadfastness of the Irish to the steadfastness of Patrick, their adherence to the faith, the Holy Trinity that was the true love of his life." [9]

This is the way I see Patrick, too—in fact, I agree with Paul Gallico so consistently that I am gratified, rather than otherwise, to find there is one minor point on which I disagree with him. That one point concerns the shamrock. The legend that Patrick used its three leaves to illustrate the nature of the Holy Trinity is, so Mr. Gallico tells us, "borne out by no evidence and never so much as hinted at by Patrick himself." Very well. But we are accepting other stories that rightly belong more or less in the legendary realm, since they have little historic support, and saying to ourselves, "Well, after all, this *might* have happened. It *could* have happened." I believe that is so in this case. What could have been more natural than for Patrick to pluck a lovely little trifoliate plant that grew abundantly in the place where he was preaching, and say to the untaught but eager people who had gathered to hear him, "Do you see what I am holding in my hand? One little plant—just one! But it is in three parts. It has three leaves, all on the same stem. And in just the same way, the members of the Blessed Trinity are all parts of the Godhead. Do you understand better now?" And the people would look at each other and whisper among themselves and then look at Patrick and smile and nod and so would he.

Let us by all means correct our mistake about his nationality and let us gratefully leave the snakes in Lérins and grant that Ireland was never defiled by such crawling creatures. But let us keep the shamrock, remembering again, as I have so often urged my readers to do, that no less a person than the great

Cardinal, Merry del Val, told us to bear in mind that "tradition, rightly controlled, even in the absence of written documents, gives us manifest proofs of the truth of our beliefs."

And then let us go back to the things we know and not tarry too long on the things we believe because we feel them, though that is a good reason for believing. Let us read more of what Patrick actually did write, noting, as we do so, how well acquainted he was with the Scriptures, how often he paraphrased the instructions of Jesus Himself.[10] Let us unite in the beautiful petition which Patrick has left us, the Prayer for the Faithful.

> "May the *Strength of God* pilot us.
> May the *Power of God* preserve us.
> May the *Wisdom of God* instruct us.
> May the *Hand of God* protect us.
> May the *Way of God* direct us.
> May the *Shield of God* defend us.
> May the *Host of God* guard us
> —Against the snares of the evil ones,
> —Against temptations of the world.
>
> May *Christ* be with us!
> May *Christ* be before us!
> May *Christ* be in us,
> *Christ* be over all!
>
> May *Thy* Salvation, *Lord*,
> Always be ours,
> This day, O *Lord*, and evermore." [11]

5

The Blessed Ramón Lull,
Founder at Miramar, Majorca,
of the First Mission Seminary

On a memorable day in the Year of Our Lord 1276, a young
Majorcan of noble birth, by name Ramón Lull, went to King
Jaime II, whom he had served as a page when Jaime was still
an infante, and asked his sovereign to "found a monastery
where a little group of Franciscans could, by prayer and meditation, prepare to preach the Gospel to the Moslems." [1] Jaime
II must have been quite unprepared for such an appeal on two
counts: his father, Jaime I, King of Aragón, was known as the
Conqueror because he had wrested control of Majorca from the
Moors and added that island to his domain and that of its ruler
to his title; therefore, his son could hardly be expected to favor
their rehabilitation. Furthermore, there was nothing about the
youth of Ramón Lull which could have prepared his monarch
for such an appeal, much less for anything which marked the
applicant unmistakably as eventually belonging to the company of the blessed.

If he were not actually dissipated, he was certainly frivolous;
in our day and age he would have been characterized as a
playboy. (It is perhaps permissible to remind readers that the
same is true of St. Augustine and even of that most beloved of
all saints, Francis of Assisi, not to mention numerous others.)
He was talented, but he frittered away his talents; beyond the
writing of light verse, he seemed incapable of making any mental effort. His parents despaired of seeing him put his pen to

better use. A position at court did nothing to give him a sense of responsibility; instead it increased his predilection for the pursuit of pleasure. Marriage to a charming girl, Blanca Picany, did not wean him from amorous adventure elsewhere. Apparently he was never to become a man of stature, but was to drift along to middle age as a trifler and a philanderer. As much as he wanted to do anything, he wanted to be a troubador.

Authorities differ as to the circumstances which brought about a sudden change, not only in his outlook, but in his entire life. According to one story, it came one evening at sundown, when he was following a girl along a street with intentions which could hardly be described as honorable. He had seen her only from the rear and, from that viewpoint, she seemed to him almost irresistibly attractive; she had a beautiful figure, she carried herself superbly, she walked with infinite grace. He quickened his step and caught up with her, already murmuring flattering phrases. She turned abruptly and revealed a face half eaten away by cancer! The sudden shock of this revelation, which seemed to be a sign that he had been mistaking corruption for beauty—spiritually as well as physically—made Lull recoil with horror from the sins of the flesh and seek the consolations of the spirit.

Another version of the story tells us that he was sitting in his room, composing one of his light love songs, when he chanced to look up and see before him the figure of the crucified Christ. He tried to persuade himself that he had only imagined the vision; but when the experience had been repeated four times, he no longer deluded himself: it was real and it had been vouchsafed both as a reproach and as a warning. It marked the end of his petty adventures.

Personally, I prefer this version and it seems to me the more credible of the two. The dark watches of the night, if spent in solitude, offer the best possible opportunity for quiet reflection. Lull would have had the time and the tranquillity to ponder the meaning of the vision between the different apparitions. It seems to me entirely logical to assume that this is what he did.

Be that as it may, something suddenly altered his way of life and of obedience. He resolved to convert infidels and unbe-

lievers to the truth of the holy Catholic faith and during the
remainder of his long life devoted himself to an apostolate
among Moslems and Jews. His choice of a special mission was
prompted by the misery he had seen whenever he passed
through the fortified city of Palma into the Arab quarter. "It
seemed to him that the statue of the Holy Virgin standing
there was ordering him to consecrate himself to evangelizing
the Saracens." [2] The Moslems still living in the Balearic Islands
were despised by the Christians who were their conquerors;
financially, they were almost ruined; socially, they were pariahs.

Ramón Lull began his apostolate by seeking the counsel and
advice of his bishop and then setting out on a pilgrimage which
took him to Santiago de Compostela, Montserrat and many
shrines in France.

"The roads are long that lead to God,"

he sang in a poem,

"But they glow with shining love."

On his return from his pilgrimage, he devoted nine years to
intensive study of Latin, Arabic, Hebrew, theology, philosophy
and the elements of natural science. During this same time he
wrote more than two hundred works of theology and religious
mysticism, which were planned as "means by which men may
learn to love God." Some of his works rank among the literary
masterpieces of the Spanish language. He also continued to
write poems, all of which were now dedicated to the Virgin
Mary. But he knew that this was simply a preparation for more
active work; and "one day he was praying on a hilltop, from
which he could see only the sky and the sea, when he suddenly
felt the light of the All-Powerful shining around him. He must
have had a similar impression as that vouchsafed Moses in the
presence of the burning bush. His mind became extraordinarily
lucid. It seemed to him that the Virgin Mary herself had come
to counsel him. In a flash of light he could see the whole world
with its uncounted hordes still awaiting the revelation of

Christ. No, writing books and pious poems was not enough. Prayers and pilgrimages were not enough. 'Go ye, therefore, and make disciples of all the nations!' The order of the Master rang in his ears." [3]

He joined the Third Order of St. Francis, set aside a sufficient sum for the support of his wife and his two children and distributed the rest of his wealth among the poor. "He lectured on mission problems at the great universities and carried on public religious debates with Moslems and Jews. He urged the establishment of missionary seminaries where future apostles might learn the languages and the customs of their flocks-to-be. He advocated the foundation of a specialized mission department in the Holy See over three hundred years before the creation of the Sacred Congregation for the Propagation of the Faith." [4]

His next step was the foundation of the College of the Holy Trinity at Miramar. The location was both advantageous and beautiful. It was only a few leagues distant from Palma and was reached by a high road which wound its way through terraced gardens and groves of almond, olive and fir trees; but it was about a thousand feet higher than the capital and the air was always fresh and invigorating. The monks who came there for instruction "went forth to every corner of Spain and the Balearics, into the Saracen villages and the Arab quarters of the cities, to explain Christian truth to the Moslems and convert them to the faith.

"Even this was not enough. The few thousand Moors remaining in Christian Spain were not the only ones in need of the Gospel. The Arab empire was still of vast extent, stretching from the Atlantic coast of Africa to Egypt in the east, northward to Syria and Asia Minor, and even, it was said, to the far-flung Indies. It represented an immense domain in which only the Koran was law and only Mohammed was venerated. It was here, to the very heart of the Islamic world, that the Good Tidings must be borne. And the time was now.

"Miramar was founded in 1276, a period when the great Christian adventure of the Crusades seemed to have bogged down in failure. Gone were the glorious days when Godefroy de Bouillon had led his valiant and exhausted Crusaders into recaptured Jerusalem. Since that July 14, 1099, the Christian kingdoms of the Holy Land had crumbled under the combined misfortunes of misrule and Moslem attack. . . . Was not this long succession of failures a sign of the will of God? . . . Had not two saints of the past century constantly proclaimed that a Crusade of Peace was worth a dozen military expeditions, that the best weapon to conquer hearts was not the sword but the mission? Ramón Lull agreed.

"Ramón believed he should seek approval of his plans at the highest level, and he took the road to Rome to open his heart to the Pope. The time seemed propitious. Not long before the Holy Father had sent a mission, headed by Jean de Plano Carpini, a Franciscan monk, into the heart of Asia to convert the Tartars and the Mongols. The Franciscan mission had in effect crossed most of the vast continent, at great risk and with unbelievable adventures, but with little success. So while the Pope listened benevolently to Ramón, the Papal advisors were less than lukewarm. Ramón's plea for schools for Arabic and other Oriental languages, for more monks to swell his nucleus of future missionaries at Miramar, fell on deaf ears in Rome. When he moved on to other Christian centers such as Paris, he still could arouse little interest in his project.

"But Ramón did not give up. His plans, he was convinced, were inspired by Christ Himself in the moment of great light on the hilltop in Majorca. Since he could get no help from men, his only recourse was to God. He left for the Holy Land. . . .

"During the long hours spent in prayer on the very spot where Jesus died that men—all men—might receive the Message of Love, Ramón Lull heard a mysterious voice speaking within him, repeating the injunction that he must embark on the great adventure. And he resolved again to do so.

"Back at Miramar he called together his community of monks, men who shared his faith and hopes, who looked upon him as their guide, a guide sent by God Himself. He spoke to them calmly but fervently. The monastery no longer needed him. The work was going along well, the senior monks had the situation in hand, and neophytes were beginning to knock at the door. The founder's task had been accomplished. Therefore he would go away. He would go alone. He would sail for Africa where he would undertake the great work which had been deep in his heart for many years. He would be missionary to the Moslems on their own soil.

"He now had a perfect command of Arabic. He had made a thorough study of the doctrines of Islam so that he could argue with the most learned doctors of Koranic law. . . . He returned to Rome for Papal permission for his adventure, then sailed from Genoa for Tunisia. He had no trouble landing, for in Tunisia, as in Egypt and other countries of North Africa, there were in all the big ports large colonies of Christian merchants. The Christians maintained cordial relations with the Arab authorities, since both groups profited by mutual trade. However, the Christians lived apart from the Moslems, kept to themselves, and kept their intergroup relationship on a strictly business basis. They carefully avoided the subject of religion for fear of causing bad feeling and being run out of the country. Their attitude was the exact opposite to what Ramón Lull had in mind.

"Ramón dressed like a sage of Islam. With his sun-bronzed skin and his gaunt build, he could easily pass for an Arab, mingle with the street-corner crowds, and take part in the religious arguments which often arose spontaneously in the market place from idlers gathered about some passing imam or Moslem savant. For many weeks he worked in this manner, speaking whenever he had the chance. He even argued with Mohammedan sages in their own schools while their students listened. He made such rapid progress that he was bound to overreach himself. And one day he did. He scored such an obvious verbal triumph over his adversary that the vindictive Moslem plotted vengeance. Any man who attacks the dogmas of Islam and who speaks so warmly of Jesus, of His life and His message, must certainly be a Christian—a *Roumi*, as they say in Africa. The vanquished debater ran to the authorities to denounce the *Roumi*.

"Ramón Lull was arrested, tried, and condemned to death

as a blasphemer of Allah and an enemy of the religion of Mohammed, his prophet. . . . A high-placed and influential citizen
of Tunis, who had heard Ramón debating with the Moslem
sages, intervened in his behalf. Whether or not the Tunisian
had been swayed by the Christian arguments, he did save the
missionary's life. However, Ramón did not escape a vicious
flogging, after which he was flung, bruised, bleeding and gasp-
ing for breath, aboard a Genoese ship sailing the next morning.
So Mohammed had been avenged and the Christian run out of
the country. Or so the Arabs thought.

"The Arabs had underestimated the courage and determination of the man of God. . . . After dark Ramón jumped overboard and swam ashore. He was too exhausted to resume his
work immediately, however. He made his way back to Majorca to gather his strength and to meditate. . . .

"So Ramón embarked once more. He sailed alone. Nobody
was eager to share his perils. They said he was mad to beard
the Moor in his own den; that the last judgment would deter-
mine who had been mad and who had been wise. King Jaime
II himself tried to deter him. The King pointed out there was
plenty of work to be done in Spain and the Balearics, and that
Ramón would have royal permission to preach in the synagogues of the Jews and the mosques of the Moors. But Ramón
was adamant. He alone knew what God had ordered him to do
during the moment of Great Light.

"This time Ramón went to Algeria. This time he disembarked boldly at Bougie. He took no precautions, made no
effort at dissimulation. He appeared in the market place and
in public squares, knowing that as soon as he started to speak
a crowd would gather, according to African custom. Once he
had an audience, he immediately began his attack on the doctrine of Mohammed.

"He was soon arrested and thrown into a miserable cell.
The Christian merchants from Genoa and Catalonia used their
influence to secure better treatment for him, and he took advantage of the bigger, lighter cell to write a long treatise in Arabic,
again attacking the Islamic religion. After six months in prison
he was expelled from Africa once more. And the day before

his ship was due to arrive in Italy, it ran into a violent storm and foundered. Ramón escaped with his life, but all his belongings were lost, including his precious Arabic manuscript. He wondered if Providence had turned against him.

"But nothing could discourage him. He stayed in Italy until he had rewritten his entire manuscript. He moved on to France to see the Pope, who was then installed at Avignon, and discuss his future plans. He attended the Council of Vienna to agitate in favor of setting up chairs of Arabic and other Oriental languages in Christian universities. Would they understand how important it was to have men without ties and without regard for their own lives who would go forth to shout the message of the gospel in the very face of the infidel? . . .

"Twice more Ramón invaded the heart of Islam. On his last journey he was an old man. . . . King Jaime II had finally understood the importance of the missions, and had given Ramón a letter to the King of Tunisia requesting a suitable welcome. Thanks to the Spanish King's backing, Ramón was able to speak for a whole year without interference from the Arab authorities. He was even able to send for some of his old pupils to come and help him.

"The old campaigner saw himself slipping into impotence. He knew that his infirmities had already won the day, yet stubbornly and heroically he continued to fight, to preach, to write, to publish more and more tracts and treatises arguing with the Moslem doctrine and proclaiming Christ."[5]

In all, he "wrote more than 300 treatises, many in Arabic, on philosophy, music, astronomy, navigation, law, mathematics, and theology. Chief of his writings was *Arbre de philosophia de amor*; he also wrote mystical poetry of the highest order, and *Blanquerna*, the first novel written in Catalan."[6]

"He knew that death was close behind him, yet he refused to look back over his shoulder. Finally, one June day of 1316, a mob aroused against him by his Islamic adversaries rushed him off his feet, beat him viciously, and left him lying in the street, believing him dead. And he would have died had not a group of Genoese sailors found him and carried him aboard their ship.

"The ship was already at sea when he regained consciousness. He was grateful to the sailors who had brought him aboard, yet he truly regretted that he was not to die on his beloved soil of Africa, a martyr to his faith. Despite the tender care lavished upon him by all the crew, he grew steadily more feeble. He died just as the headlands of his native Majorca rose above the horizon.

"Ramón Lull was laid to rest in the soil of his own island, heroic witness to the passion that burns in the heart of every missionary, harbinger of those who long afterward were to bring back to Africa the Cross and the love of Christ." [7]

6

Francis of Assisi, "The Father of Modern Missions," and His Associates, Dominic de Guzmán and Anthony of Padua

If I were asked to hazard a guess as to which saint in the whole calendar was most universally respected, admired and beloved, not only by Catholics, but by all Christians and by many whom we classify as pagans, I should not hesitate a single instant— I should say Francis of Assisi. And I should add, with scarcely less hesitation, that many aspects and episodes of his life are better known than those of almost any other saint. There is something irresistibly appealing about it: the depth and sincerity of his feeling for Lady Poverty; the complete consecration of his life to an ideal of simplicity and sacrifice, and the power to convince his disciples that this should be their ideal, also; the unsullied beauty of his friendship with St. Clare; the fellow feeling which did not limit itself to human beings, but included all creatures, even twittering birds and a vicious wolf, and went so far as to embrace the elements, which he called by endearing names; the powers of visualization which led to the creation of the crèche. All this and much more is familiar to the thousands of pilgrims who flock every year to the little chapel, known as the *Porziuncola*, near Assisi, which Francis had found in ruins and made his first hermitage and which later became the center of the community of brothers which he founded and who were known as the Friars Minor; all this is likewise familiar to thousands who can make only a spiritual pilgrimage.

But I wonder how many of these devotees also think of their favorite saint as "the father of modern Roman Catholic missions";[1] for, as far as I know, though officially approved, it is a designation which has not been generally used.

Elizabeth Goudge reminds us, in her inspired biography of St. Francis, entitled *My God and My All,* "The 'place' of the Portiuncula has such charm that it is a temptation to think of Francis and the brothers chiefly in its setting. Actually they were never there for long. They were ever on the road, traveling to distances that seem incredible when we remember that they went there barefoot, confronting dangers and difficulties that were sometimes even greater than those which met Saint Paul on his missionary journeys; for Saint Paul, traveling in the Roman Empire and speaking the Greek that was the official language in every portion of it, had a measure of protection from his Roman citizenship and could make himself understood by those to whom he spoke. But once they passed out of Italy there was no protection for the brothers, and the lingua franca was not spoken by the uneducated among them and not understood by all to whom they preached. Though in their own country the missionary journeys of the brothers were increasingly successful, beyond it they frequently ended in what the world calls failure. It could hardly have been otherwise. That they should have attempted them at all is a measure of their courage. Christ had said, 'Go ye into all the world,' and so they went, whether they knew the language or whether they did not, in childlike faith and obedience."

The instructions given by Francis to his Friars Minor—

shortly thereafter to be called the Franciscans—have been preserved in several remarkable letters. "When friars travel about the world they are to take nothing for their journey, [he ordered] *neither purse nor wallet, nor bread, nor money, nor a staff.* And whenever they enter a house, they shall first say, 'Peace be to this house.' And they are to remain in that house, *eating and drinking what they have to give them.* They are not to offer resistance to injury, but if anyone strikes them on one cheek, let them turn the other as well.[2] If anyone takes away their habit, let them have their cloak as well. Let them give to everyone who asks, and if anyone takes away anything that is theirs, they must not try to recover it."[3]

The instructions given to friars who are going among Saracens or other unbelievers are much more detailed than those given to the friars who were not going so far afield. "Our Lord says, *Remember, I am sending you out to be like sheep among wolves; you must be wary, then, as serpents and yet innocent as doves.* So those friars whom God inspires to go among the Saracens and other unbelievers may do so with the approval of their Minister and servant. The Minister is to grant permission and not oppose them, provided that he considers them suitable men to send, for if he acts unwisely in this or other matters he will have to give account to God. There are two ways in which the friars who go out can act with spiritual effect. The first is not to dispute or be contentious, but *for love of the Lord to bow to every kind of human authority,* and to acknowledge themselves Christians. The other way, whenever they think it to be God's will, is to proclaim the word of God and their faith in God Almighty, the Father, the Son, and the Holy Spirit, Creator of all things, showing that the Son is our Redeemer and Saviour, and teaching men that they must be baptized and become Christians, for *no man can enter into the Kingdom of God unless birth comes to him from water, and from the Holy Spirit.*

"These truths and others acceptable to the Lord they must teach to others, for our Lord says in the Gospel, *Whoever acknowledges Me before men, I too will acknowledge him before My Father Who is in heaven,* and, *Whoever disowns Me and*

My Words, the Son of Man will disown when He comes in the glory of the Father and of the holy angels.

"All friars everywhere are to remember that they have given and surrendered themselves soul and body to our Lord Jesus Christ, and for love of Him they must expose themselves to all enemies, both visible and invisible; for our Lord says, *The man who loses his life for My sake shall save it in life everlasting. Blessed are those who suffer persecution in the cause of right; the Kingdom of Heaven is theirs. They will persecute you just as they have persecuted Me. If they persecute you in one city, take refuge in another. Blessed are you when men hate and revile you, and when they cast you off and censure you, and reject your name as something evil, and speak all manner of evil against you falsely because of Me. When that day comes, rejoice and exult over it, for a rich reward awaits you in heaven.*[4] *I tell you, My friends, there is no need to fear those who kill the body, but have no means of killing the soul. See to it that you are not disturbed in mind. It is by endurance that you will secure possession of your souls. The man will be saved who endures to the last.*"[5]

To this long letter, dwelling on the spiritual aspects of their mission, Francis adds some explicit directions regarding obedience.

"I also require the Ministers under obedience to request the Lord Pope to appoint one of the Cardinals of the holy Roman Church to be governor, protector, and corrector of this fraternity. In this way we shall be under discipline and subject at the feet of the same holy Church and firm in the Catholic Faith, and shall observe poverty, humility, and the holy Gospel of our Lord Christ as we have solemnly vowed."[6]

It would, of course, have been unthinkable that Francis should send his friars out into the world without yearning to go far afield himself and that the Holy Land should be his most natural objective. In 1212—that is, within two years of the time when his Order had received papal recognition—he embarked from Ancona for Syria with only one companion. "But a tempest ran the ship aground on the coast of Slavonia, preventing all the passengers from continuing the journey.

Francis knew that another ship would not set sail for the Orient for at least another year, because in those times boats navigated slowly by means of oars and sails. So he beseeched the owner of a boat bound for Ancona to take him and his companion aboard.

" 'I don't want any extra mouths to feed,' replied the seawolf. 'We barely have enough provisions for the trip.'

"But the two friars were not men to be frightened by the spectre of hunger. That evening, they stowed away in the hold. Meanwhile, a good man, a native of the coastal city, consigned a supply of victuals to another good man of the crew for the poor friars who, when the ship was far out to sea, were able to emerge from their hiding place.

"The owner at first grumbled, but later he had to bless those unwanted pilgrims because during the crossing, which took a longer time than had been calculated because of a storm, the sailors ate all the rations and it was the provisions of St. Francis (who always ate so little) which saved the crew from starving. Those provisions seemed to be touched with magic; no matter how many were distributed, they sufficed each day: the Lord multiplied them for love of Francis.

"A good knight does not fear failure. Francis was not discouraged over the failure of his first Crusade. Instead, he returned to his country with a greater ardor for martyrdom, with a greater desire to carry the Gospel to where it was unknown and hated. Therefore he chose Morocco, another great Saracen center, where the Arabs, repulsed by Spain, had grouped themselves for reinforcement around their Sultan, Mohammed-Ben-Naser, called 'The Mill Watcher.'

"In June, 1213, Francis left with a few companions. . . . But the saint was unable to reach Morocco; he became gravely ill and once more he was forced to return to Italy. . . . Once again the will of God had halted him on the road of the Crusades. And still the thirst for martyrdom grew in his heart." [7]

That he would, through God's grace, somehow and sometime reach the Holy Land and preach the gospel to the infidels, he could never have doubted, since it was not only his soul's sincere desire, but his manifest destiny. However, before the time came for him to go there, Pope Innocent III had summoned a general council to the Lateran in order to proclaim a new crusade for the liberation of the Holy Places from the Moslems; and Francis, as the founder of a religious Order, was commanded to be present. "The Church in unprecedented numbers had responded to his call. The Pope's appeal had been a splendid triumph, in its eloquence, its mystic vision and its passionate sincerity. Seldom in history has intellectual and moral greatness been wedded to such greatness of occasion, as when this great pontiff expounded to the assembled prelates of all Christendom the mystic parallels of the ninth chapter of Ezekiel, dwelling on the meaning of the symbol Tau, that he, the man clothed in linen, was ordained to place upon the foreheads of those that grieved for the abominations of the world. He described the miseries of the Holy Places and the apathy and sin of the Christian nations, that were to be re-inspired by faith for the tremendous undertaking. The resolutions of this Council have caused it to be called the great reforming Council of the Middle Ages; the Crusade was to be proclaimed, the Curia purged, the Clergy purified of old abuses; if these designs had been put into execution possibly the later schism might have been avoided. Unfortunately for mankind, it failed to execute its resolutions, and within but a few months the great Pope was dead, in the vigour of his manhood and the fullness of his opportunity." [8]

In the course of his stay in Rome, Francis met a Spanish nobleman, Dominic de Guzmán, who himself was seeking permission to found an Order of preachers. Each immediately recognized in the other a kindred spirit and "the friendship between the two men, and between their Orders, is one of the great friendships of history." [9] Maria Sticco, in *The Peace of St. Francis,* gives a charming account of their meeting.

"Dominic, the older of the two, looked graceful and gentle in his tunic, black and white like the swallows; Francis, the younger, but already worn out, was dressed in his tunic which was the color of larks. They did not know each other, but Dominic had seen Francis in a dream as the man destined by God to revise the destinies of Christianity and at their first encounter they understood each other without saying a word. They were standing on the Aventine Hill where Dominic founded the two first great convents of his Order, and Rome was spread out before them . . . the whole panorama here and there dotted with meadows and woods. . . . Under the bridges, the Tiber flowed like time.

"The two great reconstructors confided their lives and ideals to each other. . . .

" 'I come from Spain,' said Dominic. 'I have been studying since my childhood: the University of Salamanca unveiled to me the verities of theology and the beauty of science, the sister of faith. I spent ten years among the worse heretics of Provence. I have known the evils of error, the danger of knowledge without God. I stood at the side of Simon of Montfort, like a priest at the side of a knight; I fought with the word of the Gospel before the soldiers fought with the sword; I prayed and fasted while the inevitable battle raged. From my knowledge of the heretics I have learned that the evils of the century stem from the pride of intellect which is blindness and servitude. Only the truth will make us free. What can you tell me of yourself, brother?'

" 'I was a merchant, a man of the world and a sinner: I studied little and read little save for the ledgers of the shop and songs of love and chivalry and ballads and other vanities until the merciful Lord touched my heart, and gave me the Cross to read. I knew no heretics, I came to know lepers. And then when the Lord entrusted the friars to me, no one showed me what to do but the Most High Himself revealed to me that I should live according to the Holy Gospel.'

" 'My holy friars also live according to the Holy Gospel and they pray and study in order to combat the astuteness of the world.'

" 'Mine are simpletons and unlettered and have no book but the crucifix.'

" 'Mine must possess nothing save the common cloister and the cell which is theirs today and no longer theirs tomorrow.'

" 'My friars have no place on which to lay their heads, and their cell is my heart.'

" 'My most simple brother, how can a community sustain itself without having care and solicitude for the things needful to the body?'

" 'O Father Dominic, the Lord has revealed to me that if we will tightly embrace holy poverty, the world will follow us and will nourish us copiously since God has placed this pact between us and the world: that we set a good example to the world, and God will provide for our necessities.'

" 'We too are poor: we are naught but the dogs of the Lord and with the lighted torch of the faith we sow terror among packs of heretic wolves, scattering them.'

" 'We are the jongleurs of God and we wish to keep Him happy with our praises, with our countenances happy even in tribulations, and thereby we wish to make men understand that to serve God is to reign, and that to serve Him is needful, but in gladness.'

" 'We strike the roots of heresy and extirpate the weeds that poison.'

" 'We have no valor for cutting others down but only to let ourselves be cut down willingly, for if the seed die not the earth brings forth no fruit.'

" 'God is truth and sin is born of our ignorance.'

" 'God is love and ignorance is born of our want of love.'

" 'I would fain, O Friar Francis, that your Order and mine should become one, and that we live in the Church with the same Rule.'

" 'We are two wheels of the same cart, and mine is always the smaller.'

" 'Brother,' said the blessed Dominic with great reverence, 'deign to give me the rope with which you are girded.'

"Francis refused out of humility, but St. Dominic insisted with so much charity that he won, and placing his hands in the hands of the other, he commended himself to his prayers.

"Thus, the Spanish saint and the Italian saint embraced under the great sky of Rome."

The same year that Francis and Dominic met in Rome, Dominic convened the first Chapter in Bologna; that he had only one more year to live did not matter now. Through the

Order of Preaching Friars which he had founded, the work he had begun would go on. Before his birth, his mother had dreamed that "through these *Domini Canes,* these Dogs of the Lord, Dominic would go forth with a flame in his mouth to set alight the world." [10] The flame was now burning brightly.

Five years later, Francis at last started again for the Holy Land. "He sailed for the East from Ancona on the Feast of St. John the Baptist 1220, taking with him twelve brethren, Peter Cataneo among them. They arrived at the camp of the Crusaders on the eve of an attack upon the fortress of Damietta, and Francis, ashamed and deeply grieved at the open profligacy of the Christian army, warned the princes that the attack would be unsuccessful. They laughed him to scorn, attacked and were repulsed with a loss of six thousand slain. A truce for the burying of the dead was sought and granted, a circumstance of which Francis took advantage in order to pass over to the Sultan's camp.

"He was accompanied on this perilous enterprise by Illuminato. On the way they met two lambs, which afforded them great consolation in the light of the promise: 'Behold I send you forth as lambs in the midst of wolves.' Awed possibly by the friars' strange appearance, the Moslem guards let them pass through and they were brought, as they desired, into the presence of the Sultan, Malek-el-Kamil." [11]

"The Sultan's features were swarthy, and he was dressed in gold-colored robes. He sat cross-legged on a pile of cushions, holding a curved scimitar in his hand. Around his neck were numerous pearl necklaces, and delicate white plumes waved above his turban. The walls and the ground were covered with fine rugs, and a sweet-smelling perfume rose out of golden vessels." [12]

"To him and his Court Francis expounded the Gospel of Christ in the *lingua franca,* possibly his favourite Provençal. The Sultan was probably diverted by the strangeness of the occurrence, but he recognized in the herald's bearing the signs of no ordinary faith, and caused him to be courteously treated.

"There was a second audience. This time before the Sultan's

throne was spread a carpet covered with crosses. 'If he treads upon them, we will convict him of irreverence to the holy symbols of his creed; if he does not, of discourtesy to me,' the Sultan said. Francis incurred the former charge by stepping forward without hesitation. 'You must remember there were three crosses,' he said boldly; 'we have the true Cross; what you have must be the thieves'.' The Sultan was delighted and pressed him to remain with him.

"But Francis's condition was that the Sultan and all his Court should embrace the Christian faith, or put to the test the truth of the two creeds. Let a great fire be lighted into which he and the Moslem priests should enter, or, if the latter were afraid, he would enter it alone. 'If I am burnt up, impute it to my sins; if I am saved, acknowledge Christ to be God and Saviour of all.' " [18]

Harold Goad concludes his account of the interview there, but Maria Sticco continues it and gives it a thrilling sequence. "The sultan, who had never found a man ready to throw himself into the fire for his soul, presented him with gold, silver, silk cloths, previous objects, commanding him to take what he wished. St. Francis naturally refused, to the growing astonishment of the sultan who, in order to test him fundamentally, offered him all sorts of honors and pleasures and Francis firmly replied no to all the flatteries and blandishments.

"Then Melek-el-Kamil convoked the more authoritative and religious personages of the encampment to get their opinion of the two prisoners. And the opinion was that they be beheaded without mercy, because they preached against the law of Mahomet and he, as a custodian of the law, ought not permit such sacrilege.

" 'Christians,' said the Sultan of Egypt to the two friars, 'my doctors counsel me to have your heads cut off, but I will never send to his death one who would give his life for my salvation.' He let them go free then with a decree permitting Francis and his fellow friars to roam undisturbed through the Saracen lands, including Palestine, and go to the Holy Sepulchre without paying tribute.

"St. Francis took advantage of this and, always trying to

evangelize enroute, he visited Bethlehem, Jerusalem and Mount Calvary, visits which were destined to bring most important fruits to the Catholic Church. But since the purposes of his crusade (conversion of the infidels and martyrdom) were not being realized, and from Italy disturbing news arrived soliciting his presence, he decided to return to his native land.

"Before leaving, he again went to see Melek-el-Kamil who said to him, 'Friar Francis, willingly would I be converted to the faith of Christ but I fear to do so because if my Saracens knew it, they would kill me, you and all the friars. Since you can do much good and I must settle some important questions, I do not wish to provoke your death and mine, but do teach me how I can be saved and I will do it.'

" 'Lord,' replied St. Francis, 'I am returning to my country, but after my death I will send you two of my friars from whom you will receive the baptism of Christ. Meanwhile, release yourself from every impediment so that the grace of God may find you prepared for faith and devotion.'

"Francis promised this because he felt most deeply grateful to him. Seven years later, Francis died on the bare ground. Another twelve years went by, and the sultan fell ill in his royal palace and, suffering on his rugs and pillows, he waited for the fulfillment of the promise made to him by the Italian pilgrim. His border guards were ordered to be on the lookout for two friars dressed in the habit of St. Francis. And one day two brothers did come from the sea, because St. Francis had inspired them in a dream, and the guards immediately sent them to the dying sultan who rejoiced as if the countenance of the saint whom he had benefited stood once more before him. He was baptized and died as Christian among the Saracens, because the Lord has promised that there is no sinner so great who will not be saved if he truly love the Order of St. Francis with all his heart. So say the 'Little Flowers.' " [14]

Meanwhile, in another direction and under other leadership, the Franciscan missionary movement was steadily going forward. Just before Francis started for the Holy Land, he had summoned six young friars and told them that God had commanded him to send them among the Saracens to preach their faith and fight the law of Mohammed. They had rejoiced in their selection and, while he was carrying out his crusade, crossed Spain and halted at Seville, the last bulwark of Arab rule in Europe. They had been obliged to leave the head of the band, Friar Vitale, in Aragón because of his illness, but the others began preaching in front of the mosque, where they were immediately arrested and sent to the sultan, Abu-Jacub, who "entertained no bellicose plans against Christians, indeed he entrusted the command of his army to a Christian prince, Don Pedro, Infante of Portugal, who because of quarrels with the king, his brother, had unblushingly passed over to the service of the Mohammedans. Instead of imprisoning the five missionaries, Abu-Jacub entrusted them to Don Pedro who received them most respectfully in his palace. The friars took advantage of their freedom to preach the Gospel publicly, and one day the sultan ran into Friar Bernardo who, standing on a cart, was inveighing against Mohamet. The sultan ordered the five missionaries to be seized and expelled from the country. Don Pedro put them aboard a ship leaving for Ceuta, warning them to sail for Italy from there. Instead, a short time later, they were once more seen preaching on the roads of Morocco and the sultan had them imprisoned, and then dispatched to Ceuta. But the heroic band, vowed to martyrdom, returned to Morocco. Once more, Don Pedro took them in tow and for fear that their stubborn resistance might prejudice the native Christians, he had them interned on Moroccan territory under close guard. The five, however, managed to escape surveillance and re-entered the city. One Friday—the Mohammedan Sabbath—they began to preach on the public square through which the sultan was bound to pass. This repeated and open defiance infuriated the sultan; he had the missionaries arrested and submitted them to an interrogation to which the heroic youths responded with the steadfastness of the ancient martyrs. Then he tortured them, making them roll on a carpet of broken glass and finally, driven to ferocity by their very patience, he lopped off the heads of all five with his scimitar.

"Don Pedro composed the bodies of the martyrs and sent

them to Coimbra. The pious procession accompanied them to the church of Santa Croce, where they were buried with the reverence of the people." [15]

The emotions aroused by this burial were fired to more than reverence and, in one case at least, marked a turning point in a remarkable life. While on their way to Morocco, the five friars had been entertained by a young Augustinian scholar, Ferdinand de Buglioni. When their mutilated bodies were brought back to Coimbra, their funeral made such an impression on the young student that his courses suddenly seemed meaningless and he took the difficult and unusual step of leaving the Canons Regular of St. Augustine to join the Franciscans. We know him better as St. Anthony of Padua.

He, too, was defeated, first by shipwreck and then by illness, from reaching Morocco. But eventually he landed at Messina, where he lodged with the Friars Minor and, hearing that Francis had returned from Syria and had summoned a Chapter General to the Portiuncula, took the road to Assisi.

Francis at this time was in a state of collapse, physically exhausted and spiritually distressed over the many questions that had arisen regarding changes in the Rule which the growth of the Order had unmistakably indicated, but to which he found it difficult to reconcile himself. He retired to his hut, hoping that he might meditate and pray in solitude, but inevitably many of the brothers visited him there and his attention was arrested by one who was a stranger to him.

" 'Who are you, son?'

" 'I am Brother Anthony. I became a Friar Minor after seeing the five beheaded Brothers whom you sent to Morocco.'

"Francis regarded him thoughtfully. 'You are going to be a great light in our Order, Brother Anthony.' And he blessed him." [16]

No one else seems to have suspected his great powers and shortly thereafter "he was sent to a little hospice near Forlì, in Emilia, where he was given duties that were chiefly menial. Within a year, however, his brilliant gifts were discovered quite by accident. At an ordination ceremony at Forlì, the special preacher engaged for the occasion failed to appear.

None of the others present would agree to fill the gap and oblige with an extempore sermon. To get out of his predicament, the Father Provincial briefly ordered Antony to preach. His performance astonished the audience, who saw at once that Antony had all the gifts of a first-rate speaker: poise, delivery, conviction, personal charm, amazing memory, mastery of theology and scripture. The immediate sequel was his appointment as preacher to the whole of Italy. It was a period when the church never had greater need of preachers to combat the prevailing heresies and, as it happened, few of the first Franciscans were effective controversialists.

"From that hour, the Forlì hospice saw no more of Antony. He was always on the road, traveling ceaselessly from the south of Italy to the north of France, devoting all his time, talents and energy to the work of preaching. The people's response was his greatest stimulus. The churches could not hold the crowds who came to hear him. A platform had to be set up for him out of doors. Soon the streets and squares could not accommodate the people and the platform had to be carried outside the town, or city, to a plain, or a hillside, where twenty, thirty, forty thousand would gather to hear him. At the rumor of his coming, shops were shuttered up, markets suspended and the law courts closed. During the night before the sermon, the whole countryside became alive with flitting lights as people began to converge from all sides to the venue. It seemed that to those who had once come within the sphere of Antony's influence, nothing whatsoever could rival the interest of his sermons." [17]

"Suddenly, at a time when the Founder of the Order, weakened by fever and incipient blindness, was more and more withdrawing himself from apostolacy to contemplation, in Anthony a spiritual force arose, moving all northern Italy. No phenomenon is more extraordinary in the history of the Order than the emergence of this shy, unnoticed friar into the glory of the apostolic life of effluent grace and miracle." [18]

Although, apparently, the ties between Francis and Anthony did not become as binding in a personal way as those between Francis and Dominic, Francis' first favorable impression of

Anthony was sustained as long as he lived. He recognized Anthony as one of the great men of their Order, addressed him in their correspondence as "Brother Anthony, my Bishop," and willingly entrusted to him the direction of the House of Studies in Bologna, which had been founded during his absence in Syria and about which he had entertained some doubts lest it violated the spirit of the Rule. Only Anthony was able to still those doubts.

Like Francis, Anthony is too little known for his achievements in the missionary field. "The well-known representations of him suggest the cloistered contemplative, but the world was his cloister and the two notes of his lifework were militant activity and ceaseless travel. He has become so monopolized by the Italians, and particularly in Padua, that it is generally forgotten that he was a Portuguese. An aristocrat by birth, he has become the special advocate of the poor and the downtrodden. A scholar who had no living rival as a biblical expert, called by his contemporaries 'Hammer of the Heretics' and 'Living Ark of the Covenant,' he has become the patron of the illiterate, the finder of lost trifles, the saint of the trivial appeals. One of the most effective preachers the world has ever known is now mostly invoked against the most petty, almost the comical, little ills of life." [19]

It is true that most people think of him only as the famous finder of the lost, and I should be the last to underestimate him in this capacity, as I have called on him at frequent intervals, over a period of many years, to help me locate articles that were lost or strayed, if not stolen, and never once have I failed to receive a prompt and helpful response. Therefore, no one can convince me that his designation as Saint of the Lost is a misnomer and, apparently, that highly intelligent and very distinguished woman, Elizabeth Morrow,[20] felt the same way about him, though she was a non-Catholic, for she was the author of the following beautiful lines:

"Walking Elysian fields the saints forget
The salt of human tears. What went before
Grows faint and far; the most unfortunate

Cry of the heart falls cold; they heed no more.
Only Saint Anthony can never rest,
Searching the depths for what has slipped or gone,
So long as men pray he must be oppressed
So long as men lose, he must labor on,
His face forever turned from Paradise
Lest he should miss that single sparrow's fall;
He finds the strayed sheep with his faithful eyes;
He holds in sight the lonely prodigal:
Saint of the lost who cannot sleep nor stand
While one child wanders from his mother's hand."

After all, why should we feel that the designation "Saint of the Lost" is an inappropriate one when we consider how many lost *souls* Anthony saved and how his great talent as a preacher furthered the work of "the Father of Modern Missions"?

7

Ignatius, the "Knight of God," and Xavier, the "Greatest Missionary Next to St. Paul"

Montmartre is not one of the sections of Paris which I am most apt to frequent. Night clubs have never attracted me, even when I was young, and noisy restaurants have done so less and less as I have grown older. Moreover, unkempt groups of men and women, endlessly sitting at sidewalk cafés with half-drained wineglasses and coffee cups in their hands—if they were not wildly gesticulating as they wildly talked—have never impressed me as being seriously involved with their artistic ambitions, abilities and achievements; if they really wanted to paint and write, or if they had already succeeded as artists and authors, they would be spending most of their time in their studios and libraries. And as I have taken it that the main tourist sights of Montmartre are supposed to be night clubs and restaurants and sidewalk cafés and that these are what the outsider is generally invited there to see, I have assiduously avoided it.

There are, however, two really noteworthy sights, one of which is well known and usually appreciated, though it owes no small part of its recognition to the popularity of Charpentier's opera, *Louise,* whose most striking *mise en scène* is the panorama of Paris as seen from the open square before the Church of the Sacred Heart. The actual view, of course, is infinitely more impressive and beautiful than the operatic version of it, as many persons have now happily discovered, even if the church itself had previously no special appeal for them; and, once on the *place,* they have been moved to go to the church, too. It was because I wanted a young granddaughter to see both that I did go to Montmartre the last time I was in Paris; and, as my lameness prevented me from doing as much standing and walking as she and my other companion very naturally wanted to do, once I had persuaded them to go there, I returned to our waiting car, which our driver had parked on a surprisingly quiet side street, in front of a small and relatively unpretentious church.

The driver engaged me in conversation, delighted, or so he said, that he had a client who was interested in sights other than night clubs and who could converse with him in his own language. Then he asked me if I knew the name of the church beside which we were waiting and I told him I did not. "St. Denis!" he said proudly. As I had always associated St. Denis with the cathedral where many of the kings and queens of France are buried, which is located not in Montmartre, but in the suburb named for the saint, I did not respond with the immediate recognition and enthusiasm which he evidently expected; so he added helpfully, "You did not perhaps realize, Madame, that we are very close to holy grounds. It was in this church that Ignatius of Loyola and a small group of fellow

students at the University of Paris, Francis Xavier and Peter
Favre among them, met on the Feast of the Assumption in
1533. Favre, who was a priest, celebrated Mass and, afterward,
they all pronounced a vow on which they had agreed before-
hand." [1]

"And the vow was—?"

"To renounce family ties and worldly goods, keeping only
enough of the latter for a journey to Jerusalem. But if war
with the Turks stopped shipping for a year, or if the guardian
of the Holy Sepulchre declined to accept their services, they
were to go back to Rome and place themselves at the disposal
of the Holy Father as missionaries." [2] The driver paused for a
moment and then he added, in a tone that bespoke emotion
and increased mine, "So it was at this little meeting, here in
this little church, in which you are the first of my clients to
show an interest, that the Jesuit Order was born."

I shall have to confess that, up to this time, though I had
enjoyed the privilege of acquaintance with a few Jesuits, my
contacts with them had been social rather than spiritual. I had
come to recognize the fruits of their insistence on general culture and specified learning; but the most significant aspect of
their history, as far as I was concerned, was their almost superhuman ability to survive and surmount the injustice and severity of their expulsion from one country after another. Now I
wanted to learn more about that little group which had foregathered in that quiet and inconspicuous church more than
four hundred years ago and, especially, about Ignatius of Loyola, the ringleader, and Francis, his special friend.

The story of their lives, like that of their destinies, is closely
interwoven;[3] but since Ignatius is the elder, we should begin
with his. Fortunately, it is easier to trace than the stories of
many other saintly lives; for not only have countless books and
articles been written about him, but he himself dictated large
portions of his story to various secretaries. His parents, Don
Beltrán and María Saenz de Licona y Balda, were high-ranking
Spanish nobles, and he was born about 1491 in their castle of
Loyola, long their ancestral stronghold, which is located in a

beautiful green valley among the beautiful green mountains of
the Basque province of Guipúzcoa. He was christened Iñigo,
after a Spanish Benedictine saint; but he later took the name
of Ignatius out of personal devotion to St. Ignatius of Antioch.
Iñigo—or Ignatius, as we shall call him from the beginning,
as that is the name he chose himself and by which he has come
down to us—was the youngest of a large brood, eleven according to some authorities, thirteen according to others, and was
orphaned at the age of fourteen, when an elder brother became
the head of the noble but impoverished family. His scholastic
education was superficial and his early years seem to have been
given over largely to the pursuit of pleasure, unfortunately not
always innocent pleasure, for pilfering, gaming and "affairs of
gallantry" were among his confessed pastimes. However, he
also excelled in "feats of military prowess" and, as a youth,
took service, first with the King's Treasurer, Juan Velásquez,
who was a family friend, and later with Antonio Manrique
de Lara, the Duke of Najera, who was Viceroy of Navarre.
Even as a boy, the courage of Ignatius was phenomenal; and
when the French invaded Spain and laid siege to Pamplona,
he was one of the few who stood out against surrender. During
the siege of the fortress, his thigh was shattered by a cannon
ball and so badly set, directly after the battle, that resetting
was required after he was taken home on a litter by the belea-
guering French, whose admiration had been roused by his bravery. It is recorded that "he bore the pain with fortitude" and
certainly he accepted the handicap of permanent lameness with
cheerful resignation; but the tedium of convalescence was
harder for him to endure and he strove to relieve it by reading.
The ancestral castle did not have much of a library. In fact,
according to some authorities, it contained only two books,
a life of Christ by the Carthusian Rudolf of Saxony and Jacobus
de Voragine's *Golden Legend*. For lack of anything else to
peruse, Ignatius began poring over the lives of the saints, as
related in *The Golden Legend,* and found these unexpectedly
arresting, especially the biographical sketches of St. Francis of
Assisi and St. Dominic. As he pored, he pondered and, at first

vaguely and then more clearly, he began to visualize himself as a knight in the service of God, rather than that of any earthly prince.

As soon as Ignatius was well enough to undertake the journey, he went on a pilgrimage to the famous shrine of Montserrat near Barcelona, made a three-day confession, gave away his knightly apparel and hung up his sword on the altar of Our Lady. All this might be set down as savoring slightly of a beau geste, in keeping with a rather flamboyant temperament; but his next step was taken in deadly earnest: he went to the nearby village of Manresa and made a three-way division of his time. Part of it was spent in active service at a hospital, where he volunteered as a menial worker; part of it at the Dominican Priory, where he read *The Imitation of Christ* by Thomas à Kempis; and part of it in a cave, "where he employed himself in ascetic practices worthy of any of the desert fathers"; and all of it in the self-searching and study which had manifold and important results.

"Everything that had gone before had been at most but a preparation for that irruption of the divine into his life which was about to transform him. Manresa saw the birth of his life's work; it holds the key to his entire development. Ignatius himself, whenever he was asked anything about his life, always answered with reference to Manresa. In Manresa, Ignatius came face to face, as it were, with the Being of God; there the Eternal hammered his soul mercilessly into its providential shape. There the truth about the diverse effects of diverse spirits that he had glimpsed upon his sickbed took on existential reality, and he became immediately and painfully aware of the conflict between good and evil of which his soul was both the terrain and the prize." [4]

But meanwhile, "Ignatius was assailed, in his cave, by frightful temptations. In the literal sense of the word, hell broke loose about him; the powers of evil raged and stormed, seeking to crush him under the weight of their wrath. At the same time he was afflicted by every form of the spiritual malady of scrupulosity, which tortured him to the point of desperation. . . . Ignatius spoke of his problems to various spiritual persons, but none was able to help him, as none had dealt with the adversary at such depths. In the end he triumphed over his scruples only by resolving firmly not to confess again sins which he had confessed before—to treat the past as really past." [5] For the rest, he derived the greatest help in his temptations from his reading, especially his reading of Thomas à Kempis' *Imitation of Christ*. "All his life he kept it beside him and read it over and over again. This is not difficult to believe, for the *Imitation* has something of the quality of daily bread: it never wearies the spiritual palate, and always nourishes. Ignatius's love for this humble work speaks in his favor; only a real Christian can be so attracted to Thomas à Kempis's sober teachings, wholly devoid, as they are, of artifice or equivocation.

"The *Imitation* produced a profound change in Ignatius. He realized now that holiness consisted of inner purification rather than in external mortification, as he had thought before. Gradually, therefore, he relaxed his excessive austerity. . . . From this time forward, Ignatius no longer confused the supernatural with the unnatural, or a love that was purified with a love that was merely benumbed.

"By this victory over negative asceticism, Ignatius achieved far greater spiritual depth. More than anything else, he now desired to attain to joy in God. And later, whenever he found a tendency to excessive mortification, he always opposed it." [6] To Francisco Borgia, Duke of Gandía, who was impatiently awaiting a propitious moment to detach himself from the world and become a militant missionary, Ignatius wrote:

"1) 'As to the hours to be spent in interior and exterior exercises, spend just half the time . . . devote the remaining half to study, the governing of your estates, and spiritual conversations, always managing to keep the spirit quiet and peaceful and ready to receive God. . . . It is a far greater virtue to be able to enjoy God at various occupations and places than at one alone.'

"2) 'As for fasting and abstinence . . . do not weaken the body, for when it is feeble, the internal organs cannot function properly. . . . We should love and care for our body as long as it helps our soul . . .'

"3) 'As for scourging our body for Our Lord, it is better to leave it alone. . . . Instead of trying to achieve some benefit from drawing blood, look closer for God . . . in tears provoked by contemplation of our own or of others' sins, or of the mysteries of Christ in this life or the other, or of the love of the Divine Persons. . . . Any one of these sacred gifts should be chosen in preference to corporeal acts. . . . With a sound mind in a sound body, everything becomes more sound.' " [7]

It so happens that the passage I have quoted, regarding *The Imitation of Christ,* has had a very special and very personal appeal to me: my mother always kept a copy of this book on her desk, close to a lamp and an easy chair, and read in it every night before she went to bed. I have followed her practice for nearly thirty years and have long since found, as Nigg so rightly says, that the book has in it something of the quality of daily bread—without which we cannot live.[8] I did not previously know, however, that one important aspect of its influence on Ignatius was its effect on his views regarding self-mortification, and this was one of far-reaching results. As far as I know, he was the first of the saints to recognize his body as the temple of his soul and to share this recognition with his followers. It was one of his greatest contributions to progressive Christianity.

There were many other manifestations of growing grace at Manresa. It was here that he "had his first taste of heavenly joys. Visions came upon him, unsolicited, irresistible, as they have always come upon the great visionaries of Christian history. Mostly they were trinitarian visions; as he himself relates, one day 'his understanding began to be elevated as though he saw the Holy Trinity under the figure of three keys.' Again, in his spiritual diary, he noted: 'I saw the divine being, or essence, in the form of a sphere, a little larger in appearance than the sun.' " [9]

It was also at Manresa that "Ignatius received the great illumination of his life. . . . He was on his way to the church of St. Paul, about one mile from Manresa, and he sat down for a moment at the roadside, looking toward the river that flowed below. 'As he sat, the eyes of his understanding began to open. He beheld no vision, but he saw and understood many things, spiritual as well as those concerning faith and learning. This took place with so great an illumination that these things appeared to be something altogether new.'

"This wholly unexpected experience was pivotal for Ignatius's whole development. He himself used the strongest possible terms to describe it, saying that it had made of him 'another man,' with a 'new understanding.' All the spiritual insights he had received during his whole life, he said later, could not compare with this single illumination. And he told Laynez[10] once that he had learned more in that hour than a hundred professors could have taught him. Ignatius, indeed, should be numbered not among the official theologians of the Church, but rather among the great visionaries who are granted a spiritual understanding of the mysteries of the Christian faith. The art of the discernment of spirits, first perceived but not yet learned at Loyola, was now gloriously consummated. Everything appeared new to him: this lapidary experience encompasses the whole of that 'illumination of existence' which modern philosophy vainly strives for. As for Ignatius, it caused him to fall on his knees in boundless thanksgiving before the nearest wayside cross.

"But his new knowledge had to be given form, lest it dissolve again into uncertainty. It took Ignatius almost ten years of inner preparation to achieve that goal. Meanwhile, the impression he had received was so powerful that he was compelled to put his thoughts on paper. He filled a whole notebook in this way—this was the first draft of the Spiritual Exercises." [11]

"This marvelous work is a drillbook of spiritual self-mastery. Under the guidance of a religious master-at-arms, the disciple is to exercise himself for four weeks in attempts to gain, by strenuous effort of will, a vivid consciousness of man's sinfulness, and of the life and saving work of Christ. The world as a battleground between his Lord and the powers of evil is to be made real to his imagination; and the great facts of salvation are to become part of his mental imagery. Never was there a more remarkable or a more successful attempt to awaken, control, and direct mental pictures. In the order which Ignatius was later to establish each member had to pass through the discipline thus prescribed; and its effects on most minds must have been an unforgettable quickening of the spiritual imagination by which what is usually fantasy was directed into definite pictures of great Christian verities. Loyola would use the visions of the spirit to the full; yet control and direct them absolutely." [12]

"The final version was to come much later, but in their original conception the Exercises are the fruit of the Manresan period. The truth of this statement is in no way affected by Ignatius's own statement that 'the Exercises were not composed all at one time, but things that he had observed in his own soul and found useful and which he thought would be useful to others he put into writing. . . .' " [13]

The famous Act of Contrition seems to belong to the earlier part of the stay at Manresa and the Prayer for Compliance to God's Will to a later period. It is, therefore, perhaps appropriate to quote them together as a further revelation of development.

ACT OF CONTRITION

"Pardon me, *O Perfections of my God,* for having preferred imperfect and vile creatures to *Thee!*

"Pardon me, *O Justice of my God,* for having outraged *Thee* by my crimes!

"Pardon me, *O Holiness of my God,* pardon me for having so long stained *Thy Sight's Purity* by my sins!

"Pardon me, *O Mercy of my God,* for having despised so long *Thy Mercy's Voice!*

"In deep sorrow and contrition, I cast myself at *Thy Feet:* have mercy on me: amen."

FOR COMPLIANCE TO GOD'S WILL

"*O Lord,* so great to all *Thy* servants: Dispose of my life, of my liberty, of all that pertains to me. O my *Creator:* Speak to *Thy* creature! Behold my soul before *Thee:* my will is as a scale in a state of perfectly equal balance, which shall waver to one side or the other only when *Thou* placest in it the weight of *Thy Will* or *Wish*. I ignore all natural inclinations. My will is suspended, and in a state of perfect indifference. I have but one will and desire: to obey, to please *Thee*. Enable me closely to approach to Thee, to lose none of *Thy Words*, to be better disposed for receiving of the Gifts of *Thy Divine* and *Supreme Goodness:* amen." [14]

Ignatius remained at Manresa for an entire year. Then he undertook another pilgrimage, this time much farther afield than the first: he went to Palestine by way of Venice and Rome, for, by now, he knew he would never again be satisfied with a horizon which limited him geographically. But he likewise realized that, to make the most of this, he must also widen his horizon scholastically. He returned to Spain and, at Barcelona, without shame or self-consciousness, enrolled in a school where he was put in a class with small children; his book learning was still so inadequate that he could not keep up with the more advanced students. But he learned fast and, from Barcelona, he went on to the excellent university at Alcalá de Henares and from there to the still greater university at Salamanca where he emerged, triumphant, from two bouts with the Inquisition. Then, at last, he believed himself ready for the Sorbonne and left for Paris.

He was nearly thirty, of course much older than most of his fellow students, and he remained in Paris nearly seven years before he earned his coveted degree as Master of Arts. But this seniority did not prove an impediment to friendships and one of these was with another Basque, by name Francis Xavier, whose mother was "the heiress of two ancient and noble families of Navarre" and whose father was a learned professor of law at the University of Bologna. "Francis himself as a boy was polite, gay and attractive. He was dark, athletic, ambitious, eager and quick to learn, and looked forward to a life at the court, or, like his older brothers, in the camp. After his earlier education in Navarre, he went at nineteen to the University of Paris, where he spent eleven years, first as a student of liberal arts, then as lecturer on philosophy. The young professor was recognized as gifted with brilliant intellectual ability. He was also a social favorite; but found himself between two fires in the matter of religious faith. On the one side was Protestantism, represented by the leaders and advocates of the new-born German Reformation; on the other Catholicism, stirred by the Spanish Reformation and by the fierce passions of the Inquisition, then under full headway in Spain and still moving in other countries. And on the Catholic side was Loyola, between whom and Xavier a strong attachment sprang up, and whose influence finally restrained young Francis from going Protestant." [15]

It is easy to understand that, despite the difference in their ages, Ignatius and Francis discovered that, in many ways, they were kindred spirits; and though Ignatius did not immediately succeed in arousing the interest of Francis in the Spiritual Exercises, this was only a matter of time.

Meanwhile, they must often have sung together the charming song composed in the thirteenth century by a fellow Basque, whose name had already been forgotten, but whose message lived on.

> "O little lark, you need not fly
> To seek your Master in the sky.
> He's near our native sod.
> Why should you sing aloft, apart?
> Sing to the Heaven of my heart,
> In me, in me, in me is God.
>
> "O travelers, passing in your car,
> Ye pity me, who come from far
> On dusty feet, rough shod.
> You cannot guess, you cannot know,
> Upon what wings of joy I go
> Who travel home with God.
>
> "Ships bring from far your curious case.
> Earth's richest morsels are your share,
> And prize of gun and rod.

At richer boards I take my seat,
Have dainties angels may not eat.
In me, in me, in me is God.

"O little lark, sing loud and long
To Him who gave you flight and song,
And me a heart of flame.
He loveth them of low degree,
And He hath magnified me,
And Holy, Holy, Holy is His name." [16]

When the meeting, with which this story began, took place at the Church of St. Denis, not only the vows of Dominic and Francis united them; their very hearts and souls were in unison.

As we have already learned, their primary hope and that of their companions was to set out for Jerusalem; but they had foreseen that circumstances might prevent this and were not unduly discouraged when their earliest journeyings ended otherwise. Ignatius went first to Spain to settle personal affairs and then to Venice, where the little company, now grown from six to ten members, gathered to meet him. Leaving him there, the others went on to Rome and were favorably received by Pope Paul III, who authorized the ordination to the priesthood of Ignatius and six of his companions, including Francis. This was good news with which to return to their leader. But since conditions in the Mediterranean still made a voyage to the Holy Land impractical, Ignatius decided that it was not the will of God he should go there, whatever the others should eventually do. Meanwhile, they would all go to Rome together and put their company, which they now called the Society of Jesus, at the disposal of the Holy See.

When the proposed Constitution was presented to the Pope, he was so impressed with it that he exclaimed, "Here is the finger of God!"—a great contrast to the discouraging reply that Dominic received when he presented the Constitution of his Order to Pope Innocent III. Part of Paul III's enthusiasm may have been due to the significant fact that to the three customary vows of poverty, chastity and obedience, a fourth was added—

special obedience to the Pope. It is also significant that the Order referred, as it still does, to its director as its general. From the beginning, the Jesuits considered themselves as Soldiers of Christ.

That Ignatius should be the first general, despite his protests, was a foregone conclusion; that he should spend practically all the rest of his life in Rome was less self-evident. Under the circumstances, some disappointment would have been natural; but none was voiced in his Hymn of Thanksgiving.

A Thanksgiving

"*O Lord God! Thou* art infinitely wise: I adore *Thee, Who* has borne with my ignorance.

"*O Lord God!* Thou are infinitely just: I adore *Thee, Who* has not chastised my iniquity.

"*O Lord God! Thou* art infinitely powerful: I adore *Thee, Who* hast deigned to spare my weakness.

"*O Lord God! Thou* art infinitely good: I adore *Thee, Who* hast pardoned me all my malice and my sins.

"*O Lord God:* I thank *Thee* that the Angels', who are of *Thy Justice,* avenging swords, have not slain me.

"*O Lord God:* I thank *Thee* because the Saints, *Thy* friends, have prayed and made intercession for me, who was *Thine* enemy.

"*O Lord God:* I thank *Thee* that *Thy* heavens, *Thy* stars, *Thy* sun, have not refused to shine on me. I thank *Thee* for having placed the whole of creation at my service: I have caused it to groan beneath the burden of my sin—and yet it has not risen up against me. I thank *Thee* that the very earth has not opened beneath my feet to precipitate me into the lowest depths of hell, where I indeed deserve to be eternally.

"I behold before me, O my *God,* the mystery of the infinite abyss of *Thy Mercy.* I return *Thee* thanks for having preserved my life until this day, for having granted me repentance for my sins.

"*O Lord God:* How great has been, how incomprehensible remains, *Thy Pity* for me! Amen." [17]

These are not the words of a thwarted man, but of one who is triumphant; and there is every reason why Ignatius should have felt that he had not failed, but succeeded in his lifework as a Knight of God. Under his leadership, the Company grew so rapidly that it was necessary to restrict the number eligible for membership and for some time this stood at sixty, though it was later enlarged. When Ignatius died, it had risen to a thousand, divided into twelve provinces, with over one hundred houses scattered over every part of the known world. For, though he did not go forth himself, he sent out his captains and his lieutenants far and wide; and the greatest of these was Francis Xavier. Ignatius had supplied the vision of a missionary life for his followers; but it was Francis who made it into a reality.

"Of Xavier many miracles we hear,
Ignatius did one greater—Xavier." [18]

For Francis went not only to all the places Ignatius had dreamed of going, but to many, many more. It has been truly said that "the story of his journeys is an epic of adventure."

". . . On April 7, 1541, his thirty-fifth birthday, he sailed aboard the *Santiago*—the Saint James—with two other fathers and the new Governor General of Portuguese India. The Portuguese colonial empire at this time was of great extent and prestige. From Lisbon to the Cape of Good Hope, from the Cape to India, from India to Malacca, from Indo-China to Japan, there was no port of importance that did not interest the Portuguese. Their trade was more than flourishing. From Mozambique they took gold dust and ivory, from Muscat and Oman on the Persian Gulf they shipped the goods of Central Asia. Goa, Ceylon, and Nagapatam were open doors to the treasures of India. Through Malacca and the Malay Peninsula they traded with Indo-China. In the Moluccas they established trading posts for the Spice Islands. Macao, near Canton, was the Portuguese center for commerce with China and Japan. It is difficult to conceive how such a small nation was able in less than half a century to dominate with its military and trading posts a seaboard of some eleven thousand miles. Love of money alone was not enough to explain this remarkable display of energy. Also important was heroic patriotism and religious fervor such as the desire to serve God in the far lands, like that which filled the heart of the young Navarrese in the service of the Portuguese king when he set sail for Goa, capital of the Portuguese colonial empire." [19]

After a year's voyage, six months of which were spent in Mozambique, Francis "arrived in Goa in May 1542 and went on from there to Cape Comorin in the south of India. Here he spent three years working among the pearl-fishers, or Paravas, of the Fishery Coast. From there he went on to the East Indies, to Malacca and the Moluccas, and, finally, in 1549 he set out for Japan. . . . Thus in ten years he traversed the greater part of the Far East. When one considers the conditions of travel, the means of transport, the delays and difficulties which beset him at every stage, it is, even physically, an astounding achievement. It is even more remarkable when one considers that he left behind him a flourishing church wherever he went and that the effects of his labors remain to the present day." [20]

Francis carried on a voluminous correspondence, much of which has fortunately been preserved. I have chosen a letter to the Society at Goa from which to quote:

"Last year, dearest brethren, I wrote to you from Cagoxima concerning our voyage, our arrival in Japan, and what had been done in the interests of Christianity up to that time. Now I will relate what God has done by our means since last year. On our arrival at the native place of our good Paul,[21] we were received very kindly indeed by his relations and friends. They all of them became Christians, being led by what Paul told them; and that they might be throughly confirmed in the truth of our religion, we remained in that place a whole year and more. In that time more than a hundred were gathered into the fold of Christ. The rest might have done so if they had been willing, without giving any offence to their kinsfolk or relations. But the bonzes admonished the prince . . . that if he allowed his people to embrace the Christian religion, his whole dominion would be destroyed. . . . For the law of God was contrary to the law of Japan, and . . . any who embraced that law would repudiate the holy founders of the ancient law of their forefathers. . . . Considering that the law of God was opposed and hostile to the law of his fathers, let him issue an edict forbidding, under penalty of death, that anyone in future should become a Christian. The prince was moved by this discourse of the bonzes, and issued the edict as they had requested.

"The interval after this was spent in instructing our converts, in learning Japanese, and in translating into that tongue the chief heads of the Christian faith. We used to dwell shortly on the history of the creation of the world . . . for instance, that God was the Maker and Creator of the universe, a truth which they were entirely ignorant of, and the other truths necessary for salvation, but principally the truth that God had taken on Himself the nature of man. . . . We translated diligently all the great mysteries of the life of Christ until His Ascension into heaven, and also the account of the last Judgment. We have now translated this book, for such it was, into Japanese with great labor, and have written it in our own characters. Out of this we read . . . to those who came to the faith of Christ, that the converts might know how to worship God and Jesus Christ with piety and to their souls' health. And when we went on to expound these things in our discourses, the Christians delighted in them very much, as seeing how true the things were which we had taught them. The Japanese are certainly of remarkably good dispositions, and follow reason wonderfully. They see clearly that their ancestral law is false and the new law of God true, but they are deterred by fear of their prince from submitting to the Christian religion.

"When the year came to an end, seeing the lord of the town to be opposed to all extension of our religion, we determined to pass to another place. We therefore bade farewell to our converts; they loved us so much that they . . . were very sorrowful at our departure. . . . We then went to another town, where the lord of the place received us very kindly; there we remained a few days, and made about a hundred Christians. . . .

"I charged Cosmo Torres with the care of these converts, and went on with Joam Fernández to Amanguchi, the seat of a very wealthy king. . . . The city contains more than ten thousand households; all the houses are of wood. We found many here . . . very desirous to become acquainted with the Christian law. We thought it best to preach twice a day in the streets and crossroads . . . speaking to the people about the Christian religion. Some of the noblemen also invited us to their houses, that they might hear about our religion with more convenience. They promised of their own accord, that if they came to think it better than their own, they would unhesitatingly embrace it. Many of them heard what we had to say about the law of God very willingly; some, on the other hand, were angry at it, and even went so far as to laugh at what we said. So, wherever we went through the streets of the city, we were followed by . . . boys of the lowest dregs of the populace, laughing at us and mocking us with some such words as these: 'There go the men who tell us that we must embrace the law of God in order to be saved, because we cannot be rescued from destruction except by the Maker of all things and by His Son! There go the men who declare that it is wicked to have more than one wife!'

"We had spent some days in this office of preaching, when the king . . . sent for us. . . . He asked us wherever did we come from? why had we come to Japan? And we answered that we were Europeans sent thither for the sake of preaching the law of God. . . . Then the king commanded us to explain to him the law of God. So we read to him a good part of our volume; and . . . he listened to us diligently and attentively . . . then he sent us away. We remained many days in that city, and preached to the people. . . . Many of them listened to the wonderful deeds of Christ with avidity, and when we came to His most bitter death, they were unable to restrain their tears. Nevertheless, very few actually became Christians.

"Finding . . . the fruit of our labors was small, we went on

to Meaco, the most famous city in all Japan. We spent two
months on the road, and passed through many dangers. . . .
When we arrived at Meaco, we waited for some days that we
might obtain leave to approach the king, and ask of him . . .
permission to publish the divine law in his kingdom. But we
found all ways of access to him . . . closed. As we discovered
that the edicts of the king were generally thought little of . . .
we laid aside our design of obtaining from him any such license
and I determined . . . to find out how disposed that city was
to receive the worship of Christ. But as the people were under
arms, and under the pressure of a severe war, I judged that the
time was most inopportune for the preaching of the Gospel. . . .

". . . We returned to Amanguchi, and we presented to the
king there the letters and presents which had been sent as
signs of friendship by the Governor of India and the Bishop
of Goa. The king was very much delighted . . . and offered us
a great amount of gold and silver. These gifts we sent back, and
then asked him if . . . he would give us leave to announce
the law of God to his people. . . . This he granted us with
the greatest goodwill.

"He . . . affixed edicts in the most crowded places of the
city, declaring . . . that the law of heaven should be announced in his dominions; and that it was lawful for any, who
desired to embrace it. At the same time, he assigned an empty
monastery for us to inhabit. A great many used to come to us
to this place for the sake of hearing about the new religion. We
used to preach twice a day, and after the sermon there was
always a good long dispute concerning religion. Thus we were
continually occupied either in preaching or in answering questions. . . . Those who asked us questions pressed them so
well home, that the answers we gave enabled them thoroughly
to understand the falsehood of their own laws and founders,
and the truth of the Christian law. After disputes and questionings for many days, they at last began to give in and betake
themselves to the faith of Christ.

"The first of all to do this were those who in the discussions
. . . had shown themselves our most strenuous adversaries.
. . . These new Christians told us with the greatest faithfulness

the mysteries, or rather the absurdities, of the Japanese religion.
. . . There are as many as nine sects in Japan, and they are
very different one from another in their teaching and ordi-
nances. When we got to know the opinions of these sects, we
began to look up arguments by which to refute them. So we
used to press hard by daily questions and arguments the sorcerer
bonzes and other enemies of the Christian law, and we did this
so effectually, that at last they did not venture to open their
mouths against us when we attacked and refuted them.

"When the Christians saw the bonzes convicted and silenced
they were of course full of joy. . . . On the other hand, the
heathen, who were present at these discussions, were greatly
shaken in their own religion, seeing the systems of their forefathers giving way. The bonzes were much displeased at this,
and . . . they began to accuse them severely for leaving their
ancestral religion to follow a new faith. But the others answered that they embraced the Christian law because . . . it
was more in accordance with nature than their own, and
because they found that we satisfied their questions while the
bonzes did not. . . .

"The Japanese have a very high opinion of the wisdom of
the Chinese, whether as to the mysteries of religion or as to
manners and civil institutions. They used to make that a principal point against us, that if things were as we preached, how
was it that the Chinese knew nothing about them? After many
disputations and questionings, the people of Amanguchi began
to join the Church of Christ. . . . In the space of two months
quite as many as five hundred have become Christians. The
number is daily being added to; so that there is great cause for
joy, and for thanking God that there are so many who embrace
the Christian faith, and who tell us all the deception of the
bonzes, and the mysteries contained in their books and taught
by their sects. For those who have become Christians used to
belong, one to one sect, another to another; the most learned
of each of them explained to us the institutions and rules of
his own way of belief. If I had not had the work of these converts to help me, I should not have been able to become sufficiently acquainted with, and so attack, these abominable reli-

gions of Japan. It is quite incredible how much the Christians love us. They are always coming to our house to ask whether we have anything at all which we wish them to do for us. All the Japanese appear naturally very obliging; certainly the Christians among them are so very good to us that it would be impossible to exceed their extreme kindness and attentiveness.

"May God in His mercy repay them with His favor, and give us all His heavenly bliss! Amen. [Amanguchi, July 1551.][22]

The cheerfulness which had distinguished Francis as a boy remained an attractive and outstanding characteristic and illumined the sound common sense of his riper years. In writing to a personal friend, he said, "When you have a lot of engagements, and can't discharge them all, comfort yourself by doing what you can. And give many thanks to the Lord that you are in a place where the many engagements come to you, and all in the service of the Lord God, and keep you from being idle, even if you wish to be." This is advice which everyone laboring under present day tension—as most of us are!—would do well to read, mark, learn and inwardly digest. The life that is too full is greatly to be desired over the life that is too empty, and many of us, who feel hurried and harried all the time, are apt to forget this. Even if we remember it, we do not always do so with thanksgiving that we are in a place where many engagements come to us, or comfort ourselves with the thought that we have done the very best we could in discharging them all.

Moreover, Francis' advice to "men laboring under disheartening circumstances and among an indifferent and hostile population" is applicable to many whose lives are cast in pleasanter places. "If the folk love you and get on well with you, you are doing great service to God. Learn to forgive their weaknesses very patiently. Put it to you [say to yourself] that if they are not good now they will be some day [!]. And if you don't accomplish with them all you wish, be contented with what you can do. I do so." Alas! We are not prone to forgive very patiently the weaknesses of other folk, even those who love us. The lesson of the mote and the beam is one of the hardest to learn.

In more exalted vein is Francis' hymn which begins, "My God, I love Thee!" The letters, whether to his disciples or his friends, are almost entirely factual. The hymn, though underlined with fact, is an outcry of deep emotion:

"My God, I love Thee! not because
    I hope for heaven thereby;
Nor because those who love Thee not
    Must burn eternally.

"Thus, O my Jesus, thou didst me
    Upon the cross embrace!
For me didst bear the nails and spear
    And manifold disgrace.

"And griefs and torments numberless
    And sweat of agony,
Yea, death itself—and all for one
    That was Thy enemy.

"Then why, O blessèd Jesus Christ,
    Should I not love Thee well!
Not for the hope of winning heaven
    Nor of escaping hell!

"Not with the hope of gaining aught,
    Not seeking a reward;
But as Thyself has lovèd me
    O Everlasting Lord!

"E'en so I love Thee and will love
    And in Thy praise will sing—
Solely because Thou art my God
    And my eternal King!" [23]

It has been said that "St. Francis Xavier was perhaps the most famous missionary who ever lived, apart from the Apostles themselves. . . . Against enormous odds, he succeeded in making a considerable number of converts among all classes. [Some authorities place this as high as ten thousand a month and, according to the statistics of the time, more than forty thousand were baptized in four years.] Not content with these labors, he intended to approach the Celestial Kingdom itself but was overtaken by death before he could carry out his plan." [24] "He died abandoned with but one companion, without the sacraments or Christian burial. But within a few weeks his body was recovered and found to be perfectly incorrupt. It was brought to Goa and received there with a devotion and an enthusiasm which showed that the people had already recognized him as a saint. . . ." [25] Nearly four hundred years later, Pope Pius X— himself since canonized—proclaimed Francis Patron Saint of all Missions, thus giving official sanction to what had long been general popular recognition.[26]

Part III
THE WORLD WIDENS

8

Francis Solano, "Wonder Worker of the New World"

I

ST. FRANCIS SOLANO has been called "The Wonder Worker of the New World" and "the most spectacular apostle who ever walked the American earth." Both designations are appropriate; neither is exaggerated.

Like so many other outstanding Spanish missionaries of the Middle Ages and the Renaissance—Dominic, Ignatius, Xavier, Borja, Lull—he was the scion of an aristocratic family and, as in the case of two of the others, the name given him in baptism had been chosen in the hope that he might merit the special protection of his patron saint, Francis of Assisi—a hope that was unquestionably fulfilled. And in this case, even the surname seemed prophetic. The family coat of arms "featured a splendrous sun entangled in a network of seven serpents. In old Spanish, 'solano' means 'the wind which blows from the sunrise.' Fray Francisco Cabre, struck by a series of coincidences, asks: 'Did it [the escutcheon] not presage that *this* great Solano was to become the felicitous Sun of Peru, land of the sons of the Sun?' "

Very probably it did. As I have often said before and am quite likely to say often again, what we call coincidences are more often than not part of a divine pattern, and the warp and woof of this pattern were favorable by background, birth and breeding. Francisco Solano's father, Don Mateo Sánchez Solano, had been chosen governor of Montilla, the capital of an Andalusian marquisate, by his fellow citizens, "because they respected him for an integrity that carried over into civil as well as religious life." [1] Francisco's mother, Doña Ana Jiménez, was known as "la Noble," not because of her exalted rank, but because of her "excellence and piety. . . . The Solano home was one of Spain's best, wherein the security and education of the children [there were three sons] were the first considerations of the splendid parents. Long before Francisco's enrollment in school, he had formed many of the ideals and attitudes which were to accompany him through life." [2]

His formal education began at the Jesuit Seminary at Montilla, where he went as a day pupil. He was personally attractive: a straight, tall boy with dark coloring and remarkably fine eyes, even for an Andalusian. He proved popular with his classmates and outstanding as a student of literature and the sciences. But his greatest asset, culturally speaking, was undoubtedly his talent for music, which found joyous expression in two media: he had a naturally good singing voice, which was carefully trained, and he learned to play the violin, which quickly became his chosen instrument. He was fond of gardening, a fondness which, like his love of music, was to prove lifelong; and we are told that he discovered one of the best times for singing was when he was alone in the garden "planting and cultivating the flowers that bloomed so luxuriantly in Andalucía, or when he was weeding and watering the fruit trees, which stood, row upon row, in his father's *huertos* [orchards]. . . . Of course, he did not at all think of himself as alone. Our Lord was always there. No one knew this better than Francisco. Talking with God, which is prayer; playing his small fiddle while he rested; or singing to His glory while he worked at the digging, planting and watering which kept his growing body fit—all these things brought the boy an immensely desired closeness to God.

"Francisco graduated first in his class. He was the pride of the *colegio,* as much for his great spirit as for his intellectual gifts and achievements. If his admiring and devoted professors had hoped that his future would brighten their ranks, they

were too conscientious to bring any pressure upon him. They
recognized him as one of the unquestionably chosen, and were
well aware that his remarkable erudition would never tend to
incline him to any of the careers which were now open to him
in the world. Though they must have been sorely tempted, they
were too enlightened to presume to intervene in the destiny of
this pupil whose life was already irrevocably in God's hands.
Their natural and rightful zeal for the acquisition of a member
so eminently qualified to uphold the high standards of their
brilliar ' Society was secondary to the divine plan, which they
realized would be manifested soon enough. They knew that
since 'such a vocation cannot come without God, it has no need
of our counsels nor of our approvals and, moreover, that it is
a dangerous impiety to oppose ourselves to the Divine Will.'
So the fine Jesuits who had guarded and instructed his youth
were content to let our Lord lead Francisco Solano where He
would. They gave the young man their blessings and bade him
farewell with the assurance that all their prayers and love went
with him.

"On Francisco's part there were no perplexities, questions
moments of indecision. The whole of his twenty years had been
a preparation for the religious life. His intelligence and its
cultivation had only deepened his natural humility, his love
of concord, his devotion to his fellow man, his appreciation of
the simple beauties which may be captured in this world
through selflessness. The great treasures of nature, music, and
the literature of inspiration which he had made his own were all
means of praising God with the felicity that is His due. These
priceless gifts, lovingly shared with one's brothers, spread and
intensified the happiness which impelled one, in gratitude, to
search out opportunities for the personal sacrifice that alone
could adequately express what was in one's heart.

"Nothing good had ever been withheld from Francisco, and
he was incapable of withholding anything of himself from God.
. . . Francisco's heart and his will had never desired other
than the chance to give it all back, along with his very being,
to the Giver of all, and, for love of Him, to the millions of His
earthly sons to whom, for His own inexplicable reasons, He had

granted fewer and lesser favors. These were the poor, the sick, the ignorant, the evil. Had not Francisco always possessed the most holy example for what he knew he must surely do in behalf of these, his 'brothers in Christ'? Moreover, had he not been dedicated, even before his birth, to that same San Francisco de Asís who had ever made the most tender use of the flowers, the songs, and all the little creatures of nature in praise of their Creator, his Master? The very name borne by this scion of the noble Solanos had marked out his inevitable and irrevocable path. Such were the things which now led him straight to the portal of Montilla's Franciscan monastery.

" 'What do you seek, brother?' With these words Fray Francisco Angulo, the Father Guardian of La Recolección, opened the fateful interview that had been requested by young Solano.

" 'Padre, I humbly beg the habit of my Father, St. Francis, that I may serve God and save my soul.'

"La Recolección had been founded in Montilla in the year 1516. For half a century it had been an integral part of the life of the town, and a source of true sanctity. The house was renowned for its strict regimen, which closely reproduced the perfection of the Order's primitive days when its great founder had given the consummate example—which the friars of La Recolección followed unremittingly—of obedience, absolute poverty, chastity, apostolic charity and supernatural sacrifice. . . . The Montilla Franciscans, however, did not satisfy themselves with 'enclosing inside their hearts' these virtues that were their precious, special offerings to the Crucified. For the glory of God, they also went forth joyfully from La Recolección to preach St. Francis' 'Paz y Bien' throughout the surrounding countryside. In this way they came to know their people well, and would certainly have been acquainted with Doña Ana Jiménez, that fine lady who also called St. Francis, 'my Father.' Nor would they have been unaware of the remarkable piety and excellence of the son she had placed under his protection. Nevertheless, the Father Guardian regarded this young man before him with the utmost calm, according him exactly the same attention he would have given any other appli -

cant. All must be warned of the seriousness and magnitude of
the responsibilities entailed by the privilege they sought.

" 'Have you thought well? Take notice that the life of the
religious in our *conventos* is exceedingly hard. You will not be
able to enjoy many human satisfactions that another mode of
life would procure for you. Have you thought well, Francisco?'

" '*Sí*, Padre, I have thought well and I am not counting on
my own weak forces to keep me faithful to my vocation, but
only on the aid of God's grace.'

"This reply should have satisfied Father Angulo as to the disinterested desire for the religious life, the humility and the
soundness of spiritual insight of almost any honest-seeming
youth. But it did not follow that it automatically opened the
doors of La Recolección to Francisco Solano. There were certain tests to which the young applicants were invariably subjected, and no exception was made in this case. Francisco submitted himself to this ordeal with eager good will and perfect
simplicity, and, as might be expected, gave complete satisfaction
to the judges.

"It was sometime during the month of April, 1569, that his
lifelong patron, St. Francis, with a joy that would be eternal,
received into his great family the second-born son of Doña Ana
la Noble." [3]

II

Perhaps it was because Francisco Solano was a musician
rather than a writer that so few documents have come down to
us that can authentically be attributed to him, though unquestionably there must have been others which are lost, strayed or
stolen. But fortunately his first biographer, Padre Córdoba y
Salinas, knew him personally and has left us a description of
him as he appeared when a novice at La Recolección.

"He distinguished himself over those of his time in humility,
abstraction, inviolable silence, prompt obedience and the total
mortification of all his inclinations, and in such a manner that
he could well have said with St. Paul: 'The world is crucified
for me and I for it.' . . .

"The year of probation and novitiate completed with such a grace of virtues that they lighted up his soul as stars light up the firmament, he was admitted to the Order, making his profession on the Day of St. Mark the Evangelist after special preparations and penances with which to make of his person an offering and a sacrifice pleasing in the eyes of God. . . . The calendar date of Francisco's profession, which was April 25, 1570, seems most significant, for on that day we read in the Gospel according to St. Luke: 'And He said to them: "The harvest indeed is great, but the laborers are few. Pray therefore the Lord of the harvest to send forth laborers into His harvest. . . ."'" [4]

Francisco spent three years of theological study at La Recolección before going elsewhere. Then he was sent to the convent of Santa María de Loreto, near Seville, to begin a course in philosophy. And it was here after at least three years of study that he finally celebrated his first Mass, on the feast day of his patron saint—October 4.[5] The celebration took place not in the great church itself but, by his own humble choice, "in the tiny, primitive chapel of Our Lady of the Olive, which stood in its shadows." [6] His mother, whose health was failing and who had lost her sight, was not able to be with him, except in spirit, and this was a source of great grief to them both; but his father and many of his close friends were present to share in the exaltation of his great moment.

Until then, aside from his spirituality, it was his musical achievements that made him most noteworthy. He had assisted in all the offices and duties of the cloisters at La Recolección; and at Loreto he had immediately been appointed choirmaster and, as "a leading Gregorian enthusiast of his time" he had "spared no pains" to give perfect renditions of ritual music. Now his eloquence as an orator began to make itself manifest and he was sent hither and yon to preach the Gospel. Don Mateo died while he was on one of these missionary trips, and it was a source of sorrow to him that he had not been a solace to his father in these last hours, as it would have been to any devoted son; but when he was transferred to still another convent, this time to Arrizafa, near Córdoba, he was given permission to break the journey by a visit to his mother, Doña Ana, on his way to his new post.

"He set out on bare feet and in the shabby habit he invariably selected for his apparel, to walk the dusty roads which wound over and around the hills, dipping into and out of the fertile valleys of Andalucía. Through its green orchards and across its pleasant, sun-dappled streams, he took his way—back to his birthplace. . . .

"He came at last, weary and smudged with the dirt and heat of the road, to the door of his childhood home—to the door that opened below the splendid graven sun which formed the Solano coat of arms.

"His mother was in the garden. There among the flowers he had cultivated as a lad, the travel-stained *fraile* approached her quietly, that he might not startle the blind old lady from whom he had received his physical form, his earliest lessons, and his love of virtue. Before him he saw the fragile being who, having implored their father, St. Francis, for her little son's lifelong protection, had also willingly blessed the separation that had placed him in St. Francis' service forever. This lonely, aging mother, cut off now from sight of the beloved face and the verdant beauty which surrounded her, was another who knew what it meant to sacrifice all for love.

"She had not known that he was on his way to her, but she needed no more than his first low-pitched syllables to tell her who it was. What surcease of grief must have come in that moment, what joy for both these gentle, devoted hearts! How comforting to Doña Ana's to hear that her son would be lodged close at hand in La Recolección for several days before continuing on to his new station. Already her spirits were reviving from her recent sorrow." [7]

He lingered for a few days at Montilla and, with the permission of the superior at La Recolección, went into the streets to beg for alms, thus following literally in the footsteps of his patron. He also performed the first of the many miracles with which he is credited, healing first a sick child and next a crippled mendicant. Then he went on to Arrizafa where, very shortly and over his strong protests, he was appointed Father of Novices. . . .

"The Order, desirous that its novices in other foundations might benefit from Francisco Solano's inspired guidance, directed his transfer, with no modification of functions, to the Convento de San Francisco del Monte. This house was situated within the first range of the Sierra Morena mountains, several leagues distant from any other human habitation, where the solitary grandeur of the wild peaks, cliffs and gorges offered aids and no distractions for the meditations of the Fathers and Brothers stationed there. It made an ideal spot for a novice training center." [8]

Despite the satisfaction he gave to his superiors and his novices, Francisco himself was "never really at ease" in his post as Guardian, "for he never felt it to be his true calling, nor even that he was capable of discharging a responsibility of such exactitude in a wholly satisfactory manner. He frequently renewed his petitions for release from this charge, and finally his superiors acceded to his desire. He was forthwith returned to the pulpits of Andalucía, where his sermons were again heard by the people to their great benefit. Unquestionably he missed the peace and other-worldliness of the long, quiet, sun-drenched days at the mountain retreat, but he had always recognized that his real function was in the missions. If as yet he had been powerless to win his heart's deepest desire, the dangerous and difficult mission to pagan lands, he would endeavor to substitute for it this preaching to his countrymen, an activity which was certainly not without consolations to his missionary's heart.

"It is quite likely that the greatest of all Fray Francisco's gifts was his genius for preaching. . . . When he was sent from San Francisco del Monte to preach it was his custom to stroll about the towns until he spotted a group of children gathered together in play. For the little ones he had a delightful surprise: from the big, loose sleeve of his habit, he would draw out his violin and play the melodies and rhythms always so enchanting to Spanish hearts, young or old. As soon as the penetrating sweetness of the violin had drawn a large enough company of children to satisfy him, he would put down the instrument and begin to talk to them. He might start with stories about *El Niño Santo,* and these soon led into a lesson in Christian Doctrine; or perhaps he would coach them in the principal prayers of the Church. Finally, this tall, friendly *fraile* who stood before them in the worn and rumpled robe of 'our Father St. Francis,' tucked the violin under his chin once more to play his own accompaniment while he sang the more popular religious songs which the children already knew or could easily learn.

"By this time, of course, such a novelty on their familiar streets had attracted a number of adults. As they approvingly observed the good friar's attentions to the youngsters, little did they realize that they themselves were the main objective of this effort, or that the message he carried for their ears was of an altogether different character. But as he commenced to direct his words to them, they lingered to listen. . . .

"His preaching terminated in any given place, he solicited alms as became the humility of St. Francis' true son, and then promptly set out to cover the long leagues that he must trudge back to the monastery in the mountains." [9]

III

"One of the greatest tribulations during Francisco Solano's time was the suffering that periodically swept through society because of '*la Peste*.' It would seem that 'the Pest' could mean any one of several forms of plague to which the people were then extremely vulnerable. Medicine was still in a rather primitive state of development and the science of sanitation, as we know it today, almost nonexistent. Thus there were very few controls which might be applied to disease when it appeared in epidemic proportions to ravage the nation. . . . In 1583 Andalucía crumpled beneath the mighty scourge of the bubonic plague. In no part of the distressed province had this peculiarly revolting and usually fatal affliction hit with such force as in Montoro and its environments. . . . Knowing of the suffering and terror now being sustained by the *Monto-*

renses, whom Fray Francisco had so often served as preacher, confessor and father, made it impossible for him to remain quietly in the semi-security of the Sierra Morena. He immediately sought the Father Guardian's permission to proceed to the stricken city to offer whatever aid he could, both physical and spiritual.

"This was not a sacrifice his Superior could well refuse, though his consent was given with sadness and probably very real fear. For actually, this permission approximated a death sentence for the beloved brother who was now his subject. However, God's will must surely accord with so compassionate a gesture, and at least Fray Francisco would not be entering the death trap of Montoro alone. His friend, the good Fray Buenaventura, had petitioned the privilege of being his companion on this dangerous mission of mercy.

"In Montoro the two Franciscans found that frightful conditions prevailed. This most dreaded of diseases had achieved terrorizing proportions. Deaths were so numerous that those who were still unstricken, and so able to give aid, found it impossible to secure sufficient supplies for the interment of each day's new avalanche of corpses. Furthermore, so few priests had survived that there was no means of guaranteeing the Last Sacraments to console and prepare the souls of the dying. But with the appearance of these two men of God in the habits that proclaimed them to be the sons of St. Francis, hope also walked into Montoro. . . .

"They were given the direction of the hospitals. If they could not manage to conquer *la Peste,* they could still bring a semblance of order out of chaos by ministering to the doomed, who would know the blessed solace of a Christian death through their offices. . . . Without a moment's delay, these great-spirited Fathers attacked their gigantic work for the stricken in an atmosphere of calm and imperturbable cheerfulness. . . .

"It must have been a heart- as well as a body-breaking struggle, this heroic undertaking which burdened them night and day with all the labors and responsibilities of doctors, nurses and sanitary crews, but if so, they took no notice of that. Rather,

seeing their diligence frequently successful in saving lives which
would indubitably have been lost without their unceasing attentions, they praised God and knew great joy. And when, as
also happened, they understood that despite all their care,
fatigue, love and prayers for the recovery of one of these poor
unfortunates, the end was at hand, Fray Francisco contrived to
make even death an occasion of happiness. Tenderly he heard
the confession of the dying one and administered the Sacraments which eased the soul and gave it confidence of eventual
salvation. . . .

"Those who recovered were no less the beneficiaries of final
loving attentions, final rituals from their healer and father, Fray
Francisco. For when he was satisfied that the convalescents had
made a full recovery, he accompanied them to the banks of the
nearby Río Guadalquivir and gave them the baths by which
he might be assured they would not return to their homes only
to spread the infection among their dear ones. Then he provided them with new clothing. When those who had been so
desperately, so perilously ill, stood before him cleansed of
la Peste and restored to normal life, as it seemed, miraculously,
while their hearts overflowed with gratitude—then, truly, it
was the hour of thanksgiving. At this point the jubilant fraile
lifted on high the great cross which he bore through the town
at the head of the procession he always arranged to conduct
the cured to their own doors. . . .

"With so many imperative calls upon the time and strength
of the two Franciscans that they had even been almost completely without sleep, there was probably little opportunity
for them to enjoy many moments in each other's company.
Nevertheless, at first, Fray Francisco undoubtedly took much
comfort and encouragement from the knowledge that his labors
were shared by the understanding spirit and the heroic cooperation of Fray Buenaventura. We say 'at first,' because it was not
long before the good brother Samaritan sickened—one more
victim of la Peste!

"If Fray Francisco attended all so lovingly, we know what
must have been his devotion to this cohermano who had been
his companion in every risk and self-denial. But the battle was

lost, all the same—and as he held the dying Buenaventura in his arms until the end, it must have been difficult indeed to smile through the tears in praise of Him Who always knows what is best for His poor children. . . .

"Certainly the end of the suffering was not yet in sight. The next to go down under the contamination was Francisco himself. . . . While he prepared himself for a holy death, our Lord was preparing something else entirely—the new fields on earth which were to be cultivated for Him by Francisco's faithful and heroic labors!

"In a comparatively short time, then, he recognized that the plague was releasing its grip. To the amazement of all, he made a rapid recovery and was soon back on his rounds again, caring for others. He remained at his post until *la Peste* finally died out completely, then bade the grateful *Montorenses* an affectionate adiós and took the lonely road back to the peaceful solitude that enveloped San Francisco del Monte." [10]

However, we have no sooner associated him with one center, than we are told he has been sent to another. The next in sequence was the Monastery of San Luis, dedicated to Louis, the King of France, founded during the reign of Ferdinand and Isabella and located near Granada. Here he asked that he might be put in charge of the infirmary and since there could be no question of his suitability for the post, his request was granted. But as the work at the convent was not sufficiently onerous "to suit his spirit and to prove his powers" he extended his activities to embrace the hospital of San Juan de Dios in Granada and the city jails.

"But he soon saw that all this labor by which he had, in part, meant to secure his own humble obscurity was only increasing the veneration in which he was held by his brothers; and, as a matter of fact, his fame for heroic virtue had already spread throughout the whole of Spain. He felt that somehow he must separate himself from this atmosphere of adulation, if this could be done without withdrawal from the life of self-immolation and sacrifice which was now a necessity to him.

"Pondering the possibilities, he quite naturally found his thoughts turning once more to the advantages inherent in the life of a missionary to Africa. In that vast, dark and desolate continent might he not be able to pursue his work in the manner now both natural and imperative for him, while also hiding his deeds in the isolation that distance and the wilderness would automatically provide? Surely he had many precedents for this inclination among those who had worn the habit in which he himself had now passed almost half of his years. Hadn't their founder St. Francis wished to dedicate himself to the spiritual conquest of Africa? Indeed, he had longed for martyrdom there. When this was denied him, had he not animated his earliest sons to undertake the same cause? The five heroes whose bones had lain close to Francisco Solano at Arrizafa— martyrs of Morocco—had been his intimately contemplated evidence of the founder's intense concern for Africa. He knew that the first five to die for Christ in the land of the Musselman had likewise inspired the great dream of emulation in St. Anthony of Padua. Francis of Assisi had been cheated of the privilege of shedding his blood in the infidel's country; illness had sent St. Anthony back after his arrival at the same destination. Why could not Francisco Solano substitute for his beloved Father and Brother in the attainment of the intentions of both?

"Fired by this ambition, he sought the necessary permission. In his case, it was obedience which was to prove the direct obstacle. His solicitation for the African apostolate was refused by the Franciscan Father General. In the long view, however, God's hand would be seen in this most disappointing denial.

"Felipe Segundo, who had now occupied the throne of Spain for some thirty-two years (or since Carlos V had abdicated in favor of his son in 1556), had continued his father's commendable work for Spain's native American subjects, seeking to protect them by just laws,[11] and dutifully insisting upon the many religious missions which would guarantee their Christianization. In the latter cause, at least, he had displayed even more diligence than Charles himself. Such concern on the part of the monarch had worked to the inestimable benefit of his subjects—both the indigenes and the Spaniards—now dwelling in America, particularly in the section known as New Spain.[12]

There was still, however, much to be done for the vast reaches of wilderness which constituted the viceroyalty of Perú.[13] The mere fact that the land incorporated in this unwieldly division had been discovered and conquested somewhat later than New Spain was one of the reasons why Perú now stood in greater need of missionaries than did the former, better consolidated colony, where the Franciscans had been laboring with magnificent results for sixty-five years.[14] But other factors contributed to the special difficulties presented by the South American region.

"In the first place, its peoples—except for the Incas and those who had been dominated and influenced by this great highland race—were broken up into countless tribes of decidedly less intelligence and social development than that which distinguished the Mayas, the Aztecs, the Tarascans and other Indian stocks of Mexico. These South American Indians had, therefore, proved less sensitive to reason and even to the example of the missionaries who had so far labored in vain to reach and convert them. . . . That this should have been possible, brings to our attention another extreme handicap in the colonization of Perú—the disadvantages of its geography. The towering heights and icy slopes of the Andes, which served to slice off the narrow Pacific coastal plain from the vast interior reaches of the viceroyalty, were more than sufficiently difficult to conquer. But this was a simple matter compared to the thousands of steaming miles of reptile-infested jungle, the tropical and subtropical wastelands that stretched away in three directions from the eastern base of the Andes to cover by far the greater part of an enormous continent.

"Hundreds—even thousands—of *frailes* could not hope to traverse all of such a terrain (especially on foot, as the Franciscans, at least, were required to do),[15] let alone make contact with the cunningly elusive savages, who could hide themselves for generations, if it pleased them to do so, in the swamps and thickets which were almost impenetrable for Europeans. The forests were so dense and so extensive that they might easily have provided cover for millions more Indians than actually inhabited Perú.

"But Felipe II was determined that all of these obstacles must be overcome. He believed it was the sacred obligation of Spain to complete the full Christianization of America—and thus to fulfill the promise of the great Queen Isabel to Pope Alexander VI, in return for which her nation had been granted its claim to the New World. The ruler of Spain therefore persisted in importuning the religious Orders to send forth new missions. He was particularly determined that these should be composed largely of Franciscans, whose American labors, from the beginning, had been seen to be the most fruitful.

"At San Luis, Francisco heard the reports of his king's latest urgent demands on this score—and they stimulated new hope. Why should not *he* be one of those to answer the American call? Such an act would serve his personal ends quite as well, or even better, than his rejected plan to proceed to less distant Africa. The works of evangelization and charity combined to form the central objective of his earthly existence. In view of the pressure which had lately been increased in the sovereign's appeals to the Order for a fresh supply of missionaries in behalf of Perú, it was possible that his superiors might reverse their prohibition and permit his departure from Spain. And how altogether suitable if he could go out from San Luis, the *convento* founded during the reign of Spain's great Catholic queen, to forward the fulfillment of her vow and to promote a work which, more than any other, had distinguished her most meritorious reign! He therefore renewed his petitions for a mission apostolate to the pagans—specifically, for permission to join that Franciscan company which was scheduled to embark for Perú early in the new year.

"At last, to his great joy, his request was granted. He was free to proceed to America! His lifelong desire for the labors of a missionary in the far places of the earth would soon be a reality. Joined to this felicity would be the blessing of escape from the veneration which so weighted his spirit at this time that he had begun to regard his fame as a threat to his usefulness in his native land. As a safeguard against the possibility of a recurrence of this problem in Perú, he now welcomed the opportunity of serving under the orders of Padre Baltasar de

Navarra, who was the *Comisario* for the province of Tucumán. Fray Francisco knew that this region was the most sparsely colonized of all the viceroyalty; that it had not even yet been fully explored. This would take care of his need for solitude, or at least separate him from the undesired attentions of his own kind.

"There were many pagans in Tucumán, of course, nomads who roamed the mountain- and forest-locked haunts of their ancestors, by such means managing to keep well beyond the power of the white men who had overrun the coastal regions. The Indians' attitude was natural enough; the tragedy lay in the fact that in hiding from the white men they were also hiding from the white men's All-Powerful God—or thought they were.

"Tucumán was the place which could be expected to offer the greatest obstacles and difficulties for evangelical labors, and the most extreme personal hardship. Does it seem, then, a strange or unnatural choice? To Francisco Solano it was the *only* choice that could satisfy his deepest needs, and he made it with eagerness and joy.

"Soon it was time to face the reality of the moment toward which it now seemed Francisco Solano's whole life had been pointed—the moment of departure. The years of waiting for the mission assignment had been long, very long. But now they were over; and suddenly time had been cut short. There was barely enough left for the good-bys that he knew almost certainly would be final. He must say farewell to his Franciscan brothers, the only companions of his adult years; to Spain, always the loveliest country on earth for those born within her borders; to the wonderful little mother who had now lived quite alone in the dark night of her blindness for at least a decade. Such partings could not have been easy. Nevertheless, with Adiós on his lips and in his heart, he circled Andalucía, impressing her beautiful panoramas upon his memory. This trip soon brought him home to Montilla and the farewell between mother and son which must be made to suffice for the rest of their lives. . . .

"During this journey of love and farewell, he passed through the cities and towns in which he had fought for the bodies and souls of his countrymen wherever he had found sickness or sin. He gazed upon the corners and plazas where he had sung and played his violin for the children, where he had thundered the word of God to their parents. And very soon, as it seemed, he had seen it all and taken his leave of all; for now, time really had run out!

"The ship which was to carry Francisco Solano across the vast Atlantic was under the orders of Don García Hurtado de Mendoza, fourth Marqués of Cañete and Perú's new Viceroy. With the rest of a large Franciscan mission, numerous *caballeros*, and seven hundred soldiers, Fray Francisco went aboard at Sanlúcar de Barrameda, on February 28, 1589. The definite departure from Spain was effected from Cádiz on the eighth of March, just two days before Solano's fortieth birthday." [16]

IV

The voyage lasted three months before the travelers saw land again. Then they sighted a small island [17] and, though they were still far from their eventual destination, the captain agreed to anchor for a day, in order that those who wished to do so might go ashore. A boat was lowered and for several hours went back and forth, carrying happy passengers.

Probably none of them enjoyed this pleasure trip more than Francisco Solano. Although he had worked in hospitals and preached to crowds, his life on the whole had been one of quiet and seclusion, with a background of culture and religion. He had grown up in an enlightened and pious home and, when he left this, it had been to enter a convent. Since then, he had changed his headquarters five times, but each time for another convent; his close companions had always been other priests, never soldiers, sailors and adventurers. There were, to be sure, a few missionaries besides himself aboard ship, but these were more or less swallowed up in the motley crew. Francisco had been able to serve as the ship's doctor and chaplain and that had given him a measure of reward; but inevitably he had found the crowding, the noise, the turbulence, the worldliness of the ship something of an endurance test. A desert or a jungle where there was at least fresh air and quietude would have been less of one. It was not strange that he wanted to linger on the beach as long as he could; what he did not realize was that he and several others had lingered longer than they should. The captain, who evidently did not count noses very carefully, thought that all the excursionists were back on board; he weighed anchor and sailed away.

This happened at dusk and it was not until two o'clock the following morning that the oversight was discovered. Rather tardily, the captain missed a familiar figure, his favorite *fraile*, and hastily sent the little boat out again. Meanwhile, the refugees, with the exception of Francisco Solano, had become the prey of terror; they visualized possible cannibalism and probable starvation. Francisco visualized only a welcome chance for martyrdom, the opportunity for which he was so avidly seeking. It was with the greatest difficulty he refrained from shouting with joy, and then only because his terrified companions pointed out that if murderous savages were within earshot, they would hear him and then everyone would certainly be killed. Inevitably it must have taken some time after the rescue for him to be restored to their good graces!

The episode would hardly be worth mentioning were it not for the fact that it seems to be the only recorded instance of a failure on Francisco Solano's part to think of others before himself, and this is perhaps a wholesome proof that he was quite human, after all.

The next stop was the beautiful Colombian city of Cartagena—whose ramparts are a wonder to this day—where the vessel did put in before cruising along to Puerto Bello, where they disembarked. Then came the trek across the Isthmus through the jungle to Panamá City; and here the *frailes* remained for several months, before they found transportation to Perú. However, this meant resumption of congenial life in a convent and service in a hospital, even though it also meant a postponement of missionary adventures, and Francisco was able to possess his soul in patience.

There is apparently no record of the name of the ship on

which he continued his journey, though we know that its master
was Juan de Morgana. It carried eighty Negro slaves among
its hundreds of passengers; and as these poor creatures were
pagans, Francisco was able, then and there, to begin his work
as a proselyter. Moreover, he was soon able to prove, by actions
as well as words, that he really had their physical and spiritual
welfare at heart. The vessel had not gone far past the next
Colombian port—the present Buenaventura—when a frightful
storm arose and the seemingly stout ship proved considerably
less than seaworthy; having run into a reef near Gorgona
Island, it promptly began to fall apart. Its lifesaving equipment
consisted of a solitary boat and into this the captain hastily
began to herd the passengers he considered most prominent.
Like the captain with whom the *frailes* had crossed the Atlantic,
Juan de Morgana had conceived a tremendous admiration for
Francisco, and tried to hustle him to the craft which might
carry him to safety. Resolutely, the friar declined to budge.
The slaves were his sacred charge; he would stay with them to
the end. If the thought crossed his mind that here was his
chance for martyrdom after all, it did not dominate his
thoughts, as it had on the island beach. It was of these poor
Negroes and their salvation that he was thinking. He was determined that if they were destined to die, they should not do so
unbaptized.

The floundering ship split in two sideways and its prow sank
swiftly out of sight. But Francisco, who was in the stern, continued to baptize the slaves and to comfort with prayers and
confessions the surviving Europeans. "With the passing minutes, they were amazed to note that there was little change in
the position of their half-ship. They looked to Francisco for
comfort and found him serene; and though their bodies were
tried by the waters in which they stood and the hunger which
assailed them, they listened to him in a sort of fascinated trance.
As he stormed heaven with his ceaseless prayers, he was the
focus for them all, the rock to which they clung. Finally, he
announced abruptly, in tones of firm conviction, that now none
should be downcast, because he could assure them that on the

third day the boat would return for them! . . . At daybreak on . . . the *third day*, the blessed boat came alongside their tortured bit of ship, which still miraculously floated." [18]

But rescue was one thing and sustained life another. They did not know which of the scanty herbs and roots and fruits which they found were wholesomely edible; and they made the mistake of eating some which they called *manzanillas*—because of their resemblance to little apples—and this mistake resulted in several deaths. It also led to the decision that hereafter they would depend on Francisco's pharmaceutical experience to guide them more wisely, and there were no further fatalities.

But obviously they could not go on like this forever and they took counsel as to the best means of escape. "It appeared that their only chance lay in sending a few of their number to Panamá in their battered boat for help. That the expedition could reach this port seemed next to impossible, for it would have to cover four hundred miles or more on the open seas in a frail craft under a blazing sun, or perhaps in tempests such as had destroyed their sturdy galleon. But it soon became clear that this was a risk which must be taken if they were not all to perish.

"It was finally decided that Padre Baltasar de Navarra was the one to head this attempt. As Superior of the Franciscan contingent headed for Tucumán, his solicitations would have the most authority. Besides, his experience in New World negotiations had been considerable. Therefore, when the pitiful little boat had been readied to the best of the company's ability, this brave Franciscan and some equally valiant seamen put out upon an ocean whose moods could not be foreseen, to take their chances in behalf of the rest. Fray Baltasar, well aware of Fray's Francisco's ascendancy over the castaways, left everything in his charge, promising to return as soon as possible in a seaworthy ship and take them all away from these wretched *tierras*. . . .

"The weeks dragged on and on until it seemed that each had been a year; a deep depression enveloped the camp. The inadequate diet had weakened them all. This physical debility combined with the general discouragement to create a mood in which it was impossible to maintain whatever confidence they had formerly held for their eventual rescue. It was useless, if not ridiculous, they said, to keep the watch on shore for a boat that was almost certain never to appear. The approach of Christmas with its poignant memories of home and of the gay festivities, the rejoicing of other years, aggravated the over-all misery until, for some, life became nearly insupportable. Hope was dead or rapidly expiring, but not their bitter lamentations. . . .

"The heroic *fraile* had withdrawn from these lamentations that he might renew his spirit in prayer. His own unfaltering heart was so filled with love for the Precious Babe Whom he implored for the salvation of his companions that he did not notice that quiet had descended upon the camp. This had occurred gradually as one by one its occupants had retired to seek the sleep which could obliterate for a while the misery of their sorrow. And now, suddenly, Fray Francisco experienced, as a gift from the One Whose birthday he alone was honoring with no less joy because external conditions were so poor, a wonderful inspiration! In a flash this great night was lighted up with glory, for it was now given him to *see* just how and when their problems would be solved and all this wretched clamor dissipated in happiness!

"Leaping to his feet, he fairly bounded out of his hut and into the midst of the camp, crying loudly that the sleepers must all arise at once. This was *La Nochebuena,* the night when songs of jubilance must be sung in praise of the Babe! After they had accorded *El Niño* the honor that was His due from every Christian soul this night of nights, he, their *padrecito,* was prepared to reveal a most splendid surprise! Yes, after a suitable acclamation of the Good Tidings which had come to earth on that first *Navidad,* he would announce some news that had just been vouchsafed him from on high which closely concerned their fortunes.

"There was something electric in his words and manner which caused the people to arise from their incommodious improvised cots and make all haste, in a wild scramble from the brush-walled *chozas,* to join the animated *fraile.* One look at

his great shining eyes and they, too, became infected with the
jubilance which possessed him. Someone started to sing, and
for hours the wilderness rang resoundingly to the hymns and
carols of rejoicing with which they glorified their Blessed Infant
King, *El Niño Jesús*. And as they sang their hearts were so
miraculously lightened and lifted that perhaps many even forgot the exciting promise with which the priest had routed them
from their pallets and dispersed the brooding that had become
habitual. But Fray Francisco had not forgotten. When their
Lord had been fully praised and their own hearts restored in
glad gratitude, he judged the moment to be propitious. Then
it was that he made his almost incredible announcement:

" 'Listen my sons and open wide your hearts to hope! Within
three days you shall sight the ship that comes from Panamá
to bring us succor and bear us out of our captivity!' " [19]

Over and over again, in the lives of holy men, we find that
some special number has played a significant part in their history. (The famous novena of Junípero Serra is perhaps the
best known of these, but there have been many others.) This
was the second time that Francisco had placed his faith in three
days as marking a limit for delivery and both times he was
right. I do not attempt to explain this—perhaps some other
chronicler can. I only know that it happens.

"At daybreak on the third day the little community was,
to the last member, gathered at the water's edge. All eyes
searched the horizon, where, shortly now, their deliverers must
appear. Suddenly there came an 'explosion of enthusiasm.'
Far out where a moment before there had been nothing, a
tiny white fleck trembled between the blue of the sky and the
blue of the sea—and it was indubitably lengthening in line!
Thus they identified the breeze-filled mainsail of their rescue
ship!

"As little by little it emerged into its full form before their
shouts and tears, the crescendo of their jubilance touched
delirium. And once again, amid the cries, the laughs, the sobs
that rent the air and filled it with bedlam, Francisco Solano
stood silent, by far the humblest man among them.

"Fray Baltasar had redeemed his word. The vessel which

momentarily grew larger and more beautiful before their eager eyes had been dispatched by their king's representative in Panamá, whose heart had been deeply moved by the *Comisario's* story of the suffering on Gorgona. Moreover, as they would soon know, the ship was fairly bursting with provisions to satisfy every need of the half-starved company. When at last it rode close before them, dropped anchor, and sent its *tripulantes* over the side in the small craft which was soon carrying them aboard, they saw the extent of the generosity which had supplied all and more than was necessary. Then it was that they fell upon their knees before Fray Baltasar and Fray Francisco in appreciation of what these two Franciscan titans had worked in their behalf. . . ." [20]

As soon as they were revived by the nourishing fare which the rescue ship had brought them, the travelers embarked on it for the last lap of their sea trip—that is, to the Peruvian port of Paita. Because of adverse winds and currents, whicn made a voyage farther south long, tedious and very difficult, it was not customary to sail beyond Paita. The final part of the journey was made overland on foot, and it is impossible to escape the conclusion that this was also tedious and very difficult and it was certainly long—over five hundred miles as the crow flies. But the little group pressed on with fresh determination and courage and came to the end of their wanderings at the convent then known as Máximo de Jesús de Lima, which still flourishes today as El Convento de San Francisco, where they were hospitably received.

v

Lima, which owes its name to the Spaniards' mispronunciation of Rimac, the river beside which it is located, was already a city of great importance in the New World, the seat of an archbishopric, a viceroyalty and a university. It was the city of gilded coaches, of great processions, of riotous games, of walled gardens, and images of saints niched at every street corner; also, of a well-organized branch of the Inquisition. Its first call to fame was founded on the riches which flowed through it. But something about its atmosphere must also have been peculiarly conducive to sanctity, for Rosa de Lima, Martín de Porres, Toribio Mogrovejo and Francisco Solano were contemporaries.

Lima had been chosen for his capital by Francisco Pizarro, the conqueror of the Incas, in preference to Cuzco, the original capital, because of its greater accessibility to the sea and its more favorable climatic conditions;[21] and since it did not come into being haphazardly, but was carefully planned from the start, it served as a model for practically all future cities founded in Perú by the Spaniards. From the beginning it was embellished with many notable buildings, among them El Convento Máximo de Jesús, the earliest foundation of the Franciscans, who had established their first province on the South American continent in this city. Although later Francisco Solano was to become closely associated with it, he and Padre Baltasar de Navarra remained there only a few days before starting for Tucumán.

"The first attempts to plant Spanish towns in Tucumán had been thwarted when they were attacked and destroyed by the Indians.[22] However, the city of San Miguel Tucumán (established in 1565 after the early failures) escaped the fate of its predecessors, and the diocese of Tucumán was erected there in 1570. The greatest impediment to the missionaries' work in Tucumán was its isolation. There were no roads in the province, and in many places not even trails. As the approach was still customarily made from the West Coast, this suggests that the freezing rigors of the Andean crossing and the 'green hell' of the Gran Chaco must still have been less hazardous than travel up from the Atlantic seaboard. Whatever way it was done, it was a heroic undertaking. After the towering Andes had been conquered, there were then the uncharted jungles to negotiate. Through these fearsome enclosures our friars, lacking either a map or instruments of guidance, now picked their way aided only by the constellations. At certain points along the way there were separations for them, since they had been individually assigned to widely scattered stations.

[Francisco] "exhausted by his long march (and obviously unaccompanied at this point), sat down upon the bank of a brook to rest and enjoy the scenery. Very soon he noticed that the murmur of the light wind which stirred the tree boughs above his head and the tinkle of the rivulet at his feet seemed to harmonize in a soft 'symphony of the *selva*.' This inspired him to turn to his beloved violin and search out upon its strings the chords which corresponded to the blended tones of the breezes and the running water. Tentatively, his bow began to reproduce these harmonies of nature until the player had picked up the full theme and tempo which had attracted his music-loving heart. Carried away by the beauty of his improvisation, his playing became more confident and louder until it dominated the sounds which had inspired it.

"We wish we might have been present to witness this dramatic scene—the tall, intent figure of the *fraile* in the worn, likely tattered, habit—a somber splotch silhouetted against the verdant greens of a tropical forest on the bank of a singing stream, his brilliant dark eyes brooding above the violin he played in solitary abandonment to the lovely inspiration which possessed him. We also wish we might have heard this 'symphony of the *selva*' that flowed so majestically from Francisco Solano's finely mastered instrument on that day in the year 1590.

"Fortunately, however, this enchanting scene had a witness —the music, a listener; for this is how knowledge of the incident descended to us. As the priest played, an extraneous note cut the atmosphere close beside him: it was the whiz of an arrow. He [the musician] however, did not turn his head to see who it might be, nor did he suffer any break in his playing. And now, step by slow step, an Indian who had been attracted by the singing of the violin emerged from the undergrowth. He observed Father Solano closely for some minutes. The solitary man whose fascinating music bore the sounds readily recognized by the forest dweller incontestably wore the face of the Indians' common enemy—the European. But also, surprisingly, it was a face upon which both humility and peace were unmistakably graven. He carried no weapons, *this* white man! And his strange, shabby garment somehow increased his friendly appearance. Little by little, he [the Indian] forgot his initial caution, and finally walked openly to the friar's side and sat down to enjoy the remainder of the concert.

"Fray Francisco took no outward notice of this unknown auditor, but, that his confidence might be fortified and also to give him pleasure, protracted the extemporaneous work until it became quite clear from the aborigine's immobility that he had been completely disarmed by the violin. When the Franciscan finally lowered the instrument and bow, he turned with unaffected delight to greet the brave, exactly as he might have hailed any well-loved friend. Taking both hands of this amazed Diaguita (who, as it happened, was the *curaca,* or chief, Tayaquín), he asked protection and hospitality *in the clearly enunciated syllables of the local dialect!*

"Had the missionary who made good his escape from acclaim in the civilized places of earth by coming into these remote fastnesses afoot, known that he possessed the gift of tongues? This we cannot say, but we can affirm that henceforth the fact would be regarded as one of the most startling of his many prodigious distinctions. It is unknown whether his encounter with Tayaquín occurred before or after the fifteen-day period he had spent in mastering the difficult and varied dialects of the region. All his biographers mention that this was the total extent of his study, and that within this remarkably short time he had acquired a facility in the Indian tongues in which he would minister almost exclusively for the ensuing several years.

"But let us return to the forest scene, the inception of the friar's most significant friendship with the Diaguita chief. Conqueror and conquered already walked hand in hand as brothers, and the Indian who had hidden his tribe in the deep forest where the foreigners could not discover it now conducted one of them to his hideout.

"As all the *frailes* were seeking the best means of inducing the Indians to establish themselves in suitable Christian *pueblos,* it was natural that Francisco Solano should see in Tayaquín's family the nucleus of just such a foundation. Before long Tayaquín had consented to accompany him to the Spanish settlement at Nuestra Señora del Talavera de Madrid to meet and make his peace with the civil and ecclesiastical authorities, who reciprocated this gesture of good will by receiving him courteously and respectfully.

"And now Tayaquín had a great idea of his own. As a public profession of his new Faith, he suggested that he erect a church on the spot where he had first encountered his dear friend. Enthusiastic at the thought that the site of the contemplated shrine, which was just about halfway between the Spanish town and the tribal headquarters, might become an invaluable link between the two races and a symbol of their brotherhood within the Faith of Christ, the missionary joyfully agreed. Together he and Tayaquín now left Talavera to set their hands to this commendable project. Their excitement was so intense that, once arrived at the location which would one day become the town of Cochangasta, they fell to work entirely unaided to collect the building materials which abounded in the vicinity and to throw up the walls of their little chapel. In time the Spaniards would come to see, to admire—and finally, to make their own settlement nearby. Thus the little temple built by Fray Francisco and his friend Tayaquín did indeed fulfill their dream by becoming a point of spiritual convergence for the two races of the district—and the solid cornerstone of its destined future.[23]

"Naturally, there were still thousands upon thousands of Indians in Tucumán who had not yet been in contact with missionaries. Many of these now despised their Christianized brothers who had gone over to the Faith of 'the enemy' as traitors to their own race." [24]

Forty-five chiefs, with more than twenty thousand savages under them, plotted to attack Francisco's settlement on the occasion of the Holy Week observances. When the Christians saw the hordes bearing down on them, they resigned themselves to certain death. Francisco calmly confronted the attackers, armed only with a crucifix. He walked out before them and preached a simple and affectionate sermon of the type through which he was accustomed to introduce the pagans to the love of Christ.

"Whatever had happened to give his words power to penetrate the understanding of every faction there present, only God Himself could have explained. But what every witness *did* know was that nearly twenty thousand aborigines of Tucumán immediately abandoned the warpath; that nine thousand of them now fell at the feet of Fray Francisco before the Cross Triumphant, begging for forgiveness; and that the nine thousand were baptized before the setting of the sun.

"The diligent apostle did not content himself with ministering to his own converts. As soon as he was confident that their feet were firmly placed upon the Christian path, he set his own to another immense tour. His original idea is supposed to have been to close a loop of all the widely separated Franciscan missions throughout the country to the east of the Andes, while evangelizing and instructing the natives he might encounter in the great wastes that stretched between the heroically founded stations.

"In the Gran Chaco there would be no welcoming missions into which one might limp to receive even the meager comforts one or two established brothers might be able to offer. There were now no missioners in the Chaco, nor any white men—and no friendly Indians! Into this inhospitable terrain the inhabiting tribes had fled before the advancing Spaniards to an existence which was miserable even by the standards of savages. The conditions were so hazardous to life that perhaps it could only be preserved by violence. In any event, the natives concerned themselves with little more than their eternal intertribal wars, hunting and fishing. In such circumstances we cannot help but wonder what Francisco really expected to accomplish.

"We can relate what he did, what he achieved, as well as the many logically predictable things which did *not* happen to him in the Chaco. The cannibals did not eat him, nor injure him in any manner. Instead, they gazed with astonishment upon this fearless white man who approached them in simple friendliness and addressed them in their native tongues! Being able to understand perfectly all that he said, they were then somehow vouchsafed the wit to start listening to his argument. This soon had them extremely interested, and before long, convinced. As for what he did thereafter, that, too, was quite simple. He baptized them. By the thousands, he baptized them. But he did not stop with Baptism. He tarried long enough with each group of these appalling people to civilize them!

"Fray Francisco now returned to La Rioja, his old station. In making this journey, his bare feet closed the circle of his incredible tour for souls that had covered two thousand miles of jungle, mountain and desert wastes, the vast and, until his passage, totally uncivilized heart of the South American continent which is now divided between four great republics.[25] And though his biographers are not very specific about the number of years consumed 'by the great evangelization' of this sector, it would seem to have been some seven or more." [26]

In 1595, Francisco was elected *Visitador* for the Franciscan establishments in Tucumán. Since this would mean the end of his personal missions among the Indians, Francisco was by no means pleased and begged his superior to relieve him of the burden. However, "the election was sustained, which proved to Fray Francisco that it was God's certain will. He therefore put aside his own desires and obediently accepted the obligation. To fulfill his duties it was necessary to set forth upon another trip, this time to visit each of the monasteries and reductions which had been confided to his care. For two years he devoted himself to the *conventos,* serving them well in everything, but best of all as a model of religious perfection for their emulation. As the close of his term of office approached, he once again implored for his release, that he might go back to his beloved *Inditos.*

"This time he gained his freedom from the post of *Visitador,* although he was not granted the rest of his wish. He had been named Father Guardian of La Recolección de Santa María de los Angeles, a monastery which had just been erected outside the walls of Lima. La Recolección, known in our day as 'de los Descalzos,' is still venerated by the Limeños as one of their most precious relics because the holy and erudite Francisco Solano once made his home within its beautiful old walls." [27]

VI

He had spent twenty years in Tucumán and he loved it. "For him the legendary magnificence of Lima's rich churches and the honors awaiting him there would never be comparable to the attractions of the rivers and mountains he had come to love during his struggles over and through them for the salvation of his poor Indians, whom he loved more dearly still.

"Francisco Solano traveled alone, barefoot as always, making the long trip to Lima by way of Chuquisaca, now the city of Sucre in Bolivia. By this route the maps tell us that the distance is in excess of fifteen hundred miles; and from San Miguel de Tucumán merely to Chuquisaca, it is some six hundred, in part through territory as difficult as any the priest had encountered on the other Chaco trip. When he arrived at Chuquisaca, the Father Guardian of the monastery found it almost impossible to credit the fact that Fray Francisco had managed to traverse such dangerous terrain without a companion or a guide of any sort.

"After a few days' rest, the friar set out again, climbing the spectacular *cordillera* into Potosí, where he arrived at the *convento* on the fourth of October, just in time to celebrate the feast of St. Francis. At the special *almuerzo* at which the brothers honored their founder and also gave thanksgiving for the safe arrival of their brother from Tucumán, the Father Guardian of that establishment announced a dispensation of the customary reading and the rule of silence in the refectory with the words, 'Brothers take your joy in the Lord!' He then proposed the singing of a hymn to St. Francis, but this was not well received, for it appeared unseemly to many of the *frailes* that there should be any such relaxation of the regulations.

"Fray Francisco himself ordinarily observed the strictest silence; but being a 'saint in truth and possessing more experience of the world,' he regretted the exaggerated severity of the brothers, for he thought they should have had the good judgment to understand that rules may be altered upon occasion to conform with the circumstances. Therefore, despite his extreme fatigue, he at once arose from his seat and with the simplicity that was characteristic of him began to dance about the refectory while inviting his dear brothers to share in his rejoicing. This surprising exhibition jolted the entire company out of its bleak mood, and awakening hilarity, discongealed the most rigid countenances.

"Once he was established at Los Angeles, he was much sought after. To safeguard his prayers and contemplation, he had to build himself a little hut—in imitation of an Indian *choza*—on a knoll called Alberna, which rose within the monastery enclosure. In time this hermitage would become the small chapel in which is cherished today a beautiful picture of our Lord Crucified—the same, according to tradition, before which Fray Francisco was accustomed to pray, seeking, doubtless, the fortitude to embrace for the glory of God the program now imposed upon him by obedience.

"Francisco Solano had pleaded to be relieved of his authority from the time he had accepted his assignment at Santa María. He longed to serve under the direction of any other, and insisted that he really only merited a place at the feet of his brothers. But the result of all his humble objections was the new *Comisario*'s confirmation of the Guardianship.

"Father Córdoba wrote that he knew of eleven times within four months that Padre Solano re-petitioned the Commissary General to accept his renunciation of the charge at La Recolección de Santa María de los Angeles. And when his desire was finally granted, his joy was unbounded. Then, perhaps because he understood that his presence in Lima would always be a suggestion to his superiors that he was available for another prelacy, he asked for a transfer to the city of Trujillo.

"But if Francisco Solano rejoiced in the belief that in placing nearly four hundred miles between himself and the capital, he had again or definitely escaped from the post of authority that was so trying to him, he was to find out that it did not work out that way. For he had barely settled himself in Trujillo when he was named Guardian of the community there! However, as the discipline observed in this house was exceptionally strict, it is quite possible that his heart was less heavy than it had been in Lima.

"Music had its place in all of Francisco's activities. One quiet afternoon Padre Jerónimo de la Torre, another member of the Trujillo community, observed the Guardian hastening toward the church with the rebec[28] under his arm, and asked idly, 'Where are you bound, Father?'

" 'I'm on my way to play for a very attractive young lady,' the Guardian answered.

"Intrigued by this cryptic reply, Fray Jerónimo waited awhile and then drifted into the temple after Padre Solano. Concealed by an angle of the wall, he witnessed a most effective scene. After a brief adoration of the Blessed Sacrament, which was exposed on the main altar where there was also an exquisite painting of Our Lady Queen of Angels,[29] Fray Francisco began to sing *alabanzas* to the Virgin while he played the little instrument. His body swayed rhythmically to the music he made— until finally he became enraptured, his gaze riveted upon the image; and the rebec, forgotten, hung from his hand, stilled.

"In the meantime, yet another *Comisario* had arrived from Spain to take charge of the Franciscans' Peruvian affairs. This was Padre Juan Venido, who would later be consecrated Archbishop of Lima. Fray Juan found himself in agreement with the Provincial Chapter, which, by the time Fray Francisco had completed a year in Trujillo, had decided that he should, indeed, be relieved of that charge. The motive for this decision, however, was to prove immensely painful to the subject. The Chapter had recalled the Gospel warning against hiding one's light under a bushel. As Francisco Solano was surely their brightest light in Perú, he was now recalled to Lima, where he was again named Superior of La Recolección de Santa María de los Angeles!

"Although Fray Francisco's vigilance in the protection and instruction of the faithful—and especially of the beloved brothers under his care at La Recolección—was unremitting, his life was replete with moments of joy and innocent play. He made his little jokes like any other good-humored man, but the point of *his* jokes always led back to the marvelous center of his existence, which was love of our Lord, His Blessed Mother and the saints.

"Occasionally Fray Francisco would give some extraordinary exhibition for the edification of his *frailes*. One such occurred on a certain Assumption morning when the community was in the *coro* for thanksgiving devotions after having breakfasted and visited the Blessed Sacrament according to the custom of the Order. Fray Francisco's spirit suddenly experienced such elation in contemplating our Lady's great triumph, her glorious entrance into heaven to take her rightful place as Queen of the Angels, that instead of seeking his own place among the religious, he stopped before the main altar and began to sing in her praise. Only one among them failed to be edified by Padre Solano's joyful excitement. Father Juan de Navarrete, an erudite and virtuous Franciscan, was left scandalized and even sorrowful by the spectacle which appeared to him entirely unseemly. He pronounced this judgment: 'In a monastery of recollects, these noisy manifestations are incongruous. Tears would be better here than songs.'

"But the happy Fray Francisco answered his censorious brother with a short quotation: *'Mary is taken into heaven: the angels rejoice; praising, they bless the Lord.'* At that instant a strange thing happened. The somber heart of Padre de Navarrete, whose thoughts had been habitually engrossed in the spilled blood of Jesus, His cross, and His ignominious death, was penetrated by a clear ray of sheer happiness. Our Lady had wrought the transformation through which Fray Juan now experienced an elation formerly unknown, and suddenly he also burst forth in song!

"His [Fray Francisco's] importunings of his superiors for release from the post of Guardian at Santa María de los Angeles had been pursued ceaselessly ever since his return to Lima from Trujillo. To exercise authority was as abhorrent to him as it had ever been, and between the two cities he had now given it six years of obedience. Aware that the holy, prematurely old man, who was the shining light of their Order in Perú, was failing by the day before their eyes, the superiors finally concurred with his judgment, at least insofar as to acknowledge that having borne his undesired and burdensome honors wonderfully well for a number of years, he had surely earned the right to be relieved of them during the time which remained to him. He was therefore freed of the Guardianship and transferred to El Convento Máximo de Jesús (today San Francisco), Lima's oldest Franciscan foundation, to end his allotted days as a simple friar. His gratitude for this favor was almost pathetic, and his unrestrained rejoicing touched the hearts of all.

"In the spring of 1610, just a month or so after Fray Francisco's sixty-first birthday, he who had always been the nurse and physician took to his bed never to leave it again save for a few prodigious moments. When it became obvious that his last illness was upon him, he was assigned to a cell in the infirmary and placed under the special care of his old and beloved friend *Hermano* Juan Gómez. This was another cause for rejoicing, since no human being better understood or could have so completely entered into the heart of the patient as the Brother Infirmarian. Together, the dying friar and his compassionate nurse, who was most justly renowned throughout Perú for his sanctity, undertook the spiritual devotions which invariably terminated in tender and mystical transports to the Niño Jesús and His Most Holy Mother." [30]

Nevertheless, this very saintly man, while on his deathbed, had his moments of human needs and wants and, personally, I have been as pleased to hear about these as I have been to learn of his dancing. For a long while he had failed to relish his food and it had been necessary to tempt his appetite by every possible means. Then, about a fortnight before he died, he awoke at three in the morning with a craving for chicken livers. Of course, in those days, the only way to get chicken livers was to go out and kill chickens. But *Hermano* Juan Gómez bestirred himself and relayed a message to the Brother cook; and presently the necessary deed had been done and a succulent dish was set before the invalid. He sat up to clean his plate and sank back in his bed, well satisfied.

But such cheerful interludes were rare. "June wore itself out and gave place to July. But in Lima midsummer is not the season of heat and assorted discomforts which the term is apt to conjure up for North Americans. In fact, the thermometer may actually dip to coolish under the hazy July skies, for Lima stands close to the sea below the equator, which reverses the seasons. Fray Francisco, however, would have been thinking of it as *el verano*, and likely remembering in snatches those other summers of his childhood and youth in faraway Spain. This country which he had traversed so widely and to which he had given the twenty most difficult years of his life, this Perú in which he lay dying, was thousands of miles from that blessed land of his birth, Andalucía. Even so, it was summer here too, as he knew from the clamor set up by the birds that had been since his boyhood his—as well as St. Francis'—'little sisters.'

"On July 12 he was encircled by his brother religious who, in contrast to the blithe chorusing of the birds, wept inconsolably. It had not occurred to anyone to doubt the oft-vindicated prophet's prediction that his death would take place on the feast of St. Bonaventure. On July 14 they would lose the sanctifying influence of the one among them who was, as they well knew, the most tender friend and most holy Father they had ever known.

"It came at last, *El Día de San Buenaventura,* the feast of the saint for whom Fray Francisco had professed a tender devotion all the years of his life. From four o'clock in the morning, the religious took turns praying the Divine Office at his bedside. At the *Gloria Patri,* the dying man lifted his eyes to the ceiling, and, looking far beyond it, ejaculated, 'God be glorified.'

"Later he requested that they sing the *Tota Pulchra* and then the *Credo,* that 'he might die as a missionary should who has guarded and defended the Faith and so hopes for the recompense.' At the words: *'Et incarnatus est de Spiritu Sancto ex Maria Virgine,'* and while, simultaneously, the great bell in the tower pealed forth the elevation of the Host in the Mass then being sung in the chapel to honor San Buenaventura, the soul of Francisco Solano was borne to God." [31]

VII

Epilogue

"The instant Fray Francisco's death became known, the word flew from mouth to mouth, from fashionable *colonia* to shabby *barrio,* criss-crossing Lima with terrific speed. That day the capital of Perú took account of but one piece of news; dedicated itself to but one endeavor. Every street was filled with a single cry: 'The Saint has died. We are going to see *El Santo!'* At once the populace was on the move, streaming through the thoroughfares and plazas toward the focal point of its undivided interest, the Franciscan monastery which had been blessed in holding the prodigious sanctity of Francisco Solano for two years. All these people, drawn from every social class, now swarmed down upon the last earthly abode of 'El Santo,' while those who were not able to gain entrance jammed the square stretching before the main portal of the *convento* and El Templo de San Francisco. Although friars had been stationed at the gates to stem this formidable enthusiasm, the Limeños fought obdurately for a last loving look at him.

"With the fall of darkness there was some diminution of the crowd that had milled about El Máximo de Jesús all day long, and the religious gathered before Padre Solano's bier to begin an all-night vigil of prayer over his body. But by two o'clock on the morning of July 15 a mob was once more beating upon the securely fastened doors of El Máximo. One of the friars who had been posted at the main entrance undertook to quiet the commotion, offering to serve as a proxy for the whole crowd by carrying their rosaries into the *oratorio* and touching them to Fray Francisco's body. This did not appease the people, who wanted the evidence of their eyes for this greatly desired benefit. The doors had been reinforced by heavy crossbars to prevent them from being broken in by the shoving and pushing throng, but this measure was soon seen to be futile, and ultimately the friars were compelled to open the oratory to the public. Truly, Lima had never seen such a night!

"But if the uproar and clamor, though born of faith and love, made a somewhat unseemly demonstration, it should also be told that the most important of the night's events was one worked quietly in favor of the peace taught by our Lord and ever cherished by his servant." [32]

This story is related by Ricardo Palma in his *Tradiciones Peruanas Completas*:

"Among the superiors of the Augustinian and Franciscan convents, in the year 1608, some trouble arose which resulted in great enmity. And, 'as he who quarrels with the head-shepherd quarrels with his dog,' the friars of both Orders believed

themselves obligated to make the disputes of their respective
superiors their own.

"The matter reached the point where the *porteros* of both
convents received orders not to permit a friar of the opposite
community to put a foot inside the cloisters. In vain, the Viceroy and the Archbishop took sides in the quarrel, using influence and prominence in order to re-establish harmony. Such a
marvel came to be realized after the death of Francisco Solano.

"Of course, all the communities, with the exception of the
Augustinians, assisted at the funeral ceremony, and the Viceroy
took advantage of the opportunity to put an end to the scandalous hatred. He invited the two adversaries to accompany him
as he rose to kiss the shroud of the dead one. The three knelt
before the coffin and the Viceroy said: 'Padres! Enough of
turmoil! For love of this saint, who from heaven reads what is
in our hearts, let us dispense with this bickering and embrace
each other.' The two superiors embraced each other, and their
example was followed by the members of both communities.
Thus ended a dispute that had endured two years." [33]

I find this reconciliation a fitting episode to bring Francisco
Solano's story to an end.

9

The Franciscans of New Mexico
and Their Mystic Helpmeet,
María de Agreda

"The Franciscans came first" is the forgivably proud boast of
an Order otherwise outstanding for its humility. It is used as
the title for an excellent book by Fanchón Royer on the work
of these intrepid early fathers in Central America, Mexico, New

Mexico and California; and it has become almost a byword for those speaking and writing about pioneer missionary endeavor there and elsewhere. I might add that in many cases, the Franciscans have not only come first, but have stayed the longest. Fortunately, they have not been subjected to the same prejudiced evictions as the Jesuits, for example.

According to *The New York Times*, "A hundred years before the first California mission was built, Indians in New Mexico worshipped at a chain of adobe Catholic churches. Ten are still used today.

"The missions . . . began in 1598, when the first was constructed of mud and timbers on the banks of the Rio Grande at San Juan, north of Santa Fe.

"In 1621, Father Alonzo Benavides came to the New World with 26 friars, and nine years later, when he returned to Spain, most of the New Mexico missions were built." [1]

Father Benavides, the arresting character to whom this article refers, was a native of the Azores, who probably came to New Spain in 1598 and entered the Franciscan Order at the Friary of St. Francis in Mexico City. After filling several intermediary posts, he was appointed custos (i.e., Superior of the Franciscan Order) of the Franciscan missions in New Mexico and Commissary of the Holy Office for the same jurisdiction. His term as custos lasted only three years, but in that brief time, ten new missions were added. The so-called *Memorial of 1630*, of which he was the author, was the report written for Philip IV of Spain on the activities in his custodia, and Benavides was likewise the author of the revised and enlarged version written for Pope Urban VIII four years later. The two reports were prepared to inform first the King and then the Pope of "the rapid development of those missions [of New Mexico] and the scarcity of friars to minister to them" and likewise to set forth the many "wonders and miracles" with which heaven had confirmed the work of the Franciscans. They remain the most authentic and valuable source of information about New Mexico at that period. The Introduction to the first one reads as follows:

"Sire:

"I, Fray Alonso de Benavides of the Order of St. Francis, Custos of the Missions and Custody of New Mexico, declare that the events and affairs of that kingdom or, better said, of that new world, which during these recent years we friars of my Father St. Francis—the first and thus far the only ones, since no other order has entered there—have converted and pacified unto God our Lord and brought under obedience to Your Majesty, are so numerous and of such a nature that I shall find it impossible to describe them at one hearing and in a summary manner. The reason is that, with the royal assistance and protection of Your Majesty, we have discovered such great treasures, both spiritual and temporal, which the divine Majesty has seen fit to confirm with so many wonders and miracles, that the Viceroy of Mexico and my order thought it best to instruct me, as the one who has for many years governed and administered that country, to come in person to describe and represent them to Your Majesty.

"They have further instructed me to explain orally at such times as Your Majesty may be pleased to hear me, whatever, because of its brevity, this memorial has not made sufficiently clear, lest it seem verbose to the one we so much desire to serve. And I shall consider it a very great reward for the many risks, labors and journeys we have endured there, with such splendid advancement of the honor and glory of God our Lord, if only it come to the attention and knowledge of Your Majesty what great merit and prayers you enjoy in those provinces and that quite remote kingdom, which are more than twenty-six hundred leagues from here—which distance I have traveled for the aforesaid purpose in this year of 1630. I consider all this very worth while, now that I find myself at the feet of Your Majesty. My statement follows." [2]

With this preamble, Benavides then proceeds to describe, one by one, the seventeen different nations which he visited, and their habitats, beginning with "the nations that live along the road to New Mexico," whose mode of living as a whole was uncivilized, to say the least.

"Whenever we go through their lands, if they see we are few in number, they attack us. For this reason it is impossible to pass there with fewer than twelve men on horseback, all very well armed. Even then, it is necessary to proceed cautiously; and in the early part of the night a fire is lighted somewhere to divert their attention, while we advance as far as possible beyond it. Even when they see a large force, they lie in ambush by night and do whatever harm they can to the horses. Ever since the discovery of New Mexico, in journeys through these hundred leagues, there have always been battles with these Indians. Nevertheless, through the mercy of God our Lord, the Spaniards always emerge victorious. We have made every effort to convert and pacify these nations, both for the good of their souls and the safety of the road, but they are so barbarous that they refuse even to permit us to speak to them. May our Lord be pleased to grant that the time of their conversion come, as it has come for the rest.

"Having traversed these hundred leagues, we arrived at the famous Río del Norte, which owes its name to the fact that for many leagues it flows from that direction. A hundred leagues before it reaches New Mexico this river is inhabited by a nation which we commonly call the Mansos, or Gorretas, so called because they trim their hair in such a manner that it looks as if they were wearing caps on their heads.

"Because of our having preached to them on so many occasions, they have told me that they would be glad to have friars there to instruct and baptize them. This would be a very important undertaking, because, apart from the main purpose (which is the conversion of souls redeemed like ours with the Blood of our Lord) it would also insure safe passage over these two hundred leagues and at the same time serve as a starting point from which the other neighboring nations could be converted and brought to live in permanent settlements. This could be effected by stationing three or four friars there with an escort of only fifteen or twenty soldiers, thereby eliminating the need of others, since this constitutes such an expense for Your Majesty every time a journey is made to New Mexico. With this protection very many rich mining camps which are found all along this road could be settled, as well as magnificent farm sites with water and tracts of very fine land. Then one

could travel that road every year and it would not happen that
five or six years would pass without our knowing anything of
the Spanish nation here in New Mexico.

"Farther up this same river [the del Norte] there are two
friaries, that of San Francisco Sandia and that of San Antonio
de la Isleta. These have schools where reading, writing, singing
and all kinds of instrumental music are taught, and where the
pupils are well instructed in Christian doctrine and given an
appreciation of the ways of civilized life. The two friaries and
the churches are very costly and quite ornate because of the
solicitude and zeal of the missionaries who established them." [3]

The degree of civilization, even of culture, represented in
every nation except the first two, is almost unbelievable, and
any evidence of ill-will toward the missionaries is the exception
and not the rule. One such exception was in the case of the
Picuries. "These people have proved to be the most indomitable
and treacherous in that kingdom, and some of the friars have
undergone great sufferings there. Out of hatred for our Holy
Catholic Faith, they have even gone so far as to lay hands on
and ill-treat the friars. But today, thank God, they are very
peaceful and well instructed in the Faith. The land is very
fertile, yielding frequent and abundant crops. The rivers,
which contain very good water, have an abundance of trout.
The mines located there contain garnets of a very fine quality,
but there is no one available to process them." [4]

At this point, the report of Father Benavides has been ex-
panded into a delightful narrative by William H. Donahue in
his article, "Mary of Agreda and the Southwest United States."

"Fray Juan de Salas had been at the mission at Isleta for some
time when one summer a small group of Jumano Indians came
to the mission. Approaching the Franciscan, they requested that
missionaries return with them to their village so that they
might become Christians. Since he had no authority, Fray Juan
consulted his superior, Fray Alonso, telling him of the request.
The conclusion which these two men reached is expressed by
Benavides: 'For lack of friars, we did not send anyone to preach
to them, nor did they inform us who had advised them to do
this, nor did we ask, convinced that they acted like many other

nations who had also asked for baptism after hearing the truth of our holy Catholic Faith.' It is to be expected that language difficulties would have kept the conversations between the Indians and Franciscans at a minimum. So it is not surprising that the motive of the Indians in seeking the Faith was left undiscovered. Fray Juan de Salas continued with his work of patiently instructing the natives around his mission. The group of Jumanos headed back across the open plains toward the East.

"The friars, however, had not seen the last of the Jumanos. Benavides records that the Indians returned several years— always with the same request. They did this in spite of their being constantly refused. The friars longed and prayed for the time that their numbers would be great enough to spread the Gospel to these tribes that were more than ordinarily eager to listen to it. Such a time was not far off.

"By an order of the Spanish king toward the close of 1627, thirty Franciscans were to be sent to New Mexico. They went first to Mexico, and met there the new archbishop, Don Francisco Manso y Zúñiga. Before he sent them on into the missions of New Mexico, the archbishop had a story to tell, and a command to give. A short time before, he had received a letter from Father Fray Sebastián Marcilla, the confessor of a nun, Sor María de Jesús, the abbess of the convent, La Concepción, in the town of Agreda in Spain. In substance, at least, the confessor must have told the archbishop the following story which he in turn told to the missionaries. María de Jesús had claimed that she was visiting the territories about New Mexico in some supernatural manner. While in this land, far from her native Spain, she went among the Indians preaching the Catholic Faith to them. While doing this she enjoyed the gift of tongues for the Indians understood her when she spoke to them in Spanish, and she understood them when they replied in their native tongues. Marcilla had written this letter in an attempt to confirm the account that Sor María had given him.

"To this statement of Marcilla, the archbishop added a command to the missionaries of New Mexico to this effect:

"'We, Don Francisco Manso y Zúñiga, archbishop-elect of Mexico, member of his Majesty's Council and of the Royal

Council of the Indies, strictly charge the reverend fathers, the *custodio* and other religious of the said *custodia* and conversion, with this investigation, so that they may conduct and carry it out with the exactness, faithfulness, and devotion that such a matter requires. They are to advise us of the result, in the manner promised, from which no doubt there will arise great spiritual and temporal increase, in honor and glory of God, our Lord. Done in the City of Mexico, on the 18th day of the month of May, 1628. Don Francisco Manso y Zúñiga.'

"Bearing this command of the archbishop, and anxious to begin their work among the Indians, Fray Esteven de Perea, the superior [Benavides' successor] and his group of missionaries left the city of Mexico on September 5, 1628, and reached Santa Fe at Eastertide of 1629.

"When the missionaries reached the mission of San Antonio which Fray Juan de Salas had built, and where he had been working for seven years, they were to witness a strange spectacle. The delegation from the Jumano Indians, which had come to Fray Juan for several years asking for missionaries to bring them the Faith, again arrived at the mission. This time, the largest group that had ever made the long journey across the plains arrived at the mission. There were about fifty Jumanos in the group. And on this occasion they were more insistent than ever that missionaries accompany them back to their tribe.

"Since the command of the archbishop was still fresh in their minds, the missionaries were led at once to wonder what caused this large delegation of Indians to ask for priests. How had they arrived at an appreciation of the value of the Faith? The Franciscans set about finding the reason. Fray Alonso de Benavides, who was [still] at the mission at the time, related this scene in very few words when he wrote his memorial to Pope Urban VIII:

" 'We called them [the Jumanos] to the convent and asked them their motive in coming every year to ask for baptism with such insistency. Gazing at a portrait of Mother Luisa in the convent, they said: "A woman in similar garb wanders among us over there, always preaching but her face is not old like this, but young." Asked why they had not told us this before, they answered, "Because you did not ask us, and we thought she was over here, too." ' 5

"The amazement of the missionaries on having the report of the archbishop fulfilled so soon may well be imagined. They must have suspected something of an extraordinary nature at once for it was absolutely impossible that an unknown white woman should be wandering about Texas alone at that period of history. The Indians told the priests that this woman had instructed them in the law of Jesus Christ and had told them to go in search of missionaries so that they might be baptized. The Indians also said that at times the lady was hidden from them, and they did not know where she went.

"When they had obtained this knowledge, the Franciscans were eager to set out at once not only to Christianize the Indians, but also to investigate their claims to having been instructed by a strange woman who traveled among them. For this important mission, Fray Alonso de Benavides appointed Fray Juan de Salas and Fray Diego López, who had volunteered for the work. The governor sent some soldiers as protection for the missionaries as was customary. As the group traveled long miles in a general easterly direction, the missionaries found the journey long and tiring. But since they were accompanied by Indians who knew their way, there was no time lost in scouting for the right direction to follow. Having traveled several hundred miles from Isleta, this group of missionaries, soldiers and Indians was met one day by a group of twelve Indians from the Jumanos. They said that they had been told of the proximity of the missionaries by the woman who had been telling them of Christ. There still remained a few days' journey to the village of the Indians. When the group drew near to the village, men, women and children streamed from everywhere to greet the missionaries. As the missionaries drew nearer, they saw to their amazement that the crowd from the village was carrying two crosses at the head of the procession. When the missionaries and soldiers had fittingly venerated the crosses which the Indians carried, the Indians in turn came to kiss the crucifixes which the Franciscans wore about their necks. The missionaries were amazed to find the Indians acting as though they had been

Christians all their lives. The Indians also showed the greatest respect for a medal of the Infant Jesus that the missionaries carried. Having been forewarned of the approach of the priests by their lady in the blue cloak, the Indians had prepared a huge celebration for them. And with much rejoicing, the crowd led the missionaries to a bower of branches and flowers which had been prepared for them.

"When all the rejoicing had subsided, the priests settled down to teach the Faith to the Indians. In many instances they found them already well instructed. And in all cases they found them eager to learn about the truths of the Church. One day, as a great crowd had gathered around him, Fray Juan de Salas asked all those who still wished to receive Baptism to raise their hands. And, as Benavides records, not only did all the adults raise their hands, but the mothers also raised the hands of their children who were too young to do so for themselves.

"The missionaries were elated at the great docility of the Jumanos. And their elation grew more and more as messengers from all the surrounding Indian villages came to the missionaries and asked for priests to come to their village. They said that the same lady who had instructed the Jumanos had also come to them and told them to go for missionaries. Day by day, the missionaries saw the possibilities for conversions increasing. But they were unable to meet all the demands for their services. Before doing anything else, they had to return to Isleta for more missionaries. And, as we may well understand, they were anxious to return in order to report all the marvels they had witnessed.

"When, weary but bright with excitement [they] finally reached the Mission of San Antonio, they were besieged with questions by Benavides and the other missionaries. How many Indians were there in the village? Did they have a good knowledge of the Faith? How about their Baptism? The excited priests answered all the questions that were fired at them, and little by little unfolded in detail the story of all that had befallen them on their mission to the Jumanos. All doubts were removed from Benavides' mind. He was certain God had intervened in the conversion of the Jumanos and the other tribes

around them. Such extraordinary events must be reported to
the viceroy and prelates in New Spain. Since Benavides was
custos, he felt it his duty and privilege to carry this news to
Mexico. Accordingly in 1628, he decided to make the long trip
to lay before the authorities a complete report on the amazing
events occurring in the custody.

"Benavides made the difficult trip to Mexico without any
notable mishap. He was warmly received and was shown little
kindnesses in a thousand ways. When Benavides had told all
of his story, all those in authority were eager that this story
should be carried to Spain. As Benavides tells us: '. . . After
my arrival in Mexico it seemed well to the señor viceroy and
reverend prelates that I go to Spain, to report to his Majesty,
as the head of all, and to our father-general.'

"While it is true that Benavides wished to go to Spain to
carry information about the missions to the home country, his
chief motive in desiring to undertake the difficult sea journey
was that he might be able to make investigation of the nun who
was instructing the Indians in the Faith. For him the miracles
that were connected so closely with his work were of consuming
interest. He felt that great good would result to souls if he
could contact this nun. And should he be able to do this, the
impetus that her message would have for his fellow missionaries
would be tremendous. Spurred on by these motives, and having
the permission and encouragement of his superior, Benavides
set sail for Spain.

"When he arrived in Spain, Benavides lost no time in reporting to the minister general of his Order. The minister general
gave an unexpected revelation—but Benavides tells of this
important meeting in a letter which he later sent from Spain
to the missionaries in New Mexico, telling them of his success
in fulfilling the mission for which he had left them:

" 'When I arrived in Spain, which was on August 1, 1630, our
reverend father-general, Fray Bernardino de Sena, now Bishop
of Viseo, was governing the order until the general meeting. As
soon as he heard my account of the holy religious who was
preaching our holy Catholic faith in the manner that your
reverences are acquainted with, his most reverend lordship told

me at once that while he was *comisario* of Spain, before becoming general [of the Order], which was more than eight years ago, he was informed that Mother María de Jesús, abbess of her convent in the villa of Agreda (on the border of Aragón and Castile) had made some appearances in and reports concerning the conversion of New Mexico. The account that I gave him, and that which the señor archbishop of Mexico, Don Francisco Manso, had sent us there, to the same effect, aroused in his most reverend lordship such tenderness and devoutness that he wished to set out at once for the said villa of Agreda, for Mother María de Jesús herself had told him the same thing that I reported, at the time mentioned above, when he made a personal visit to her convent, since it is subject to the order and province of Burgos, and the same Mother María de Jesús had told his Reverence of it, *os ad os* [face to face]; now he confirmed it with what I told him.'

"We can easily imagine the excitement of these two men when they put together information from two entirely different sources and found it to agree perfectly. Only his pressing duties as Minister General could hinder Fray Bernardino from starting at once for Agreda. Nothing could have stopped Fray Alonso de Benavides from fulfilling the object of his mission now that the goal was so close. But he was troubled by one thing. Sor María de Jesús must have been a very holy woman to have received such extraordinary favors from God. Perhaps the humility of such a woman would prevent her from revealing her mystical gifts. Fray Bernardino also foresaw this difficulty, so he gave Fray Alonso the authority to oblige the nun in virtue of her vow of obedience to reveal to him all that had befallen her in regard to her miraculous visits to the Indians of New Mexico. With this authority, and with letters of introduction to the provincial of Burgos, the province in which the convent of La Concepción was located, and to the confessor of Sor María de Jesús, the minister general sent Benavides to Agreda as his agent.

"When Fray Alonso reached Agreda, his first concern was to get in touch with the provincial, who was Father Fray Sebastián Marcilla, and with Father Fray Andrés de la Torre, who had

recently become the nun's confessor. Together these religious
went to the convent of which María de Jesús was the abbess.
And there began a visit which would be forever impressed on
the mind of Benavides. When he wrote back to his confreres
in America, his first words about his visit were a description of
the holy nun whom he met:

" 'Before saying anything else, I state that the said Mother
María de Jesús, at present abbess of the convent of La Concepción, etc., is almost twenty-nine years of age, with a handsome face, a very clear though rosy complexion and large black
eyes. The fashion of her habit, and that of all the religious of
that convent, who number twenty-nine in all, is simple like our
habit, that is, a coarse brown sackcloth, worn next to the body,
without any other tunic, outer, or under skirt. Over this brown
habit is one of heavy white sackcloth, with a scapulary of the
same, and the cord of our Father Saint Francis; over the scapulary is the rosary. They wear no shoes or other footwear except
boards bound to their feet or some straw sandals. The mantle
is of heavy blue sackcloth and the veil is black.'

"With a quiet reserve, Benavides announced to Sor María de
Jesús the purpose of his coming and told her that the minister
general of their Order had obliged her by reason of her vow
of obedience to tell him all that pertained to the visits that she
was reported to have made to New Mexico. To this injunction
of obedience the provincial and confessor added theirs, so that
it would be abundantly clear to the nun that it was God's will
that she should disclose the favors He had heaped upon her.
Being placed under such obligation, Sor María spoke humbly
and sincerely about all that concerned her miraculous visits to
the Indians of America. This must have been doubly difficult
for her since it required that she present even her interior
dispositions.

"This is what Father Benavides learned. Even as a young
child, María was vividly aware of the startling value of a human
soul. The thought that so many souls in the world would be
lost forever caused her soul to tremble in horror. What grief
she felt when she considered the loss of souls in the remote
parts of the world where the teaching of Christ had not yet

penetrated! Spurred on by such meditation, she constantly offered her life to God for the salvation of even a single soul. With a boundless longing she wished to help souls come to God. *'En esta disposicion se hallaba la Sierva de Dios, quando un dia, despues de aver comulgado, arrebatada en extasis, como solia, la mostra el Señor por especies abstractivas maravillosamente todo el mundo.'* ('One day, after she had received Communion and had gone into her usual state of ecstasy, God revealed to this Servant of His the whole world.')

"In this transport, she saw the multitudes in the world living without the true Faith. This pierced her with sorrow and served to increase even more her prayers for those souls who had not the Faith. The Lord granted her other visions of like nature. In one of these, our Lord having showed her the heathen all over the world declared that He had a special love for the Indians of New Mexico. As her love for the souls of these creatures increased, the Lord continually revealed to her more and more about them. One time when she was praying for them, our Lord drew her into an ecstasy and took her to a strange country among a people whom she recognized as the Indians whom the Lord had shown her on different occasions. She plainly felt the difference in the climate. As a matter of fact, all her senses were affected by the change of place. Here she was among the souls whose salvation she desired above everything. The Lord told her to fulfill her holy desires by preaching His Gospel to these people.

"We can imagine the rapt attention that Fray Benavides and the other two priests must have been paying to the story of the nun. She continued. She went to the Indians and spoke to them in her native language, Castilian. They understood her as though she were speaking to them in their own language. She was given the power to work miracles in order to convince the Indians of the truth of the Faith she was preaching. The Indians accepted the things that the woman taught them and were converted. When she finally returned to her senses from the ecstasy, she was in the same place as before she went into it. This happened in 1620.

"From that time on this strange phenomenon was repeated

time and time again. These visits were still going on when
Benavides was at Agreda in 1631. María de Jesús claimed that
in all they occurred over 500 times. Sometimes three or four
visits would be made in less than twenty-four hours. On all of
these miraculous visits, she continued her work of preaching
to the Indians. Not only because of the efficacy of her preaching,
but also because of the wondrous signs that our Lord worked
in evidence of the truth of all that she taught, many Indians
were desirous of entering the Church.

"On traveling in this miraculous way through New Mexico,
the nun saw and recognized the sons of St. Francis working
there in the missions. She realized that the Indians to whom
she preached must have priests to baptize and thoroughly Christianize them. So although the tribes to whom she preached
were a great distance from the missions of the Franciscans, she
advised them to send messengers to search for the missionaries
and to request that they return with them to their people. She
gave the Indians instructions as to how to get to the missionaries. And thus it came about that these Indians eventually
arrived at the Mission of San Antonio in Isleta where Father
Fray Juan de Salas was stationed. When the Franciscans were
unable to send missionaries to the Jumanos at once, it was Sor
María de Jesús who encouraged the Indians to return periodically to repeat the request. It was she who sent the large
delegation to Isleta in 1629—the delegation which finally made
the Franciscans realize that these visits were not prompted by
any natural knowledge of the Faith as were similar visits made
by various tribes.

"What María de Jesús told him fitted so well into the way
that everything had happened in the missions that Benavides
was naturally predisposed to believe all she said. However, he
desired all possible proof that the nun had actually visited the
Indians of America. There was no question of her having been
among the Indians in any natural maner without the knowledge of all concerned. So Benavides knew that if Sor María de
Jesús was able to answer questions that he would put to her
about his mission territory, the Indians, the missionaries and

so forth, then he would have absolute proof that she had visited the missions in a miraculous manner. It would be an easy matter for him to ask questions that would be impossible of an answer by anyone who had not personally been in the country. Wishing to present to his confreres in New Mexico the full weight of this argument for Mary of Ágreda's actually being in the missions, Benavides goes to some lengths in his letter to them in describing the convincing details that she had given him.

"By this time, Benavides was overwhelmed by all the proofs for the claims that María de Jesús had made. There no longer remained any doubt whatsoever in his mind as to the validity of her claims. He was absolutely convinced. Of all the proofs for the claims of the nun, Benavides said that there was nothing that was more convincing for him than the obvious sanctity of the woman. He had formed a higher estimation of her sanctity from his conversations with her than by the miracles that were performed through her." [6]

"In 1632 Fray Alonso journeyed to Rome in the capacity of confessor to Don Francisco de Melo. He remained in the Eternal City until 1635 and while there was in frequent communication with various high-ranking officials of the Congregation for the Propagation of the Faith. He succeeded in obtaining some minor concessions from the Roman Curia, including a bull which granted him all the privileges of a 'Pater Provinciae.' It was during this stay in Rome that Benavides submitted the revised *Memorial* to Pope Urban VIII.

"Returning to Spain, he continued to work for the cause of the New Mexican missions. At the court of Philip IV he continued urging his former recommendations and added at least one new petition: that the Indians of his custody be freed from the obligations of paying tribute and rendering personal service. This request was granted by the king in January, 1635. Soon after this, Benavides began preparations for the journey back to the New World." [7]

He never reached there. A sudden change in his field of activity took him to the Friary of St. Francis in Lisbon and shortly after his arrival there he was nominated Auxiliary

Bishop of Goa, only to die in the course of the long voyage to
India. The *Memorial* he had written for his king remains his
own best memorial.

The account of María de Agreda's mystical connection with
New Mexico and the phenomenon of her bilocation is so infinitely moving that anything further about the mission story
inevitably seems like an anticlimax. But from the viewpoint
of a conscientious editor, it seems necessary to go on, especially
as nearly one hundred and fifty years after Benavides wrote his
first Memorial, another Franciscan, Fray Francisco Atanasio
Domínguez, a Mexican by birth, was sent to New Mexico "to
make a complete, detailed report on both the spiritual and
economic status of the New Mexico missions, and this entailed
the gathering of much geographical and ethnological data as
well. Moreover, he was commissioned to further the search for
new routes to connect the northern provinces, and thus open
new missionary fields." [8]

In their excellent Introduction to *The Missions of New Mexico, 1776*, Eleanor B. Adams and Fray Angelico Chavez, who
are responsible for the translation and annotation of Fray Domínguez' work, correctly call the reader's attention to the fact
that "Domínguez' description of 1776 is to the eighteenth century what the Benavidas' *Memorials* of 1630 and 1634 are to
the seventeenth." Then they go on to add: "But here the com-
parison ends. For while Benavides painted a very general picture, really a hopefully exaggerated prospectus of what was to
be done, Domínguez gives a factual statement of what has
become of these sanguine hopes almost a century and a half
later. Readers with romantic ideas of halcyon Spanish colonial
days will be disappointed by the progressive decadence found
in the missions (and in a few of the missionaries), as well as
with the material and cultural backwardness prevalent among
the colonists. To one who can place himself in a remote frontier province in a land already poor by nature, not only isolated
by oceans of land from the rest of the civilized world, but also
from his nearest neighbor, the picture is not quite so bad. Indeed, one can only feel the highest admiration for the majority

of the padres, who kept the missions going in the face of utter poverty and loneliness, and for the Hispanic folk who for generations had survived among perils and hardships that might have driven other peoples to desertion, if not extinction."

It is quite true that while Benavides gives a more general picture, Domínguez gives a more factual statement. Indeed, the detail with which he describes every mission is at times overpowering. The description of a single church sometimes covers as much as ten large pages and does not omit a single dimension. In speaking of the one at the villa (i.e., a town enjoying certain privileges of charter) of Santa Fe, he tells us: "It is almost in the center of the villa, and its titular patron is Our Seraphic Father St. Francis. It has adobe walls more than a vara [2.78 feet] thick, and the main door faces west. It is 44 varas long from the door to the high altar, 9 varas wide, and 10 high to the bed molding. It has a regular transept; this occupies 6 varas of the 44 and is 15 varas wide and 11 long varas high, for across the church at the mouth of the nave a clerestory rises to light the transept and the sanctuary. The approach to the sanctuary consists of three steps made of wrought beams (which occupy about a vara of the floor of the transept) and another beam level with the sanctuary floor, and this ascent is about a vara high. The upper end of the sanctuary is as high as the transept, and the difference in height at the back can be gathered from the height of the floor. It is in the form of a square 6 varas wide and 6 varas long, so it is not as wide as the nave of the church. There is no vaulted arch in the sanctuary, but the substitute for it will be seen later." [9]

Then he goes on and on in the same vein about the sacristy, the Chapel of the Rosary, the Chapel of Our Lady of Light and the Chapel of San Miguel. "While I am describing the church," he eventually tells us, "it will be well to recount its affiliates." So then we learn what is happening in the Third Order at Santa Fe, in the Confraternity of the Blessed Sacrament, in the devotion of the poor souls, and the table feasts. Lastly, we learn about the villa itself. If we have any grandiose ideas about this, he quickly disabuses our minds. "The location, or site, of this villa is as good as I pictured it in the beginning, but its appearance, design, arrangement, and plan do not correspond to its status as a villa nor to the very beautiful plain on which it lies, for it is like a rough stone set in fine metal."

The villa does, however, have farmland and fruits, and a section about these ends on a more cheerful note. "The harvest consists of wheat, maize, legumes, and green vegetables, and also fruits such as melon, watermelon, and apricots, of which there are small orchards."

Moreover, its outlying districts, which Domínguez names in the Census, are not without certain enlightening features; and this Census, which closes the chapter, was obviously taken with the same meticulous care as the measurements.

"Villa
"1 The lord governor and his family with 6 persons
"229 Spanish families with 1,167 persons
"42 families of genízaros with 164 persons

"Quemado
"57 families with 297 persons"

I confess that I did some skipping as I read on and on about dimensions and other statistics. On the other hand, I found some of the details about equipment extremely interesting. *"Things Belonging to the Confraternity of the Blessed Sacrament:* A white satin chasuble with narrow silver galloon, with accessories. Six cloth humeral veils. A small cape of net over mother-of-pearl ribbed silk. Two veils which Governor Mendinueta gave for the ciborium, one of blue cloth and the other of white cloth. Three cloth cinctures given by the aforesaid gentleman. Three more old cloth ones and one silk one. A blue dossal curtain embroidered in gold and silver for the little throne. A small blue ribbed silk curtain which the aforesaid governor gave for the little throne. Another, of blue and white, which a pious woman gave for the same purpose. A canopy of mother-of-pearl satin with silver fringe which the said gentleman gave. A banner of crimson velvet, now old, with an iron cross. Another of white satin, now old, with a silver cross. Two ordinary mirrors that are on the little throne. The aforesaid

gentleman gave one, and his treasurer, Don Mateo Peñare-
donda, gave the other. An umbelline which Don Diego Borica
gave. The little throne is of framework with a little gradin to
match.

"*Linen:* Brittany alb with lace. A cotta. A cambric hood
which the Lord Governor Mendinueta gave.

"*Silver and other metal:* An ordinary silver-gilt monstrance;
it is kept in a case made to fit it, as is done with others. A
thurible with its appurtenances. Key to the tabernacle for
solemn occasions. The cross which was mentioned with the
blue banner.

"Two glass vases to fit into the sanctuary lamp. A little bell.
The cross for the crimson banner. Ordinary key to the tabernacle."

Twenty-five different missions are treated separately, each
with an equal amount of detail. Then follows a chapter on the
library and archives of the Custody and one on miscellaneous
items. To these, Father Chavez and Eleanor Adams have wisely
added a section on related material which contains letters and
other documents and a comprehensive list of Franciscans and
settlers; and, in closing the remarkable book which has been
such a treasure trove of valuable information, the present editor
would like to repeat and echo the final sentence of a passage
already quoted: "One can only feel the highest admiration for
the majority of the padres, who kept the missions going in the
face of utter poverty and loneliness, and for the Hispanic folk
who for generations had survived among perils and hardships
that might have driven other peoples to desertion, if not extinction."

10

Junípero Serra, Founder and Colonizer

It would be the easiest thing in the world to prepare an anthology about Christian envoys devoted entirely to great *Spanish* missionaries; in fact, it is very hard *not* to include the lives of many, but space is lacking to give a proportionate amount of room to missionaries of other nationalities. Despite the effort to limit the number to those most outstanding, we have already followed, all too briefly, the careers of Dominic de Guzmán, Ramón Lull, Ignatius de Loyola, Francis Xavier, Francisco Solano and María de Ágreda. But there is still another whose name, in the minds of millions, "leads all the rest." This is Junípero Serra.

Like Ramón Lull, he was a Majorcan by birth and a Franciscan by choice; and like Ignatius de Loyola, he deliberately selected a name different from the one by which he was christened, and that is the one by which he is known to us. However, their reasons for this choice were not the same. Iñigo de Loyola became Ignatius because Ignatius of Antioch was his favorite saint, and the intrepid young Basque, who impetuously decided to become a knight of a heavenly rather than an earthly king, desired to pattern his life on that of the brave bishop—said to have been appointed by St. Peter himself—who converted thousands before he met a martyr's death in a Roman arena. Miguel José Serra chose the name of Junípero because he wished to have for his patron the companion of St. Francis of Assisi, known as the Jester of God, a man of such utter simplicity and celestial mirth that St. Francis himself was wont to remark, "Would to God, my brethren, that I had a whole forest of such Junipers!"

Young Miguel José—whom we are henceforth to call Junípero—had a much humbler background than his fellow Majorcan, Ramón Lull. His father, Antonio Serra, was not a learned scholar but an illiterate farmer, dependent on a friend to read aloud to him the letters which Junípero eventually wrote him, and which have since become a source of such universal admiration and inspiration. But he was industrious and devout, and he and his wife, Margarita, were both eager that their only surviving son should have the "advantages" they had lacked, just as many other underprivileged but loving and intelligent parents have been, both before and since; and though they lived in a little provincial town—Petra—educational opportunities were not lacking there: a primary school, maintained and directed by Franciscans in connection with their old church, St. Bernardino, was located close to the Serras' small but substantial house—a house which "has become famous because it once cradled a Christian hero who added a realm to the Church and a coastline to the empire." The Serras were on friendly terms with the teaching friars under whose direction Junípero "had lessons in religion, Latin, arithmetic, reading, writing, and vocal music, particularly the Gregorian Chant"—a rather comprehensive schedule for a primary school! The boy had a good voice and "on occasion was permitted to join the community choir of the friars and sing the Divine Office on the solemn feasts of the Church." [1]

But by no means all his time was spent in cultural pursuits. "Young Miguel worked with his parents in the fields, particularly at harvest time, as do the youngsters today. On a farm everyone is expected to do something and all must work for the bread they eat. Schooling was not always necessary or advantageous but work was. In the home on Calle Barracar Miguel enjoyed only the simplest things. The limited quarters of the house, the plain furniture, the rough floor, the dim light furnished by a wick burning in oil, the farmer's fare of wheaten bread, beans, cheese, fruits and vegetables in season, the Majorcan *enseimada*, or sweet cake, were the things he knew. 'What more do we want,' he wrote in later years from San Diego, 'having a little tortilla and the wild herbs of the field?' " [2]

He was satisfied with the simplest nourishment for the body; but when it came to the mind and the soul, he was more demanding. At the age of fifteen he chose the service of the Church for his career and, accompanied by his parents, went to Palma, twenty-five miles distant from Petra. There they sought out one of the cathedral canons who undertook to supervise Junípero's religious and moral progress, and a new life began for him which was to last twenty years.

"Palma, then as now the capital of the island, had some 30,000 inhabitants in an area of about four square miles. Laid out in a semicircle, it faced the open sea, with the mountains to the west, fertile plains to the north and east. Only fifteen miles away the northern sierra formed a pleasing backdrop. The city was enclosed on all sides, even along the Mediterranean, by strong fortress walls. . . . Military guards at the five gates controlled entrance to the city. Within those walls in Serra's day, and to a great extent still preserved, lay a closely built city with dark, narrow, irregular streets occasionally emerging into sun-lit plazas. In places streets on higher levels were reached by stone steps. Standing out prominently is the cathedral,[3] just above the sea wall and ancient fortifications, its flank to the Mediterranean, its façade to the west. Gothic and of medium size as cathedrals go, it is sturdy, somber, and imposing. . . .

"Miguel [Junípero] Serra enrolled as a student of philosophy in the classes conducted by the Franciscans at the Convento de San Francisco. There they taught their own students for the priesthood as well as candidates for the diocesan priesthood and secular students destined for the various professions. Miguel's professor was Fray Juan Pol.

"Too young to enter the Franciscan Order at that time, Miguel spent a year in study. He made his formal request for admission to the Order sometime after January 4, 1730, when another famous son of Petra, the Very Reverend Fray Antonio Perelló Moragues, was elected provincial for the second time. Serra was then sixteen years and three months old, The interview ended with denial of admission. Miguel, small and sickly looking, was told to wait until he was a little older. Apparently

Perelló Moragues must have made his judgment by sight only, for when he was later informed of Miguel's correct age, he gave consent for his admission to the Order. On September 14, 1730, Miguel Joseph Serra was invested with the Franciscan habit by Perelló Moragues himself in the Convento de Santa María de los Angeles de Jesús outside the city's walls. . . .

"In this convent in the year 1730-1731 the Franciscan aspirant from Petra underwent his basic training under the mastership of Fray Antonio Corrió, concerning whom we know nothing more than his name. . . .

"Not only did he [Junípero] delve into books of asceticism and mysticism, but he took great delight in reading the chronicles of the Order, of which there were many available in Spain. These chronicles contained the history of the early Franciscan movement, of the Spanish provinces in the homeland, and of the missionary enterprises in far-off countries. It was this latter group that Serra read with special interest, and the examples of sanctity and missionary zeal became for him heroic patterns to follow. He read these accounts as avidly as a modern boy would read a mystery thriller and remembered what he read, for, as he himself tells us in later years, he thanked God that he had a facile memory. And his friend and associate Palóu records how well Serra could always recount with detail and freshness what he had read in his youth.

"The novice, Miguel, particularly rejoiced when the Franciscan Order produced new fruits of sanctity followed by beatification or canonization by the Church. During his novitiate year two Spanish Franciscans were beatified, Brother Peter Dueñas and Father John of Cetinas, both of whom were martyred in 1397. Fresh in his memory was the canonization in 1726, when Serra was thirteen, of St. Francis Solanus, the Franciscan Apostle of Perú.

"His reading stirred in the young Miguel a strong desire to be a missionary and to emulate those who so appealed to him. The Spanish age of missionary conquest in the New World was a challenge to the spiritually venturesome, capable of sustaining hardship in loneliness and privation. Whether Serra ever discussed this desire with Father Corrió, we have no way of knowing. We do know that when Serra's professional studies were over, his superiors further centered his attention on books. Thus this initial burst of enthusiasm for an active, missionary life was buried under a mass of technical studies. But it never died. . . .

"After an extended spiritual retreat, Serra and his fellow-novices knelt in the sanctuary of the Convento de Jesús before the provincial, Antonio Perelló Moragues, on September 15, 1731. To the kneeling youths, the provincial addressed the following words: 'My sons, what is your petition?' They in unison answered: 'I desire to profess the rule of our Blessed Father, Francis, confirmed by the Lord Pope, Honorius III, by living in obedience, without property, and in chastity, in order to serve God better and to save my soul.' Then one by one, the novices approached the provincial, knelt before him, and placed their hands within his. Miguel Serra, now near eighteen years of age, in his Majorcan dialect and in an audible voice made this momentous promise:

" 'I, Fray Junípero Serra, vow and promise to Almighty God, to the ever blessed Virgin Mary, to Blessed Father Francis, to all the saints, and to you, Father, to observe for the whole span of my life the rule of the Friars Minor conformed by His Holiness, Pope Honorious III, by living in obedience, without property, and in chastity.' Those words pronounced, Serra was a Franciscan forever." [4]

However, he still had six years of study before him, three of philosophy and three of theology, and these subjects were pursued at the Monastery of San Francisco, headquarters of the Franciscan province of Majorca; and after these years of study, during which he was ordained first subdeacon and then deacon, Junípero became, almost simultaneously, a full-fledged priest and a librarian. Three additional years were devoted to the latter task before he became Lector of Philosophy at San Francisco; then he received the signal honor of an appointment to the de prima Scotus Chair of Philosophy at the "Pontifical, Imperial, Royal and Literary University of Majorca" which had been founded in honor of Ramón Lull and which was more informally and better known as the Lullian University.

PENTECOST BY ZURBARAN.

Museo de Bellas Artes, Cádiz, Spain

ST. LUKE BEFORE THE CRUCIFIED CHRIST BY ZURBARÁN.
Prado Museum, Madrid, Spain

PENTECOST BY ZURBARAN.

Museo de Bellas Artes, Cádiz, Spain

ST. LUKE BEFORE THE CRUCIFIED CHRIST BY ZURBARÁN.
Prado Museum, Madrid, Spain

ST. MARY MAGDALENE
BY RIBERA.

Prado Museum, Madrid, Spain

ST. PETER BY FRANCISCO PACHECO.

Provincial Museum, Seville, Spain

SILVER STATUE OF SAN FRANCISCO SOLANO.

Museo Pedro de Osma, Lima, Peru

CONVENT OF LOS DESCALZOS.

MARIA DE AGREDA.

Convent of San Francisco, Lima, Peru

SAN FRANCISCO SOLANO. ARTIST UNKNOWN.

Infirmary of the Convent of San Francisco, Lima, Peru

ST. DOMINIC BY BERRUGUETE.
Prado Museum, Madrid, Spain

ST. DOMINIC BY J. S. GUTIÉRREZ.
Provincial Museum, Seville, Spain

ST. IGNATIUS OF LOYOLA BY VALDES LEAL.

Provincial Museum, Seville, Spain

ST. IGNATIUS OF LOYOLA BY JUAN DE LAS ROELAS.
Provincial Museum, Seville, Spain

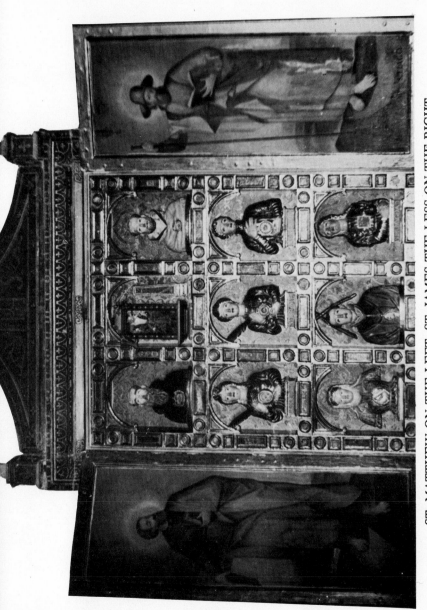

ST. MATTHEW ON THE LEFT; ST. JAMES THE LESS ON THE RIGHT.
ARTIST UNKNOWN.

Church of Santa Ana, Avila, Spain

ST. FRANCIS OF ASSISI BY ZURBARÁN.
Provincial Museum, Seville, Spain

ST. ANDREW AND ST. FRANCIS BY EL GRECO.
Prado Museum, Madrid, Spain

ST. ANTHONY OF PADUA BY A DISCIPLE OF BERRUGUETE'S.

Prado Museum, Madrid, Spain

Along with Junípero's greater responsibilities and opportunities matured a friendship with a fellow Franciscan, Palóu, which
became an integral part of his life. As Palóu himself wrote,
many years later, "From the year 1740, when he received me as
one of his students, until the year 1784, when death separated
us, I was the object of his very special affection, an affection
we always mutually shared, more than if we had been brothers
in the flesh." And when at last Junípero, who had hardly dared
to hope that his missionary dream might come true, was permitted to embark for New Spain, "his joy was the greater that
Fray Francisco Palóu, his closest friend and former student, was
going with him." [5]

"Down to Palma's harbor went Junípero and his companion
Francisco, accompanied perhaps by some of their brethren,
where they boarded an English ship which was going as far as
Málaga. Hardly were they on board when Doctor Serra turned
to Professor Palóu and said these memorable words: 'From now
on let us stop using all these titles of respect and superiority in
regard to each other; no longer will we use the titles "Master"
and "Your Reverence," for we are now in every respect equals.
Call me Junípero and I shall call you Francisco.' [6] Then and
there Junípero broke completely with the past. Protocol was
thrown into the Bay of Palma and the age-long courtesies of
the classroom and cloister were exchanged for the more familiar,
fraternal relationship of the frontier. Aristotle and Scotus and
Virgil would still form part of the professor's mental equipment, but for his success in winning the hearts of the barbarians
of the Sierra Gorda and the more primitive, marginal peoples of
the California coast he would need more of the spirit of Christ,
St. Francis Assisi, and St. Francis Solanus. Self-sacrifice would
be more urgent than learning. [7]

"As the unnamed vessel sailed from the Bay of Palma out
into the Mediterranean, Majorca gradually faded from view.
. . . The captain [of the ship] had probably come from Mi-
norca, a British possession since 1713 according to the terms of
the Treaty of Utrecht, and was on his way to England. Most
likely the vessel was a cargo ship; at least there is no mention
of other passengers. For both Majorcans it was probably their

first sea voyage. Their time was their own and they could arrange their daily religious program aboard. Normally it should have been a pleasurable cruise, but a storm arose at sea caused neither by wind nor by weather. It arose on deck.

"The vessel's skipper, whose memory has come down to us nameless save for Palóu's epithet 'stiff-necked heretic,' was interested in more than the tack of his vessel and the quota of his cargo. He had dabbled in theology and continuously inflicted his unstudied theological lore on his Majorcan passengers. The captain, Palóu tells us, disturbed Serra and him while they were reciting their office together and insisted on arguing religion. With a smattering of broken Portuguese picked up in his voyages, he tried to communicate his theological ideas to the Spanish-speaking padres. Musty Bible in hand, the captain started to give his lessons to the friars, not realizing that Serra was an expert with five years of experience in testing budding doctors in theology. Palóu insinuates, and Serra vouches for the fact, that they volunteered nothing but that they were provoked into replies. Serra became interested in this 'postgraduates' course and quoting chapter and verse from memory, he would ask the captain to look up the corresponding page in his Bible. When this became difficult or embarrassing, the captain replied that the page must be missing.

"But this did not defeat the obstinate skipper. Several times the irate man threatened to throw Junípero and Francisco overboard and proceed directly to London. Who would know the difference? Palóu considered the threat serious. On one of these occasions, matching threat for threat, he told the captain that if he did not deliver the friars safely to Málaga, since they were traveling under the protection of his passport, there would be international repercussions. 'Our king will demand indemnity from your king and you will pay with your head.' No one was thrown overboard. . . .

"Reaching Málaga on Sunday, April 27, the Feast of the Patronage of St. Joseph, Serra and Palóu had their first view of the southern coast of the Spanish peninsula. . . . Land must have been a relief after the two unusual weeks at sea and the two friars immediately went to the Franciscan convent of San Luis of the Province of Granada. . . .

"Fray Juan Jurado,[8] the superior at San Luis and a professor emeritus, received them most hospitably. Palóu states that within half an hour after arriving at the convent Serra joined the community in the recitation of compline and evening prayers, showing Serra's devotion to religious community exercises and his love for monastic regularity. 'Thus he followed the community exercises during the five days we remained there.'[9] However, 'when the humble Father realized the excessive regard in which he was held by that superior, he decided immediately that we should leave the friary and go aboard a small Spanish vessel which was to take us as far as Cádiz.'[10] Serra and Palóu sailed on May 2 or 3. . . .

"Disembarking at this rendezvous for missionaries from all over Spain, Serra and Palóu went for their lodging to the Convent of San Francisco, located in the northeast section of the city, only two blocks from the bay. . . .

"At San Francisco the two friars met their Father Commissary, Fray Pedro Pérez de Mezquía, a veteran missionary of Texas and the Sierra Gorda, a member of the College of San Fernando. There was a round of introductions and embraces between the two Majorcans and the volunteers from the other parts of Spain who had arrived before them. Eleven had come from the north, four from the region of Madrid, six from the eastern coast, and five from western Andalusia. But this was not the full quota for the mission. A few friars at their first sight of the sea reconsidered the step they had taken. Many friars who came from remote country convents in the interior of Spain obtained their first view of a world emporium and the deep blue Atlantic when they arrived in Cádiz. Some retraced their steps home to Father Guardian and Provincial; the unknown and the unexperienced were not for them. Such had been the situation here and it had resulted in five vacancies in all. Serra learned that Father Pérez de Mezquía wished to take with him the complete number of missionaries allowed by the king if it were at all possible, and so he reported that there were more volunteers in Majorca and suggested that if time were left, they should be notified. The commissary acted on Serra's advice and sent letters patent to Palma inviting three more missionaries to join the group: Fathers Juan Crespí, Rafael Verger, and Guillermo Vicens, who, like Serra, was a native of Petra.[11]

"Four long months of patient waiting in Cádiz were still ahead before the sailing for the Indies. It was thus that Cádiz had become a missionary city, a Franciscan port of embarkation where hundreds upon hundreds of missionaries were lodged in the course of centuries waiting to be shipped to their distant mission fields, some as far away as the Philippines.

"When an apostolic college or a province needed new missionaries, the respective superiors in the Indies appointed a commissary from the area to go to Spain to recruit them. His first act was to make known his request to the Council of the Indies at Madrid through the Franciscan Commissary General. The Council of the Indies, after consulting the king, stipulated the number of missionaries allowed for the enterprise and determined the sum of money for all necessary expenditures, covering the time from which the missionaries left their convents in Spain until they arrived at their college or province in the New World. The Council of the Indies notified the Board of Trade at Cádiz of the arrangements made and of permissions given.

"Once the royal permission had been given, the commissary traveled about Spain or sent out letters inviting missionary enlistments from colleges and monasteries. As often as not, the men they gathered represented a cross section of the Spanish homeland, from Galicia to Andalusia and from Extremadura to Catalonia. From the moment a friar left his convent he was in the royal service and in the royal pay. *All missionaries went to the Indies as agents of the state as well as emissaries of the Church.*[12] The individual friar brought with him to Cádiz a certified letter from the superior of the convent he left containing a statement as to the place and time of departure. This he gave to the guardian of the convent where he stayed. The superior at Cádiz notarized this with the date of the missionary's arrival, and it was presented to the officials of the Board of

Trade. Allowances were made for the transportation of books and clothing from the missionary's place of origin to Cádiz, the distance being calculated on the basis of the mail routes in vogue. Thus the distance from Palma of Majorca to Cádiz was computed at three hundred and nine leagues and on that basis Serra and Palóu were allowed seven reales a day at the rate of eight leagues of travel a day.

"At Cádiz itself the friars were maintained at royal expense for the length of their stay. The local superiors kept a record of the friars' sojourn and expenses and presented vouchers to the Government for reimbursement. Thus Serra and Palóu were allowed two reales a day for maintenance between May 5 and August 24, 1749. While the friars remained in port waiting for embarkation, they usually lived in the convents of their Order and followed the daily round of religious exercises. However, a housing problem did exist. It frequently happened that the number of friars exceeded the possibilities of conventual hospitality, with the result that some had to be lodged in the auxiliary posts across the bay and even in private dwellings. Such friars, no doubt, had a little more freedom of movement and their religious conformity depended on their sense of duty. It was a condition that commissaries did not like but which, because of conditions, they were forced to tolerate.

"Matters concerning sailing were arranged by the commissary and the Board of Trade with the shipmasters of the area. Detailed commitments were made in regard to the quality and number of cabins, food for the journey, and safe deposit at the destined port in the Indies. At times various adjustments had to be made and delays were frequently long.

"The missionary went forth as an ambassador of Christ and as an emissary of the Catholic Church but, according to the arrangements of the time, his function was carried out under Spanish auspices. To compensate for the privileges the Spanish nation had acquired under the *real patronato*[13] granted by the pope shortly after the discovery of America, the king was obliged to provide all those external arrangements and activities calculated to maintain and spread the faith in the Indies, east and west. Whatever disadvantages this method offered, it was the most effective means at the time for unbroken missionary endeavor. *The New World was Christianized through it.*[14]

"At Cádiz, the missionaries gathered by the commissaries were presented to the officials of the Board of Trade who noted down their vital statistics, offices, and physical characteristics. . . . In the Archivo de Indias at Seville there is an extant document, a bulky one hundred ninety-six folio pages, concerning the mission going to Mexico under Father Pérez de Mezquía, which describes all the official acts of the preparation of the mission of friars for San Fernando in the year 1749, the mission of which Serra and Palóu were members. Every cent is accounted for and no physical feature of a friar that had any distinguishing value was overlooked. . . . The physical description and vital statistics of the four men who were to bound so intimately in the American mission field are officially given there as follows: Father Junípero Serra, lector of theology, native of Petra in the Diocese of Majorca, thirty-five years old, of medium height, swarthy, dark eyes and hair, scant beard. Father Francisco Palóu, lector of philosophy, native of Palma, twenty-six years old, of medium height, swarthy, dark eyes and hair. Father Juan Crespí [whose name the port officials misspelled as Chrispín], a native of Palma, twenty-eight years old, short of stature, sallow skin but somewhat florid complexion. blue eyes, and dark hair. Father Rafael Verger, lector of philosophy, native of Santañyi, twenty-six years old, of regular stature, fair complexion, face pock-marked, somewhat florid, with a scant beard.

"It is unfortunate that we have no letter of either Serra or Palóu written from Cádiz describing their stay in this port and their reactions to the colorful city . . . [but] one very personal letter Serra did write immediately before leaving Cádiz, filled with spiritual beauty and missionary enthusiasm. This was [the one intended as] his farewell letter to his parents, the only complete letter of the first thirty-five years of life that has come down to us. In it the Majorcan missionary-to-be is revealed in the fullness of his mind and heart, in middle life, ready for spiritual conquest of the New World. Padre Parras gave us a colorful painting of the external world in which the departing missionaries moved. Serra depicted the world of the spirit, the motives, aspirations, and resolves of the missionary's soul." [15] As his parents were illiterate, the letter was addressed (as others which have not come down to us had been) to Junípero's friend and associate at San Bernardino in Petra, Francisco Serra, to whom he entrusted the charge of reading it to his parents and other members of his immediate family.

"Most Dear Friend in Jesus Christ, Father Francisco Serra:

"Dear, intimate friend: Words cannot express the feelings of my heart as I bid you farewell nor can I properly repeat to you my request that you be the consolation of my parents to sustain them in their sorrow. I wish I could communicate to them the great joy that fills my heart. If I could do this, then surely they would always encourage me to go forward and never to turn back. Let them remember that the office of an apostolic preacher, especially in its actual exercise, is the greatest calling to which they could wish me to be chosen.

"Since they are advanced in years, let them recall that life is uncertain and, in fact, may be very brief. If they compare it with eternity, they will clearly realize that it cannot be but more than an instant. Since this is true, it will be very much to the point and most conformable to the holy will of God if they will not emphasize the very little help that I could give them with regard to the needs of this life. Rather should they strive to merit from God, our Lord, that if we see each other no more in this life, we may be joined forever in future glory.

"Tell them that I shall ever feel the loss of not being able to be near them as heretofore to console them, but since first things must come first and before all else, the first thing to do is to fulfill the will of God. It was for the love of God that I left them and if I, for the love of God and with the aid of His grace, had the strength of will to do so, it will be to the point that they too, for the love of God, be content to be deprived of my company.

"Tell them to heed the advice of their confessor as to what instructions he shall give them concerning this matter. They will realize then in all truth that God has come into their home. In holy patience and resignation, bending to God's holy will, they will possess their souls, for in so doing they will attain eternal life. Let them attribute what they now lament to no one but to God, our Lord. They will learn to see how sweet is His yoke, and that He will change for them the sorrow they may now experience into great happiness. Now is not the time to muse or fret over the happenings of life but rather to be conformed entirely to the will of God, striving to prepare themselves for a happy death which of all the things of life is our principal concern. For if we attain that, it matters little if we lose all the rest. But if we do not attain that, nothing else will be of any value.

"Let them rejoice that they have a son who is a priest, though an unworthy one and a sinner, who daily in the holy sacrifice of the Mass prays for them with all the fervor of his soul and on many days applies the Mass for them alone, so that the Lord may aid them; that they may not lack their daily bread, that He may give them patience in their trials, resignation to His holy will, peace and union with everyone, courage to fight the temptations of the evil one, and last of all, when it is God's will a tranquil death in His holy grace. If I, by the grace of God, succeed in becoming a good religious, my prayers will become more efficacious, and they in consequence will be the gainers.

"The same I say to my beloved sister in Christ, Juana, and to my brother-in-law, Miquel. Let them not be concerned about me now, but rather let them commend me to God that I may be a good priest and a holy minister of God. In this we are all very interested and this alone matters. I recall the occasion when my father was so ill that extreme unction was administered to him. I, being a religious, was at home at the time, and thinking that he was going to die, we two being alone, he said to me: 'My son, let me charge you to be a good religious of your Father, St. Francis.'

"Now, dear father, be assured that those words are as fresh in my memory as when they proceeded from your lips. Realize, too, that in order to become a good religious, I have set out on this course. So do not be disconsolate when I am carrying out your will, which is one with the will of God. I know, too, that my mother has never ceased to commend me to God in order that I may be a good religious. Now, dear mother mine, if perhaps God has set me in this course as a result of your prayers, be content with what God disposes and ever say in life's tribulations: 'Blessed be God. May His holy will be done.'

"Let my sister Juana recall that not so long ago she was at the very door of death when God, through the merits and intercession of Mary Most Holy, restored her to perfect health. Had she died, she would not be concerned one way or the other whether I would be remaining in Majorca or leaving it. Let her rather give thanks to God and conform herself to what He disposes, because what He does is the proper thing. Moreover, it may be quite true that the Lord gave her good health precisely so that she might be able to be the consolation of our good, aged parents now that I have had to depart. Let us give praise to God. May God love us all and keep us close to Him.

"My brother-in-law Miquel and my sister, Juana, I sincerely entreat you as I entreated you on a former occasion to live together in great peace and harmony. I asked you to endeavor to show respect for, to bear with, and to console our old parents and to take most diligent care to bring up your children. I entreat all to be conscientious in attending church, in going to confession and receiving Communion frequently, in making the Stations of the Cross, in a word, in striving in every way to be good Christians. I trust that since you have not forgotten to commend me to God so that I may have His assistance, you will not fail to do so likewise in the future. Thus while we continue to supplicate God for one another, I for you, and you for me, the same Lord will aid us in this life by giving us His holy grace, and after that the life of glory.

"Good-by, my dear father! Farewell, dear mother of mine! Good-by, my dear sister, Juana! Good-by, my beloved brother-in-law. Take good care of little Mike [who was then eight years and seven months old] and see to it that he becomes a good Christian and a studious pupil and that the two girls grow up as good Christians. Trust to God that your uncle may yet be of some service to you. Good-by and farewell! . . . .

"From this house of the Holy Mission in this city of Cádiz, August 20, 1749.

Your cordial friend in Christ,
FRAY JUNÍPERO SERRA
Most unworthy priest.

Father Palóu sends Your Reverence repeated regards and kindly give the regards of both of us to Señor Guillermo Roco and the members of his household." [16]

The long period of waiting for transportation across the Atlantic finally came to an end, but the passage was almost as protracted as the stay in southern Spain. "The crossing from Cádiz to Veracruz took an exceptionally long time—ninety-nine days. Even the vessels of the preceding century had been accustomed to do it in less. On board the *Nuestra Señora de Guadalupe* were twenty-one Franciscans and six Dominican friars, who were to endure extreme discomfort. The ship's slow progress reduced its food stores dangerously, and even the water ran out before the sighting of Puerto Rico, the first chance for replenishment. Fray Junípero overcame his thirst as always he would triumph over his body. When asked later whether he had not suffered intensely from lack of drinking water, he said: 'Not particularly. I soon discovered that to eat little and talk less is a remedy for this distress.' " [17]

The voyagers remained for eighteen days in Puerto Rico before continuing on their way to Veracruz. There are conflicting reports as to exactly how they began their activities in the beautiful port of San Juan; but there is no doubt that some sort of a missionary program was promptly organized and that there was an overwhelming popular response to this. "Another phase of life at San Juan recorded by Serra was the friendly intercourse between friars and laymen in the old fortress town. Local ties are strong when you meet fellow-countrymen on distant, foreign soil, especially if they are from your own native town or district. As soon as the missionaries landed, several Spanish gentlemen, apparently of wealth and distinction, came to greet them and to ask if there were any Majorcans among them. Fathers Serra and Palóu identified themselves as such and there was mutual rejoicing. Paraphrasing St. Paul's words, the friars and laymen must have recalled that they were natives of no mean island. These laymen immediately offered 'various and splendid gifts.' The Majorcan friars accepted nothing for themselves, but the laymen sent the gifts to the community as a whole in the form of fruits and preserves and money with which to buy meat for their table and candles to light up their rooms. Serra observed that there was no olive oil in Puerto Rico, as in Majorca, to illumine the houses. 'They honored us greatly and treated us royally,' wrote the exuberant and grateful padre. Finally, a third Majorcan gentleman appeared, Juan Ferrer by name, who was a nephew of the Franciscan definitor of Majorca, Botellas. He was superintendent and manager of the royal warehouse at San Juan. Serra declares that he too 'treated us very splendidly and gave us numberless gifts.' He certainly was well placed, if any one was, to do so!" [18]

Presumably, their missionary zeal was so great that Junípero and Palóu were able to leave San Juan and its delightful amenities and seek out other worlds to conquer without too much regret; but this time they had more than a "stiff-necked heretic" with whom to contend: there was a mutiny among the sailors and the *Villasota* (their next ship) was buffeted with such fearful storms that she had to put back to port before she was actually out of sight of land, only to encounter even worse storms when she finally got under way. It was a month before the already historic harbor of Vera Cruz was reached and Junípero stepped on land "at the most desired end of a long and tedious voyage." He could, however, boast that "during the ninety-nine days' voyage, he had not been seasick even once. We have this on his own declaration in a letter, perhaps as a note of consolation to his aged parents. Serra, to become noted as a tireless land traveler, was also a good sailor." [19]

Franciscans, as well as Dominicans, were already established in Vera Cruz, so the missionaries were suitably welcomed at their respective monasteries, and Palóu, who was felled by a sudden and severe illness, was tenderly cared for; but if there were as many wealthy, aristocratic and hospitable Spaniards in this city, eager to ply the missionaries with gifts and feasts, I have found no mention of it. Consequently, they were able to start for Mexico City without undue delay. Their route was by the Camino Real, but we are reminded that we should not misinterpret this term, which was used to designate thoroughfares throughout the Spanish dominion. "Travelers hardly ever used these roads for pleasure. They were roads in so far as they led somewhere. They served the interests of the king in consolidating his dominions, in furthering commerce, and in propagating religion. By acclaim of one and all these Royal Highways were described as bad, very bad. As late as 1787 it was stated in Mexico that while nothing served the public interest more than good roads, nothing was given less attention. Spain, the builder of magnificent cathedrals, powerful forts, and impressive aqueducts, did less well in the matter of roads. . . . Our immediate interest lies in the old Camino Real between Vera Cruz and Mexico City, the first road in America traversed by Serra and his confreres in 1749. It stretches from sea level to an altitude of 7,382 feet through tropical country, arid plains, high plateaus, across formidable sierras, in view of volcanos and lakes, perennial snow, and abundant sunshine. With some variations it is the road of Cortés, Humboldt, and that of the modern tourist. It is not a direct road—a physical impossibility—for high mountain barriers make it forcibly circuitous. Today you can make the trip by plane, train, bus, or private car. Serra walked." [20]

"It was no longer the custom of the friars to do their traveling afoot on the longest and hardest journeys. True, St. Francis had prohibited his first followers the comforts of four-footed locomotion, but he could hardly have foreseen America and the incredible distances his later-day followers would be called upon to cover just to reach their stations. And moreover, it was now the middle of the eighteenth century and it would not be long until speed itself would become a standard requirement throughout the world. However, Fray Junípero was determined to walk from the port to Mexico City as had the early Franciscan missionary heroes—even though only one of his companions could be persuaded to accompany him.

"His austerity on this occasion had painful results, for en route he suffered the bite (variously reported as that of a snake and a poisonous insect) which, becoming infected and ulcerous, was to cripple him for life. But he refused to bow before this mishap and on December 31, trudged into La Villa de Guadalupe, where he spent the night and said Mass on New Year's day in honor of the celebrated *Virgen Morena*[21] at her shrine. The same day he walked into the capital as had those stalwarts before him—Pedro de Gante, the twelve of Fray Martín de Valencia's party, El Beato Sebastián de Aparicio, and Fray Margil de Jesús—albeit much more painfully. At the College of San Fernando, he was welcomed with joy, his fame for scholarship and preaching having preceded him." [22]

We are reminded by Geiger that clarification of this use of the term "college" is needed. "Apostolic colleges are a part of the institutional history of colonial Hispanic America and of the Franciscan Order. They were founded to form a picked body of men of exalted spiritual ideals, of strict ascetic life, and of austere living—an elite corps of missionaries ready when the call was given to extend Christianity among the American aborigines or to renovate the lives of the home folk in more genuine Christian fashion. . . . The physical plant was indeed large—San Fernando had several cloisters and, besides its community rooms, accommodations for about a hundred friars. But while education went on there, the primary purpose was a special mode of living for the formation of apostolic men and able missionaries. There was a very strict routine, a program, and a purpose. There were teachers and alumni. All were banded together for the achievement of a common purpose— the etymological meaning of 'college.' In a word, it was an independent, specialized institution within the framework of the Franciscan Order to gather and train men for the apostolate of the home missions and unconverted Indian fields. The apostolate college was a completely Franciscan idea, a new contribution to the mission field. . . .

"During his first year of residence at the college, a friar was not to be sent out into a mission field nor did he have the right to vote. That year served as one of apprenticeship or a sort of second novitiate, a time of probation and trial of his fitness for the institute. Friars coming from Spain at royal expense were required to serve the college for ten years, after which time they could return to their colleges or provinces, again at royal expense and with the permission of their superiors. Because of unfitness, illness, or scandal, they could be returned sooner. . . .

"All the material needs of the friars were attended to by the lay syndic who received money for the college maintenance and paid the bills. No friar could handle money in a commercial sense. In times of illness the friar was cared for and convalesced in the college, not in a hospital or private home. Recreations were taken in common in the college patios or in walks outside the city. The color of the habit worn at all the apostolic colleges was gray, woven from white and black wool. No dye of any kind was allowed. . . .

"On their arrival at their new home, Junípero and his companion first went into the church to pay their respects to *Jesús Sacramentado*. There the churrigueresque altars, glowing with gold, may already have been set in place. Their gaudy splendor had a tropical brilliance of which the friars themselves tired in time and substituted simple classic altars, still extant and a disappointment to those looking today for adornment at San Fernando. Within the church Serra heard the sound of rhythmic prayer, for the friars were chanting their office. His first impression of San Fernando was not of the symmetry of its architecture but of the harmony of its prayers. He was pleased and a note of optimism struck his soul. 'Father,' he said to his companion, 'we can indeed consider as well employed our journey here from so far away, together with the difficulties we encountered, if only to gain the happiness of being members of a community which so slowly and devoutly fulfills the obligation of the Divine Office.' [23]

"A few steps brought the two straggling pedestrians to the portal of the college and into the enclosure where Fray Joseph Ortés de Velasco, the guardian, received them. It was a Happy New Year all around. Serra knelt to receive the blessing of the guardian and to kiss his hand. Then embraces in the Spanish custom were exchanged. . . .

"Promptly Father Ortés assigned a cell to Serra and he became a regular member of the community. Serra gave himself only a day to get his bearings, for he had come to San Fernando to prepare himself spiritually for his missionary vocation which he prized as the greatest blessing of his life. So on January 2, with a humility refreshing in one accustomed to speaking ex cathedra, he approached the Father Guardian and asked to be placed under one of the Fathers who would be his confessor and spiritual director. As spiritual Father he received Fray Bernardo Pumeda, then master of novices, a man who was versed in ascetical and mystical theology and who had received his training in the Apostolic College of Sahagún[24] in Spain. Serra, commenting on the choice, possibly to Palóu, declared: 'The superior has hit the mark; this is what I need, to make the novitiate.' . . .[25]

"Shortly after the arrival of the friars, during a recreation period when all were in the cloister garden, Father Ortés de Velasco expressed his pleasure at their coming and explained a difficulty with which he was confronted. The college had assumed the responsibility of manning the Sierra Gorda Missions in 1744, but its personnel had been sharply curtailed by the deaths of four missionaries within a short time. As an emergency measure to help out a sister college, Santa Cruz of Querétaro had supplied missionaries for six month periods. Though Ortés de Velasco realized that the rule of the college required all newcomers to remain there a year before being sent to missions, he felt that in the circumstances Querétaro should not be obliged to maintain missions not under their jurisdiction as long as San Fernando had men to supply them. He could dispense from the college rule. 'Now, who of you will volunteer for the Sierra Gorda?' Serra spoke up first, using the words of Isaiah, the prophet: 'Here I am; send me.'[26] Others present echoed their willingness and before long the guardian had more than the needed complement of volunteers. Nine were chosen, among them Palóu. However, they were not sent immediately. Querétaro had to be notified and meanwhile the Fernandinos could prepare themselves. Palóu tells us that after his assignment to his mission Serra gave himself over to even more intense spiritual preparation." [27]

Although he recognized the need for preparation, "because he had crossed the sea to carry the Gospel to the heathen, the first five months in Mexico City before he was given a field assignment were a heavy trial to Serra. He was a very holy man and willing enough to accept hardship and suffering in the name of Our Lord. But his was scarcely a social temperament, and certainly he did not feel like being sociable with the vain and ostentatious *Capitalinos*. He was particularly annoyed that the sophisticated gentry showed themselves so mindful of their 'creature-comforts' that the society ladies even persisted in having their hot chocolate served to them in church! There had never been such 'goings-on' in Mallorca. He was quite sure that the most atrocious sins and the unaffected pagans would be more endurable than the peccadilloes of these wealthy, brash and self-indulgent colonists!

"The Sierra Gorda, of legendary fame for the hostility of its savages and the rigors of its climate and terrain, was still a rugged mission field in 1750. This was the region Fray Lináz had so wished to evangelize and one of the few places where Fray Margil de Jesús had found it necessary, before departing, to '*brush off the dust against those who would not hear.*' Fray Junípero's first mission post was among the Pame Indians of the Sierra Gorda. He accepted it with the greatest joy he had yet known in the New World, his happiness heightened because Father Palóu was to be his companion in this work. Together they walked the two hundred miles to Santiago de Xalpan, arriving there on June 1." [28]

"Among the fiercest of the aboriginal tribes, the Pame Indians of the Sierra Gorda ranked high. They were cannibals, for one thing, who ate human flesh only when cooked with tomatoes and chili peppers—a sauce, incidentally, still popular in Mexico although now containing less sinister ingredients. An official report admitted that all military expeditions attempting to penetrate the thick jungles sheltering the Pames were unsuccessful, and that missionary efforts to convert these Indians had failed. And yet it was necessary to do something about a menace which had become so bold that raiding parties frequently ventured from the region of Jalpan to strike at the much-traveled highway from Querétaro to Mexico City. . . .

"Fra Junípero remained in Pame country for eight years. Amazingly enough, he was not devoured by the Indians. He was not even attacked. From the first he employed a method which became increasingly effective. *He remembered that the missionaries of the Middle Ages had taught the techniques of material civilization at the same time they were teaching the spiritual values of Christianity.*[29] As soon as Fra Junípero had settled his little group of brothers in the Pame country, he set about teaching the Indians how to cut down trees, plow the ground, plant corn, and breed cattle, sheep, and mules. The happy results of his efforts gradually became known throughout the Sierra Gorda. Not only the Pames, but other tribes discovered that the methods taught by the white missionaries led to a better and easier life than that to be had by depending entirely on the hunt and the products of the forest. The new missionary centers which sprang up were also centers for agriculture and stock-raising.

"The Spanish military leaders were dumbfounded by the success of unarmed monks in the same area that had fiercely defied Spanish muskets and cavalry sabers. Junípero and his brothers, however, did not permit their material progress to divert them from their evangelical goal. They worked hard at converting their Pames to Christianity. They translated the catechism into Pame, preached in Pame, heard confessions in Pame. They discredited the witch doctors. The old idols of the Sun Mother were overthrown, some burned, others ceremoniously presented to the missionaries.

"The good Franciscan fathers found themselves running a little communal republic in which the converted Indians worked together, shared the products of their common cultivation of the soil, and prayed together. It was a triumph. The impenetrable Sierra Gorda had become God's province.

"The spectacular success of the lame little brother influenced both his religious superiors and the Spanish lay authorities to utilize his remarkable talents as a pacifier in a field still more difficult than that of the Pames. They would send him to the Apaches. What was then known as 'Apache country' was situated roughly in what is now the states of Texas, New Mexico and Arizona. Actually Apache country constituted a vast and ill-defined region also inhabited by Indian tribes other than the Apaches who had little in common except their ferocity. The Apaches were reputed to be cannibals without the epicurean finesse of the Pames. Instead of stewing their prisoners in a pot with tomatoes and chili peppers, they merely flayed them alive, bled them well (they were not fond of red meat), and roasted them on a spit. The transference of the name of 'Apaches' to the worst bandits of the Paris underworld seems to have had some justification.

"When Junípero Serra arrived in this dreadful Apache country, the Indians had just killed two missionaries under the most frightful circumstances. This did not prevent his attempting to evangelize them—in vain. The malice of some men can defeat even the charity, the zeal, and the heroism of saints. Other missionaries were murdered by these intractable savages, whose trickery was as dangerous as their violence. One Apache tribe would come knocking at the gates of a Spanish presidio, asking protection against an enemy tribe. No sooner had they been admitted to the stockade than the Indians produced tomahawks, quivers of arrows, and muskets stolen from the French in Louisiana—and the massacre began. After several tragedies of this sort and the failure of attempts to convert the Apaches, the mission superiors recalled Junípero and his group." [30]

Though Father Junípero's mission to the Apaches was not crowned with success—and it is one of his few recorded failures —he went on with his good work in the dioceses of Mexico, Puebla, Morelos, and Oaxaca and might have continued to do so indefinitely, with fruitful results, if two unexpected events, which came close together, had not precipitated a change in his activities. In 1767 the Spanish Government abruptly exiled the Jesuits, both from the homeland and from the colonies, and, in regretfully leaving the many missions they had founded, the dispossessed followers of St. Ignatius appealed to the members of other Orders to carry on the work which they themselves had begun with such competence and devotion. No less than fifteen Jesuit missions had been established in what we now know as Lower California and the Viceroy[31] of Mexico appointed Junípero Serra Father President of this chain. Delightedly, he accepted the appointment and, with several of his friars, including Palóu, arrived on Good Friday, 1768, at Loreto, whose mission became the mother church of all the others.

Upper California was still unexplored and reports that the Indians who inhabited this region were as murderous as the Apaches had not encouraged attempts at colonization. Then a rumor began to spread that whether or not Ferdinand of Spain was interested in occupying this territory, Catherine of Russia was beginning to look at it with covetous eyes. Acting with great dispatch, the Viceroy of Mexico decided to send a military expedition farther north than any had so far penetrated and build a fortress which would prove a formidable bulwark against the enemy. At the same time, he decided that it would be a good plan to suggest that Father Junípero Serra should accompany the soldiery. A more extended chain of missions would prove an added safeguard to a more extended chain of forts—in fact, one would supplement the other. If Junípero were as successful with the Indians of Upper California as he had been with the Pames, he would do much more, or rather much besides, baptizing them; he would teach them to make the soil productive and to have due respect for the laws of their conquerors. On this point the Viceroy and the King's *Visitador* (Inspector-General), Don José de Gálvez, were in complete accord, for the latter had just made a tour of inspection and had been much impressed with Junípero's efficiency. Accordingly, he was given the title of Father President of Upper as well as Lower California. Again, he accepted the appointment with the delight of a man who is essentially an adventurer and an explorer as well as a missionary.

"The expedition would set out in four divisions, two by sea and two by land, to meet again at San Diego. Each party would be composed of artisans, farmers, soldiers and friars, together with their horses, mules, other domestic livestock and provisions. Some indispensable items, including church bells and altar furnishings, as well as mules, actually had to be 'lifted' from the peninsula missions. This was regrettable, but Fray Junípero knew it couldn't be helped: once arrived in the north, the missionaries would have put months of travel between their needs and the cities where such things might be had. And at the moment time was short enough for the much that demanded doing.

"As soon as the two ships (the *San Carlos* and the *San Antonio*) were loaded and ready for sailing, they and their standards were blessed. Gálvez, unable to go along, made a little speech, and the cannon roared. Fray Junípero sang the farewell Mass on each boat, only a few days apart, and they were off for California! It was February, 1769. In March, the first land party pulled out under the command of Captain Rivera y Moncada. That of Gaspar de Portolá would not get away until two months later. With it, after seeing to everything and attending everyone, would go the overworked, middle-aged, lame and jubilant Padre Serra!" [32]

"For the next sixteen years, until the day of his death, the little monk with the limp would be the director of this astonishing project: to rescue for civilization this wild new country, to plant the Cross along some six hundred miles of coast line. His poor leg still pained him. The ulceration refused to heal, and his limp was more and more pronounced. Other maladies were to be added to his physical handicap: chronic bronchitis and frequent serious attacks of gastritis. And the life he was forced to lead was hardly designed for a semi-invalid. . . .

"As soon as one mission was founded—they were situated one day's march apart—Fra Junípero put his system into operation. Love and gentleness were his secret ingredients. How he cherished his Indians! He spoke warmly of their natural virtues, the rare qualities which they possessed and which needed only baptism to come into full flower. He found no fault with them,

THE WORLD WIDENS : 181

which is saying much. According to him, they had only to hear of the beauties of the holy Christian religion to become converted, to become better, more civilized men than many Europeans. He suffered agonies whenever events proved him wrong; when, for example, a few renegade Christian Indians would attack some mission. He suffered even more when European soldiers, who were far from all being saints, used violence on the Indians or launched reprisals. The most surprising thing was that on the whole Fra Junípero's methods were quite successful.

"Soon each of his mission stations became a true center of European civilization. The three or four Franciscan fathers who maintained each mission taught the Indians the cultivation of soil, the raising of livestock, and even a few rural crafts. Numerically, the project really didn't amount to very much at the start: only a few hundred Indians were ready to come and live under the protection of the white men and listen to their counsel. Beyond the missions many dangers still existed, and communications between stations could be maintained only under heavy escort. Furthermore, the methods of kindness often seemed pretty absurd to the Spanish soldiers charged with pacifying the country. They believed that only force could maintain law and order. A good massacre from time to time would keep the Indians in line.

"Junípero Serra naturally opposed the military viewpoint and went so far as to protest the policy of force to Don Antonio María Bucareli y Ursúa, Viceroy, Governor, and Captain General of New Spain. Luckily the Viceroy was a true Christian who understood the great missionary's viewpoint. Yet despite the backing of Mexico City, of the sixteen years he devoted to the creation of California, Fra Junípero spent no less than six or seven of them in fighting the stupidity of lay administrators and military officers who thought only in terms of killing. Some of them were so disgusted with the Franciscan's methods and influence that they recommended to Mexico City that the whole California project be abandoned." [33]

This discouraging recommendation was based on a series of mischances that culminated in the non-return of the *San Antonio,* which had been sent off for much-needed supplies, and it marked "the worst moment in Junípero Serra's life." [34] He had accepted with Christian resignation the royal decree by which Franciscans were supplanted in Lower California by Dominicans. There is no doubt that Palóu, to whom he had necessarily delegated much of his authority as he went farther and farther north, was following his superior's wishes when he described that situation objectively and philosophically. [35] But Upper California was something else again. "He simply couldn't conceive of accepting defeat now, abandoning all these Indians whose welfare had already cost them so much effort and hardship. He had come to California to save them for God. Very well, he would depend on Him to see the holy adventure through! First, though, he used all the arguments at his command. If this expedition was to come to nothing but a huge waste of money and life, could they expect Spain to send out another? Hardly, and certainly not in time. The result would mean the loss of California to more enterprising nations, and this loss would also be the Church's loss. He even went so far as to declare that if their Commander ordered the colonists to move south, he and Father Crespí would remain behind!

"In the end, Portolá [now military governor] compromised. Rivera was dispatched to Velicatá with twenty soldiers and a pack train, but he and the others would delay nine days to give Father Serra time to make a novena for the arrival of the San Antonio. To all practical appearances, this ship was their one hope at the moment and, in Portolá's opinion, a decidedly slim one. The two frailes might refuse to go if they chose, but what could they accomplish without supplies and the help of at least a few colonists? Nothing but their own futile deaths. So they commenced the novena which was to end on March 19, the Feast of St. Joseph. Their pleas would be directed to this saint." [36]

This is surely one of the most memorable novenas in history and it has been made the subject of a charming novel entitled The Nine Days of Father Serra by Isabelle Gibson Ziegler, which I highly recommend to anyone interested in following Junípero's career. But as a matter of fact, the actual episode is so dramatic that it hardly needs the support of fiction to give it color and excitement. Day after day "dawned, each dragging on into relentless night, increasing the tension. On the nineteenth of March, Fray Junípero exhausted himself in prayer. By sheer force, he held to his hope all the long day while that of the others must have waned distressfully. Into the dusk, the lame, aging Franciscan persisted in his lookout toward sea. And then, just before the light faded completely, he had his reward. Out there on the ocean before his eyes, a ship had suddenly appeared." [37]

In the next fifteen years, Junípero Serra, with the help of his old friend and spiritual brother, Palóu, who rejoined him in 1776, founded no less than ten[38] missions and was the guiding force in the settlement of Upper California. To succeeding generations, his accomplishments, both as a missionary and as a colonizer, seemed very close to the miraculous; and indeed, there are many who are amazed that his name has not yet been formally entered in the calendar of saints. The state which was to such a degree his foundation has given him the highest honor in its power by placing his likeness in the Statuary Hall of the Capitol at Washington, where only supreme service to any state is recognized and such recognition is limited to one man. But Junípero Serra himself was destined to die without the realization of the magnitude of his achievements. Indeed, he was not even sure that the Franciscans might not be officially supplanted in Upper California, as they had been in Lower California, by the Dominicans. A seemingly well-founded rumor to this effect did not fail to reach him and in April, 1784, he wrote to his old friend, Father Lasuén: "Concerning the matter of our expulsion from these lands, we who were the first ones to announce the name of the true God, of Jesus Christ, and of His Holy Gospel, from lands in which we were the first to raise the holy wood of the cross and where today there are many thousands baptized among the living and the dead—for soon the good [Dominican] Fathers may arrive—I hope to give them a good account of more than five thousand confirmed in these lands and they will have much to think about. How much evil, thought I, must have been spoken against us at court when a Señor Gálvez who only yesterday was adamant that the Fathers who are in [Lower] California today were to get out and those of San Fernando were to return there! Now it has happened not only that we will not supplant them there but that their Reverences will supplant us here. What a thought that the College of San Fernando, until yesterday so highly esteemed for its conversions, as is known, and in whose honor a little while ago, the Illustrious Bishop Reyes in the refectory, offering a toast to it, said before the community: 'Rejoice, O College of San Fernando, who alone today has true missions among the pagans and you alone!' This is what was related to me by Father Nobóa. Is it possible that such a college in such a condition today they will leave thus [stripped]? What shall we say about this? This is indeed an hour for me in which to take stock and amend my ways. . . . Do not hide from me any news from the college, however sad it may be." [39]

Very few letters were written after that and none of which we have documentary evidence after early August of that same year. Junípero Serra had always been ailing and frequently ill; now he suffered continually and intensely. Yet he continued to travel and to labor. "And only he understood that now the end was approaching. But he was content. He had striven against insuperable obstacles in the wilderness to plant the seed of faith in the souls of men. His subjects could hardly have been worse; his results could scarcely have been better. His nine missions would be the forerunners of many more. Attended by his lifelong friend, Father Palóu, he quietly died, without a word of regret, on August 28, 1784. Grief-stricken Indians covered his tomb with wild flowers and lovingly pleaded for bits of anything that he had touched. Services for the humble priest who had created California lasted for days." [40]

11

The Ursulines of New Orleans,
Pioneer Educators of Girls

The moving spirit of the Ursuline Missionaries who first came to New Orleans in 1727 was Mother Marie Tranchepain, who had been admitted to the Ursuline Convent at Rouen the same year that Iberville began the settlement of Louisiana. At the request of Iberville's brother, Bienville, who was then Governor of Louisiana, the Bishop of Quebec, Nicholas Ignatius de Beaubois, had invited her to come to the newly opened territory for a dual purpose: maintaining a military hospital and founding a girls' school in New Orleans—the first of both in what is now the United States. The choice of her Order was a natural one; the mother of the two explorers, as well as other members of their family, had been educated at the Ursuline Convent in Quebec, established nearly a hundred years earlier by the Venerable Mother Mary of the Incarnation.

For years, Mother Tranchepain had dreamed of doing missionary work and she found the invitation irresistible. Other members of her Community were equally enthusiastic and, despite "the opposition raised against the enterprise by relatives and even by some ecclesiastical superiors, who were loath to see their respective dioceses deprived of the services of their Sisters, the Ursuline colony for Louisiana numbered, at the close of 1726, eight professed choir Sisters, one lay Sister, two choir postulants and a lay postulant. Two of those postulants were dismissed some months after their arrival in New Orleans, owing to their lack of the qualities requisite for good Ursulines.

One, however, persevered, Miss Mary Magdalene Hachard, who was richly endowed with every desirable quality. . . .

"Meanwhile, Rev. Father de Beaubois took every measure . . . to ensure the success of this enterprise. To this end . . . he caused a contract to be drawn up between the Ursulines and the Company of the Indies, under whose control Louisiana was at that time. This contract, styled a treaty, was signed at Paris, on September 13, 1726, and the Royal Patent, styled a Brevet, approving said contract, was issued five days later."

To anyone laboring under the impression that the early missionary undertakings were more or less hit-or-miss ventures, this treaty and this Patent, together with the King's formal authorization of the enterprise, should be as astonishing and as revealing as the provisions made for the Spanish missionaries, not only at the time of Junípero Serra, but also in the period of the earlier Franciscans. After a preamble, stating that the Company of the Indies considers "the most solid foundation of the Colony of Louisiana are the establishments which tend to the advancement of the Glory of God, and to the edification of the peoples" and expressing the wish "to relieve the poor sick and provide at the same time for the education of young girls," the Company accepts the offers of Sisters Marie Tranchepain of St. Augustine and Marianne of St. Angelica to take charge of the Hospital of New Orleans and outlines, in twenty-eight articles, the following conditions:

The six nuns who were to maintain the hospital and the four servants accompanying them to Louisiana would each be furnished their passage, in addition to a gratuity of five hundred francs; on their arrival, the hospital would be turned over to the nuns, who were to make themselves as comfortable as possible while awaiting the construction of more suitable accommodations; sufficient ground would be granted the Sisters for these new buildings, as well as for a poultry yard and garden.

The Negroes and Negresses, cattle, furniture, beds, linen and utensils for the hospital were to be carefully inventoried and the nuns held accountable for them; one nun was to act as housekeeper, two others were to care for the patients, a fourth would keep the school for young girls and the fifth was to be ready to fill in for any of the others who were unable to perform their assigned duties.

A plot of eight acres, on the river, was given by the Company "to there form a plantation which may in the course of time provide a maintenance for the Ursulines on account of the said hospital." Until this plantation was productive enough to support the nuns, the Company would grant each of them six hundred francs a year. If the Ursulines ceased "to take charge of the hospital, they shall be obliged to remit to those who take their place, the hospital, the plantation, and all that they will have received by inventory."

In addition to the hospital accounts of the housekeeper, which were to be balanced each month, the nuns would have their own treasurer who was to report to the Mother Superior. An exact record was to be kept "of the patients that enter the said hospital and of those who will leave it by death or otherwise."

Persons able to pay for treatment were expected to do so, but those who were too poor to do so could receive free treatment by presenting a certificate to this effect from their parish priest. Officers and employees of the Company were to receive preferential treatment in a "separate and select place" established for them in the hospital, but deductions would be made from their salaries for the benefit of the hospital.

To help make the hospital self-supporting, the Company would grant it sufficient land, as close as possible, for the establishment of a second plantation. However, as soon as the hospital could maintain itself, the Company expected to be reimbursed for the cost of the plantation.

When they could conveniently do so, the nuns would be permitted to take young girls as boarders, charging them whatever the Superior thought proper and retaining the fees paid.

As soon as their plantation was productive enough to maintain them, the Ursulines could increase their number if they wished and free passage would be furnished those who came from France; in like measure, any nun who could not "accommodate herself to the country" or for some valid reason was obliged to return to France, would be given free passage for herself and one servant, but her allowance would cease on the day of embarkation. If one of the nuns became infirm and unable to work, she would not be counted as one of the six for whom the Company was responsible, though she would be treated equally with them, at the hospital's expense, if the religious could not maintain her.

Article XXVIII concludes: "The present Treaty shall be addressed to the Council of Louisiana to be there registered, and in case of any contests about the articles which it contains, they shall be decided by the Council, to whose judgment the parties have engaged themselves to submit.

"September 13, 1726. *Signed* L'ABBÉ RAGUET.— J. MORIN.—D'ARTAGUETTE.—DIRON.—CASTANIER. —DESHAYER.—P. SAINTARD.—SOEUR CATHERINE DE BRUSCOLY, DE ST. AMAND, *première Supérieure des Ursulines de France.* SOEUR MARIE TRANCHEPAIN, DE ST. AUGUSTIN, *Supérieure* SOEUR MARIE-ANNE LE BOULLENGER DE STE. ANGÉLIQUE, *Dépositaire*"

PETITION TO THE KING TO APPROVE BY COMMISSION THE ABOVE TREATY

The Directors of the Company of the Indies very respectfully petition His Majesty to approve, by commission, the Treaty which the Sisters Marie Tranchepain de St. Augustin and Marie-Anne Le Boullenger de Ste. Angélique, Ursulines of Rouen with the assistance of Sister Catherine de Bruscoly de St. Amand, first Superior of the Ursulines of France, have entered into, on the 13th of the present month with the said Company of the Indies for the establishment of six religious of their order, at New Orleans, where they will take care of the hospital of that city and employ themselves in the education of young girls, according to their Institute.

Done in Paris, *September* 17, 1726.

BREVET OR COMMISSION OF LOUIS XV, KING OF FRANCE, IN FAVOR OF THE URSULINES OF LOUISIANA

TODAY, the eighteenth of September, one thousand seven
hundred twenty-six, the King being at Fontainebleau, it has
been represented to His Majesty on the part of the Sisters Marie
Tranchepain de St. Augustin and Marie-Anne Le Boullenger
de Ste. Angélique, Ursuline Religious of Rouen, that they had
with the assistance of Sister Catherine of Bruscoly . . . entered
into a treaty with the Directors of the Company of the Indies
. . . by which the said Sisters, on the one side, engage themselves to go to Louisiana with four other religious of their
order, to take charge of the Hospital of New Orleans and to
employ themselves in the education of young girls, conformably to their Institute; and the Company of the Indies, on the
other side, obliges itself to provide not only for the needs of the
said hospital, but also for the sustenance of the said religious
. . . in fine, they hope with God's blessing for a happy success
in their enterprise, whose charitable and pious principles promise them the King's protection, very humbly begging His Majesty . . . to approve of their establishment in the province
of Louisiana; in consideration of which His Majesty . . . has
approved the conditions of the treaty made between the Company of the Indies and the Ursuline Religious . . . the intention of His Majesty being that they enjoy without molestation
all that will be granted them by the said Company conformably
to the agreements that may have been made, or will be made
between the said Company of the Indies and the said religious,
for the purpose of which His Majesty places them under his
protection and safeguard, and for assurance of his will His
Majesty has commanded me to dispatch the present Brevet
which he has been pleased to sign with his own hand, and to
be countersigned by me, his Councillor, Secretary of State and
of his commandments and finances.

LOUIS—

PHÉLYPEAUX

The postulant, Miss Mary Magdalene Hachard, had, indeed,
shown herself richly endowed with every desirable quality, but
whether she had revealed her special gifts as a lighthearted and
observant letter writer, before she began her correspondence

with her father, I do not know. Fortunately, her letters, as well as the contract, the Patent and the correlative documents have not only been carefully preserved in the Ursuline Archives, they have also been carefully translated.[1] Nothing in the preparation of this anthology has given me greater pleasure than the presentation of several of these letters as uniformly enlightening, inspiring and utterly delightful.

L'Orient, February 22, 1727

MY DEAR FATHER:

You ask me for an exact account of all that happened on our route. In order to satisfy you, here is a kind of journal from Rouen to L'Orient, a seaport of Low Brittany.

You know it is the Reverend Father de Beaubois of the Company of Jesus who has formed the whole project of our establishment at New Orleans. You know also that our Reverend Mothers, Madame Tranchepain, Mother Superior; Madame Jude, Mother Assistant, and Madame Le Boullanger, Mother Treasurer, went to Paris long before us to contract with the Company of the Indies.

The affairs concerning our establishment having been settled, our Reverend Mother Superior departed from that city with her two dear companions to go to Hennebon, it being proper to take some measures with the Reverend Father de Beaubois. Our Reverend Mothers could confer with him only a few days. This Reverend Father was obliged to embark, taking with him a good reinforcement of worthy missionaries. I think them at present very near Louisiana.

If I appeared to leave you and all my family with dry eyes and even with joy, my heart was suffering none the less. I confess that I felt in those last moments some severe struggles. But the sacrifice is made. I am pleased with myself for having obeyed the Sovereign Master of our destiny.

On Thursday, October 24th, 1726, I left Rouen for Paris. I had for companions Mother St. Francis Xavier and Madame Cavelier of Rouen; each of a different disposition, but both agreeable companions. We passed through Saint-Denis on the 26th and arrived at four o'clock at Paris.

We hoped to remain only a few days in Paris, but the Procurator of the Missions of Canada and Louisiana told us that the vessel which was to take us to Louisiana not being yet ready, it was better to stay at Paris than at L'Orient where we would have time to grow weary.

We left Paris with Rev. Father Doutreleau and Brother Crucy, Jesuits, who are going with us to Louisiana. The 8th of December, at five o'clock in the morning, after having heard Mass, recited the prayers for travelers and breakfasted, the coach of Brittany came to take us. It cost us forty francs each to take us to Rennes, without counting the expense of board. On the 10th, we dined at Hodan. There we found a gentleman of good looks who was going our way. He wished to occupy the eighth seat in our coach, in order, said he, to pass the time more pleasantly in such amiable company. We did not welcome him; Rev. Father gave him to understand we had three hours of silence to keep morning and evening. But the gentleman answered that, if we did not wish to speak, he would converse with Brother Crucy. However, when he made himself known, we saw that it was necessary we treat him with consideration; that, being the President of Mayenne where our chests, valises and packages were to be inspected, he might save us from this inspection. We welcomed him and he treated us with much courtesy. He had the kindness to go to the Custom House and nothing was inspected. We slept at Mortagne, after having passed a rather dangerous place where the coach from Caën to Paris had been robbed eight days before.

On the 11th we slept at Alençon. I cannot tell you much of this town, for we reached it at night and left before daylight. The roads were so impassable that we were obliged to alight, our coach being deeply stuck in the mud. We did not wait for it.

We walked about a league. We were very cold, and as we found no house in which to seek shelter we were obliged to sit down on the ground. After having rested a little, we resumed our walk, and at last had the good fortune of meeting with a little cottage in which there was only a poor woman, who had already gone to bed. Our coach did not rejoin us until after ten o'clock. In spite of the fatigue we laughed often. We were cov-

ered with mud up to our ears. On the thirteenth, we slept at
Lavalle, a very pretty town where there is an Ursuline Community. The whole town was at the door of the inn to see us get
in the coach. Although it was raining very hard, that did not
prevent the people from being in the street from five in the
morning until eight, waiting for us.

At last, on the 16th, we arrived at Rennes. The Ursuline
Ladies had the kindness to send one of their attendants to meet
us. This good Sister took us into the house of one of the principal men of the town, for it was very cold. The owner received
us very well, and went with us to the coach which was to take
us to the Ursulines. Father Doutreleau took up his residence
at the Jesuit College.

Several Reverend Fathers of this college honored us with a
visit and invited us to their house and Church. While we were
visiting the College, Brother Crucy was preparing two carriages
which he had engaged to continue our route. The price of these
was twenty francs per head to carry us in one day from Rennes
to Hennebon.

Father Doutreleau had sent ahead his valet to announce our
coming to Madame Tranchepain. Our dear Superior received
us with open arms and the Superior of the Convent received
us equally well.

The day after our arrival, I saw two Ursuline Religious of
Plohermel, accompanied by the Reverend Father Tartarin,
Jesuit Missionary to Louisiana. We have another sister from
Hennebon. Thus, our Community is composed of eleven with-
out counting two servants.

Our Reverend Mothers, before leaving Rouen, had granted
me two favors. First, that my novitiate would begin on the day
of my departure from Rouen. Second, that I would take the
holy Habit of Religion at Hennebon. Having received my Certificate of Baptism, which you had the kindness to send me,
I reminded Madame Tranchepain of her promise. She listened
to me willingly and kept her word. The ceremony of my religious reception took place, with great solemnity, on the 19th
of January, 1727. I took the name of St. Stanislaus.

Our Rev. Fathers are taking with them a cabinet-maker, a

locksmith and several other workmen. As for us, my dear father, be not scandalized at it, for it is the fashion of the country, we are taking a Negro to wait on us. We are also taking a very pretty little cat that has wished to be one of our Community, supposing apparently, that there are in Louisiana, as in France, mice and rats.

I am not at all offended at the rumors circulated at Rouen, concerning me, that I have never left home and that I am often seen there. It is glorious for me to be at the same time in two towns so distant from one another.

I remember having read in the life of St. Francis Xavier that this great Apostle of the Indies and Japan was often at the same time in different places, which is regarded as a very great prodigy.[2] I am not so great a saint as to work similar miracles. I am certainly not at Rouen but at L'Orient, and I am always very gay and very contented in my vocation, well resolved to fulfill its duties to the best of my power.

Our Rev. Fathers do not wish us to say "our," as you know is said in convents, because, they say, we should soon hear the sailors making fun of us and saying our soup, our cap and so on. It so happens that since the Fathers have forbidden it, I cannot help saying it, even so far as to saying our nose. Father Tartarin often tells me, "Sister, hold up our head." All this is to make us laugh, to divert us from our fatigues.

At last, my dear father, has arrived this day, this great day, this much desired day for our departure. The wind has become favorable, and we have been notified that we must embark in an hour.

I am puzzled how we are going to be able to get on board our vessel for it is very high on the side. Rev. Father Tartarin says he will have us put two by two in a sack, and that they will hoist us up with a pulley as they do a bale. But our Captain assures us he will have us carried up more commodiously, that is, seated in an arm-chair.

Good-bye, my dear father. I beg you to write often. I have nothing dearer to me than you and my dear mother. Be assured that nothing less was necessary to separate me from your dear persons, than the glory of God and the salvation of His poor savages. I assure you that I shall be separated from you only in body, and shall always be with you in mind and heart. But as I cannot do anything of myself, I address myself to Him who alone can load you with His blessings. I pray every day for the preservation of your health and the sanctification of your souls. I ask you not to forget a daughter who will be, all her life, with the most profound respect and most perfect gratitude,

My very dear father,
Your very humble and very obedient daughter and servant,
MARIE MAGDELEINE HACHARD DE ST. STANISLAUS

New Orleans, October 27, 1727

MY DEAR FATHER:

You have expressed the wish to have an account of our voyage. Here is a general confession of all that has happened since our departure from France. You see how faithful I am to render my accounts.

We embarked on the 22nd of February in the *Gironde*. But it was decided we should not sail until next day. This gave us time to arrange our apartment. It was a partition they made for us between decks, eighteen feet long and seven or eight feet wide. We had six beds on each side, three one above the other so close that we could not sit on our beds without touching the ceiling. As for me, I was often hit, since I was one of those who slept on the top because they put up there the lightest. One of our Sisters slept down in the passage. There were no other windows than two port-holes twice the size of the hand. Moreover very often they could not be opened on account of the surges of water which, to bedew us, came even in our beds. We were obliged to arise and lie down one after the other, not being able to stay in the room more than two or three at a time. Our Reverend Fathers were still worse off than we. They had but a wretched little hole without any opening. They decided to sleep in the poop at the mercy of the rain and wind, their heads in a clothes-basket to receive the rain when it came.

We set sail the 23rd, at two in the afternoon. The weather was fine. At half a league from L'Orient, our vessel twice struck a rock. The shock was very great and caused alarm in the vessel. The sails were hoisted at the same time. This having been remarked at the port, they did not fail to inform Mr. Dufaillet that our vessel had split on a rock. This gentleman and several others came to our help. He reassured us and made them work with so much vigor, that we found ourselves in a condition to continue our route. It was then that all commenced to be seasick, and pay their tribute to the sea. The vessel was in a continual agitation and it made bounds which threw us one against the other. The soup was no sooner on the table than it was upset on the cloth, unless the precaution was taken to hold it with both hands. Even then it required a mariner, for we could hardly hold ourselves. That contributed to make us laugh sometimes in spite of the sea-sickness, which is a very violent malady; but once it is known it occasions no anxiety for it does not cause anyone to die.

The tempest was so strong that it caused the death of forty-nine sheep and a great number of hens which had been taken on board for our nourishment and that of the crew. This greatly diminished our provisions and we were reduced to rice, salt beef and bacon so unsound we could not eat it. The beans were cooked with lard, but this bad diet did not impair our health. In fine, the wind being contrary, our vessel advanced but little. This diminished also our store of water, so that we were reduced to half a pint a day. If our Captains had found the wind favorable they would have put into port at the Canaries to take in water, but the wind was not favorable, which obliged our Captain to put into port at Madeira. As soon as we were perceived, a ship's boat was sent to meet us in order to know what we wanted. Those that had come to see us, having reported that there were on board a convent of religious and several Jesuit Missionaries, this news attracted many visits. The Fathers of the Company of Jesus were the first to come on board. There was only one of them who spoke French, but they urged us to land and take up our abode with them; but we gratefully declined. Our Reverend Fathers went to dine with them. They were received cordially and treated with magnificence, and for a present they were given a ram. They brought us large baskets full of all sorts of refreshments, such as lemons, salads, preserves and other things.

Our Rev. Fathers find the church of these Jesuit Fathers very magnificent, the counter-allies and frontal of the altar are of massive silver and the walls are of porcelain. There is not a Church in France so rich in ornaments. No women were visible. They walk out only to go to Mass, and all at the same time, so that they form a kind of procession. They walk covered with large veils, and in silence unless they say their beads. There are in this Island two convents of which the principal is of the order of St. Clare. The Abbess is a Portuguese Princess. [She] wrote a very gracious letter to our Rev. Mother Superior, to invite her and all the Community to go to her convent.

The next day, a young woman from our vessel having gone to pay her a visit on the part of our Community, she was loaded with attentions and presents. Finally we stood out to sea to continue our route. The wind was not favorable, so it took us a long time to make two hundred leagues, at the end of which we discovered a piratical vessel. Everybody armed himself, cannons were loaded, and all took their posts. These preparations were useless. The hostile vessel, after having made several turns and returns, went away and left us at liberty.

But it was a sad liberty for religious to be on a vessel where it is impossible to have a moment to one's self. However, we did not neglect our spiritual exercises, in the midst of the dissipation which exists among people who think only of diverting themselves to pass the time.

If we had any consolation, it was assisting at the Holy Sacrifice of the Mass, which was celebrated each day. On Good Friday, the adoration of the Cross was devoutly made. We were the first to advance barefoot to adore the Cross. Then followed the Rev. Fathers, the officers, the passengers and the crew. In a vessel, it suffices for the officers to give the example, in order to inspire the whole crew with devotion. They never failed to ring and recite the Angelus three times a day.

After having lost sight of the hostile vessel, the sea continued to make itself feared. But we suffered still more from the length of the voyage. We redoubled our vows and prayers to obtain

more favorable weather, of which the Lord granted a few hours
at intervals. With the aid of this succor, we arrived at the Quay
St. Louis which is a port of the Island of San Domingo or Haiti.
It was there we commenced to know Messieurs the mosquitoes;
they are little insects which I can compare to gnats, except that
their stings are much more venomous and painful; they cause
blisters and violent itching. Fortunately, they appear only in
the evening after sunset until sunrise the following day.

As there is no religious house there, and as it was necessary
to go ashore in order to see to our clothes which we desired
to bleach, we took care not to refuse the gracious offer made
by the gentlemen of the Company, who came to visit us and
offered us the Company's Warehouse.

The first is named Cirou; he is still a bachelor; his conversation is very agreeable in spite of his continual application to
business. The second is called Girard, whose merit shines no
less. We took our meals at their house with a Creole lady of
the country, between whom and the best bred Parisian one
could find no difference. The remainder of the time we stayed
at their house, nearly a fortnight, we were entertained with
neatness and abundance.

Two days after our arrival, the Governor sent to inquire
after our health, and he came himself in the afternoon. He is
called Mr. Brache, a man of quality and rich as Croesus. He
spoke to us of an earthquake which had happened that morning. It was only I of our Community that had perceived it,
without knowing what it was. I regarded the movements as
an imagination which I had of being always on the *Gironde*.
The Governor intimated to us his great desire of having an
Ursuline establishment in that country. Nobody better than he
could contribute to it. He has no children and enjoys fifty
thousand francs a year. Messrs. Cirou and Girard have the same
desire for the education of the young Creoles, who usually
have good dispositions, and whom they are obliged to send to
France in order to be instructed. There is reason to hope that
some day we shall have a house of our order in this country.
In all this country there is only one priest, who is obliged to
say High Mass at the parish church of which he is Rector, and

a second Mass at Fort St. Louis, which is situated in the middle
of the sea, where there are a great number of officers and soldiers, by whom it is guarded. The Governor wished us to see
this fort, which is according to connoisseurs a thing very rare
in its kind. We found three companies of fine troops, drawn up
in order to receive us and, before leaving, they presented us
with some refreshments. At last, we reembarked on the 19th
of May, loaded with attentions and presents on the part of
Messrs. Cirou and Girard. Among other things, they gave us
a barrel of sugar, weighing three hundred pounds and as much
to our Reverend Fathers, to sweeten us, without doubt, the rest
of the voyage which was still at least five hundred leagues. We
had much calm and contrary winds, which delayed us.

We had hoped that we would arrive about the feast of the
Blessed Sacrament; but Our Lord, who had preserved the greatest trial for the end, sent us very contrary winds. These winds
conjointly with the currents in the Gulf of Mexico, pushed us
toward the island called Blanche. As we desired eagerly to see
the first land of Mississippi, we experienced great joy at our
approach to this island; but good God! what a brief joy it was,
and how dearly it cost us! Our vessel found itself all of a sudden
stranded, and this caused so many violent shocks, that we believed ourselves hopelessly lost. We took our beads and said our
In Manus thinking it was all over, and that we should there
make our establishment of religious. All the crew was in an
instant in movement, the sails were hoisted and they made
diverse maneuvers to draw us out of this dangerous place; our
ship was sunk more than five feet in the sand. This at length
determined our Captain to unload the vessel. They began with
the cannons which were tied on rafts of wood, so they could
not sink; then the ballast was all thrown into the sea; but that
did not lighten the vessel enough. Then it was decided to throw
overboard the passengers' chests which were between decks;
ours were the first; therefore, it was for us to make the first
sacrifice. Just as we thought to see our trunks thrown into the
sea, the Captain changed his mind and ordered all the sugar to
be thrown overboard. Our Reverend Fathers and we lost the
two barrels of which Messrs. Cirou and Girard had made us

a present. This not yet producing the desired effect, they threw away sixty-one barrels of brandy and a large quantity of ballast and iron which they still found. We were on the deck looking with pity on all this sad work; it was the desolation of desolations itself, to see the poor passengers, who were trembling for their trunks and regretting their sugar; for even the sailors had their little barrels;[3] not one was exempted from it; all the sugar was thrown into the sea without discrimination. Then new efforts were made to draw out the vessel, and they succeeded in doing it, which filled us all with joy. Then we again set sail.

We had hardly made a quarter of a league when our ship grounded a second time, but with such stiffness and frequent shocks that no hope remained to us except in God's almighty power. Fear was painted on all faces, even of those who had the bravest hearts. We prayed everywhere, most frequently at the feet of our amiable Superior, who told us that we ought to feel less pain than the others in meeting death since we had made an entire and perfect sacrifice of our life to our dear Lord; but He gave His blessing to the care of our Captains and the labor of our sailors and passengers who did not spare themselves. Our vessel was then once more pulled out, and what was more astonishing, without being much damaged, at least according to appearances.

After this accident the ship's boat went before us, with the sounding-line in the hand of an officer, until we were in the offing.

We arrived finally in sight of land; but, as it was unknown, only the necessity of having water, determined us to approach the shore. The ship's boat was sent ahead conducted by our second Captain; and the more we approached, the more were we persuaded the island was inhabited only by savages. However, there were not more than two hours that the boat had left when the wind became favorable. Our first Captain caused a cannon shot to be fired to signal the boat to rejoin us, and at the same time he ordered to weigh anchor to continue our voyage, hoping that the boat, having heard the signal, would return. But he was mistaken, for the second Captain, thinking it was a clap of thunder, continued on his way to land; and, the wind having soon fallen, we cast anchor to wait for our boat; we had the joy of seeing it only the next morning.

A few days after, having stood out to sea, we gained sight of Dauphine Island and of a brigantine coming toward us. As we expected only friends, this caused us much joy, hoping to hear from New Orleans. Our hope was not in vain. We learned the first news of Father de Beaubois who was awaiting us with impatience, that our lodging was prepared to receive us, while waiting for our Monastery to be finished. I assure you, my dear father, that this was the first exterior joy that we had tasted since our embarkation, and it was so heartfelt, that it made us forget all past fatigues. The wind being favorable we set sail and resumed our journey toward the Balize and entered the roadstead the 23rd of July, five months, day for day, after our embarkation, away from Rouen about two thousand four hundred leagues.

Balize is a seaport at the entrance of the Mississippi River. Mr. Duvergé [de Verges] is the Commandant for the Company; he offered us his house while awaiting boats from New Orleans to ascend the River. We accepted this offer and on the feast of St. Anne went ashore with the parts of our baggage that were most necessary. We had much trouble to land there and ran the risk of passing the night on this island where there are workmen of the Company who are occupied in building a fort under the direction of Mr. de Verges, who sent his workmen to get canoes (pirogues). These canoes are hollowed trees, and are sometimes large enough to hold sixteen persons. The three that were brought to us were smaller. We were obliged to separate into two bands. The third pirogue was occupied by Mr. de Verges and Father Doutreleau.

It was in this manner that we arrived at Balize, the home of Mr. de Verges. This gentleman is very kind, and although he is young and unmarried, he leads a regular and most solitary life, being applied without intermission to the affairs confided to him. We are persuaded the Company has few employees as worthy as this gentleman. He must have enemies, true virtue being always persecuted, or he is unknown to the gentlemen of the Company. For if he were known to them he would without doubt be more advanced, these gentlemen making it a pleasure and a duty to reward true merit.

We remained at his house until the 29th, waiting for news from New Orleans. Rev. Father Tartarin had preceded us, having left the *Gironde* some days before us to announce our arrival. Our long navigation had alarmed the whole country and many thought us lost. Rev. Father de Beaubois did not delay to send a sloop and some pirogues to take us. Recovering from a malady, he was not in a state to come himself to meet us. He intrusted this commission to Mr. Massy, brother of our postulant.

It must be acknowledged that all the fatigues on the *Gironde* were not comparable to those which we had in this short passage which is generally made in six days. What renders this so fatiguing is that it is necessary to erect every night some sort of cabin and this must be done one hour before sunset, in order to have time to make some pallets and eat supper. For as soon as the sun is set there come mosquitoes, like those we had commenced to see at the Quay St. Louis. Their comrades, which are called *"Frappes d'abord,"* are not less redoubtable. Sometimes they are so numerous they could be cut with a knife. But they are not more compassionate than the mosquitoes.

Along the river, there is no land cultivated. There are only wild forests alive with animals of all colors; snakes, serpents, adders, crocodiles, vipers, toads and others which did not harm us, although they approached very near. Our sailors, to make our pallets, stuck canes in the ground in the form of a cradle around a mattress and shut us up two by two in our cradle in which we lay down without undressing. Then they cover the cradle with a large cloth, so that the mosquitoes and *frappes-d'abord* could not find any little passage to come to visit us.

When we were at eight or ten leagues from New Orleans, we began to meet some inhabitants who vied with each other as to who could persuade us to enter their homes. Everywhere we were received with joy. Beyond our expectations, we found a number of good people who have come from France and Canada to establish themselves in this country. They promised us some boarders, and several wished already to confide them to us. Our last sleeping place was on the plantation of Mr. Massy, where we found ourselves as well as at home. We re-embarked at three o'clock in the morning and arrived at five at New Orleans.

It would be too long and even useless, my dear father, to express our joy at the sight of a land for which we had been sighing so long, and how great was our consolation on landing. We directed our steps to the house of Rev. Father de Beaubois. We soon met him coming to greet us with unequaled joy, as the long delay of our arrival had caused him much uneasiness. He conducted us to his house where he gave us a good breakfast, which was interrupted by a great number of his friends who came to welcome us and accompany us to our house. This is a house the Company rents to lodge us while waiting for our Monastery to be built. We do not count on taking possession of our Monastery and the hospital until a year or perhaps more, for workmen are not as common here as in France, and they wish to build us a permanent brick residence. Meanwhile, they are building in our residence a small apartment in which to teach the day-scholars and lodge the boarders. There are already more than thirty boarders who entreat to be received from here, as well as from Balize and the neighborhood.

The fathers and mothers are transported with joy to see us, saying they no longer care to return to France, since they have here the means of procuring an education for their daughters. This good disposition of the inhabitants renders them attentive not to let us want for anything. We have, for our best friends, Mr. Perier, the Commandant, and Madame his spouse, who are persons of merit and of amiable dispositions. This gentleman has acquired in three months the esteem of all the country. He has established a well regulated police, he declares war on vice, he drives away all those who lead a scandalous life. There is corporal punishment for girls of bad life. Persons are hung or put to the rack for the least theft. The Council is sovereign. There is no appeal.

We receive also much graciousness and kind attention from Mr. de la Chaise, General Director of the Company. He has not yet refused us anything for which we asked him. We have every reason to hope that our establishment will procure the glory of God, and that in time it will greatly promote the salvation of souls; such has been our principal end.

I have the honor to be, with all the respect possible, my dear father,

Your very humble and very obedient daughter and servant,
MARIE MAGDELEINE HACHARD DE ST. STANISLAUS

New Orleans, October 27, 1727
MY DEAR FATHER:

I received yours of the sixth of April on the twentieth of this month, the eve of St. Ursula, when coming out of a retreat. Judge what was my joy in getting news of you, my dear mother and all my sisters.

Those who told you we had been in peril during fifteen days at the roadstead of L'Orient were very much mistaken. It is true that we were for about an hour in peril, after which we shook our ears as scholars do and resumed our course.

I am pleased that you will inform me of the progress which my dear brother will make in the sciences. The most ardent wish of my heart is that he will either be a good holy secular priest, or a fervent Jesuit Missionary. I am a little displeased, however, with my brother because he has not written me. Is he displeased with me or does he think I am displeased with him? It is true that, in order to deter me, he told me, before my departure, many things which could not afford me pleasure, but I have looked upon all that as a trial and even as a mark of his affection. If I do not write to him, it is that being naturally timid I dare not take that liberty without his permission.

Although I do not yet know perfectly the country of Louisiana, I am going to give you a few details. There is here as much refinement and magnificence as in France. Gold and velvet goods are common, though three times dearer than at Rouen. Bread costs ten cents a pound and is made of Indian meal; eggs from forty-five to fifty cents a dozen; milk fourteen cents a gallon. We eat meat, fish, peas, and wild beans and many kinds of fruits and vegetables, such as pineapple which is the most excellent of all the fruits; watermelon, sweet potatoes; pippins which are much the same as the russets or *"reinette grise"* of France; figs, bananas, pecans, cashewnuts, which, as soon as eaten, seize the throat, pumpkins and a thousand other things which have not yet come to my knowledge. In fact, we live on wild beef, deer, swans, geese and wild turkeys, hares, hens, ducks, teals, pheasants, partridges, quails and other fowl and game of different kinds. The rivers are teeming with enormous fish, especially turbot which is an excellent fish, ray, carp and many other fishes unknown in France. They make much use of chocolate with milk and coffee. We drink it every day. During Lent, meat is allowed three times a week and, during the year, meat is allowed on Saturday. We accustom ourselves wonderfully well to the wild food of this country. What is eaten most and is most common is rice cooked with milk. The people of Louisiana find very good a food called *"sagamité,"* which is made of Indian corn crushed in a mortar, then boiled in water, and eaten with butter or cream.

We are here nearer to the sun than at Rouen without, however, having very great heat. Winter lasts about three months, but it has only slight white frosts. We have been assured that Louisiana is four times larger than France. The lands are very fertile, not along the river, but at a few leagues, there are prairies, fields and plains where grow a large number of trees named cotton-trees though they yield no cotton, sycamores, mulberry trees, chestnut trees, almond trees, walnut trees, fig trees, lemon trees, orange trees, pomegranate trees, and others which make the beauty of the fields. If the soil were cultivated, there would not be any better in the world. A man here, working two days, only digging the ground and sowing it with wheat, would reap more than sufficient to support himself all year. But the generality of the people here apply themselves to scarcely anything except hunting and fishing.

The Company carries on much commerce in furs and other merchandise with the savages who are persons of whom the majority are very sociable.

We observe the same seclusion as French convents. Should

we have the misfortune that Father de Beaubois were sick and could not say Mass for us, we would miss it rather than leave our convent to hear it at the Parish Church.

I shall not speak to you of the morals of the seculars of this country, not knowing them and having no desire to; but we have been told they are very corrupt and scandalous. There are not seen here any of those girls who are said to have been sent by force. None of them have arrived so far.

All our Mothers are in perfect health except Rev. Mother Superior, whom we have had the grief of seeing nearly always sick since we came here. One can well see that it is God Himself Who has chosen His subjects; for there is not one of these Mothers who is not of great merit and of perfect devotedness, particularly our Rev. Mother Superior and Mother St. Francis Xavier with whom I left Rouen. We would not be surprised to see them work miracles.

I forgot to tell you that in the danger on the *Gironde*, I promised six Masses to the souls in Purgatory, on condition that you would have them said, knowing your good heart, and that you would not refuse them to me.

I shall now stop, for fear of wearying you. I embrace you a thousand times; but, no, I cannot, you are too far away; I beg then, my dear brother, to acquit himself for me of this amiable commission.

I am with all my heart, with profound respect and perfect gratitude,

> Your very humble and very obedient servant,
> MARIE MAGDELEINE HACHARD DE ST. STANISLAUS

New Orleans, January 1, 1728

MY DEAR FATHER:

I have just heard that the vessel named *The Two Brothers* is going to leave for France. I avail myself of this occasion to wish you, and also my dear mother, brothers, and sisters, a Happy New Year.

They are working hard on our house. Mr. Perier promises to lodge us there within this year. We desire nothing so much as to see ourselves in this house, in order to be also occupied at the hospital to attend the sick, for we learn every day that it is the greatest pity to see the bed arrangement there, and that the great part of the patients die for want of help. The intention of M. the Commandant is that we should also take care of the girls and women of evil life; this is not yet determined on our side; but we have been given to understand it would do a great good to the colony; and for that they propose to build a special apartment at the end of our enclosure to shut up these people.

We keep also a school to instruct the Negro and Indian girls and women; it is further the intention of Rev. Father de Beaubois that we should take charge of some little orphan girls; and he tells us, in order to engage us to do it, that he and Mr. Perier charge themselves with all the orphan boys.

We are determined not to spare ourselves in anything that will be for the greater glory of God. I am sometimes employed with the day-scholars. I cannot express the pleasure which I find in instructing these little souls and in teaching them to know and love God.

All our Community enjoys a contentment which cannot be expressed. I beg you to believe me, with a very sincere and very respectful attachment,

My dear father,

Your very humble and very obedient daughter and servant,
MARIE MAGDELEINE HACHARD DE ST. STANISLAUS

New Orleans, April 24, 1728

MY VERY DEAR FATHER:

I have received the letters which you had the kindness to write me dated the 12th and 20th of August, 1727. You ask me for an explanation of the state of the country, the situation of our city; in fine of all that can be learned about this place. I hope to have anticipated your request by the account of our voyage and of our arrival here, which I sent you in October, 1727, and by several letters which I have had the honor of writing you.

On our side of the river, there is a levee to prevent the overflow of the river in the town; and all along the levee on the city side there is a large ditch to receive the water that runs down the slope, with palisades to confine it.

On the other side of this river, there are wild woods with a few huts in which lodge the slaves of the Company. Our residence is the finest house in the city; it has two stories and a garret. There are everywhere large windows. However, there is no glass; but the sashes are hung with fine cloth which gives as much light as glass. We have a poultry yard and a garden bounded on one side and at one end by trees of prodigious height and bulk. This procures us the visit of an infinite number of mosquitoes and another species of flies, with which I have not yet become acquainted but by sight; there are at this moment several that fly around and would like to assassinate me.

The house they are building for us is at the other extremity of the city. It will be very regularly built, and wainscotted, and with large glass windows. But the construction advances slowly. We will be happy to take possession of it and our hospital at Easter, 1729; then we shall need new help, and I pray the Lord that He may send us some good subjects.

We have been given two cows with their calves, a sow with her little ones, some hens and some Muscovy ducks. All this commences our poultry yard, in which we have also turkeys and geese. The inhabitants, seeing that we would not accept any money to teach our day-scholars, help us with everything they can. The marks of protection which we receive from the principal persons of the country cause us to be respected by everybody. All this would not continue, if we did not sustain by our actions the grand idea which they have of us.

Rev. Father de Beaubois has the finest garden in the city. It is full of orange trees which bear oranges as sweet and as large as those of Cape Francis. He gave us three hundred sour ones, of which we made preserves. Thank God, we have not yet wanted for anything. We are much better off than we expected to be, but this is neither our wish nor the intention of our enterprise. Our principal end is to draw souls to the Lord.

During Holy Week, this Rev. Father gave a retreat to us and to our boarders. Several ladies of the city repaired here assiduously. We had the Tenebrae Lessons in Music and a Miserere every day, accompanied by instruments. Easter Sunday, we sang motets in four parts; and on Low Sunday we sang the entire Mass in music. The convents of France with all their brilliancy do not do so much. All this has a good effect and helps much to draw the public. There always follows a sermon at the end, for our Rev. Father is a man of admirable zeal; it seems as if he has undertaken to convert everybody, but I assure you, my dear father, he has yet to labor much in order to succeed. For not only debauchery, but dishonesty and all the other vices reign here more than elsewhere. As for the girls of evil life, although they are punished severely by putting them on a wooden horse and having them whipped by all the soldiers of the regiment that guards our city, there are more than enough to fill a refuge.

We have twenty boarders, of whom eight have today made their First Communion; three lady boarders, and three orphans. We have also seven slave boarders to teach and prepare for Baptism and First Communion.

The custom here is to marry girls at the age of twelve or fourteen. Before our arrival many had been married without even knowing how many gods there are. Judge of the rest. But since we came here, none are married unless they have attended our instructions. Not long since, there were given to us two colored boarders, one six years and the other seventeen, to instruct them in our religion; and they will remain to serve us. Some boarders of twelve or fifteen years have never been to confession, or even to Mass. Brought up on a plantation, without any spiritual help, they had never heard of God. When we tell them the most ordinary things, they are to them as oracles.

I am very contented in this country and in my vocation, and what redoubles my joy is to see the time of my profession approach. I cannot express to you the joy I will feel to pronounce my vows in a land in which Christianity is almost unknown.

I stated in one of my preceding letters that Mr. Robert Cavelier Sieur de la Salle had come to this country, with a number of persons from Rouen, to make the first discovery.

That was all I knew about it then. Since, I have learned other circumstances which will afford you pleasure. The King, informed of this discovery, made by Mr. de la Salle, of the esteem he had acquired among the savages, and that he had found the means of being feared and respected by the Iroquois, named him Viceroy of Louisiana, permitted him to raise troops, and gave him four vessels commanded by Captain Beaujeu. The embarkation was made at La Rochelle about the month of July of the year 1684.

Mr. de la Salle brought with him workmen of all trades to found a settlement and a great number of volunteers, all select young people of good families of Rouen, and many others, including one hundred soldiers and officers.

He had intended to land at the mouth of the Mississippi; but some misunderstanding between Mr. de la Salle and Mr. de Beaujeu was the cause that they could not find the mouth of the river, and Mr. de la Salle was obliged to disembark with his troops about a hundred and fifty leagues lower, on the west between this river and New Spain, a territory in which are mines of gold and silver which yield the King of Spain a considerable profit. At that place, Mr. de Beaujeu abandoned Mr. de la Salle and returned to France.

Mr. de la Salle and his troops went further up in the interior; and, after having traversed many rivers, forests and countries, arrived near the Fort of the Illinois, a place which is named today the Little Rock.

As this brave Captain knew how to make himself feared and esteemed, it seemed that everything favored his enterprise. But one day, when he was preparing to send his brother to France, to inform the King of the state of his enterprise, he was assassinated by five of his people, through jealousy.

It was thus that the noble and glorious enterprise of Mr. de la Salle failed, and only for that perfidy he would have discovered all that country of the Mississippi, to which he had given the name of Louisiana.

Is not your city of Rouen glorified, my dear father, in the honor that it was Mr. de la Salle and his Company, almost all natives of this city, who made the first discovery of the Mississippi? I do not know if it is on this account that the savages of Louisiana hold the Normans in such high esteem. They think more of that province than any of the others, and recognize them as capable of succeeding in all their enterprises. If one should speak to them of the conquests of the Dukes of Normandy, the bravery of the Normans in the Holy Land, their conquests of the kingdom of England and others, they would be more convinced of their capability. But we are not here for that. If they desire to know, let them inquire of others or read histories.

I had written this letter thus far, so that it would be ready to send by the first vessel which would leave for France; but none having left, and today, May 8, 1728, hearing that one is ready to set sail, I end it at present. I have nothing new to relate except that for several days I have had some attacks of fever. Yesterday, I took to cure me an emetic, which is the ordinary medicine in this country. Our dear Mother Superior is always sick, but our other Mothers are perfectly well.

I pray the Lord every day to keep you all in perfect health; and I am, from the bottom of my heart, very respectfully, my dear father,

Your very humble and very obedient daughter and servant,
MARIE MAGDELEINE HACHARD DE ST. STANISLAUS

When Sister Magdeleine's letter of January 1, 1728, was written, the Ursulines, while awaiting the completion of the convent the Company of the Indies was building, had been living for a little over five months in the house assigned to them, which probably belonged to Bienville.

At this temporary convent, the first Sodality of the Blessed Virgin Mary, in what is now the United States, was founded in 1730 and it continued to function after the nuns moved to permanent quarters. In fact, it still flourishes after more than two hundred years.

Among the nuns' first charges were thirty *filles de les cassettes*—casket girls—who arrived the year after they did, to be placed in their care and boarded until their marriages. They were peasant girls of honest parentage or orphans from the

asylums of Paris and were so called because of the small chests
of clothes and linens allotted them by the French government.
Soldiers who married them were given their discharge, a plot
of land, a cow, provisions and a rifle.[4]

Although the Ursulines had hoped to take possession of their
own convent shortly after their arrival, its cornerstone was not
laid until three years later and they did not move into it until
four years after that. But it was worth waiting for. It still
stands, a French Renaissance building, for a long time said
to be the oldest in the Mississippi Valley though that claim is
now disputed by another known as Madame John's Legacy.
It is a three-story edifice built of bricks between timbers. "The
beams and rafters are rough-hewn cypresses that grew, perhaps,
on the very spot where now they support their ecclesiastical
burden; the bolts, bars, nails, hinges, and balustrades are of
iron, handwrought . . . by *brute* slaves, as they were then
designated."[5] The first orphanage of Louisiana was on the
ground floor; on the second were the cells for the Sisters. One
of the most striking architectural features is the winding stair-
case, attached to the wall, but otherwise unsupported, with a
railing of wrought iron. The entrance to the grounds faced
the river and the property covered almost two squares; what
is now the façade and entrance was originally the back of the
convent.

The nuns took possession of this convent with great pomp.
Bienville was in charge of the ceremonies and one of the nuns
wrote an account of them:

" 'Toward five o'clock . . . our convent bells rang . . . to
announce our decision. Immediately the troops ranged themselves on each side of the abode we were about to leave forever.
Governor Bienville, Mr. Salmon, intendent, together with the
most distinguished citizens and almost the entire population,
came to form our escort.

" 'After Benediction of the Blessed Sacrament . . . all left
the chapel in processional order; the citizens opening the
march, followed by the children of our orphanage and day
school, and over forty . . . ladies of the city, all bearing
lighted tapers and singing hymns. Next came twenty girls

dressed in white, who were followed by twelve others dressed as angels.

" 'The young lady who represented Saint Ursula wore a costly robe and mantle, and a crown glittering with diamonds and pearls, from which a rich veil hung in graceful folds; and in her hand she bore a heart pierced with an arrow. Her companions were clad in snow-white dresses and veils and they bore palm branches emblematic of victory.

" 'Last of all came the nuns and clergy; the former bearing lighted tapers, and the latter a rich canopy under which the Blessed Sacrament was borne in triumph. The soldiers marched on each side. . . .

" 'As soon as the procession was in sight of the convent some kind friend commenced to ring the bells . . . thus we entered the new abode amidst the chiming of bells, the fifes and drums and the singing of hymns. . . .'

"The Ursulines played an important part in the early history of New Orleans, for it was in their schools that the future mothers of the colony were educated; it was the Ursulines who took care of the orphans and nursed the sick. Year after year they remained, gaining strength with the growing city." [6]

As we have noted, the first social welfare work in the country had been undertaken by the Ursulines in their temporary abode and it continued on a much more extensive scale after they moved. "Orphan girls were taught trades . . . to enable them to obtain employment. . . . Settlers from up-river came to the convent to obtain wives from among these girls, but the nuns and the Jesuit Fathers . . . carefully studied the character, disposition and references of applicants. These settlers were required to follow the custom of entering into a marriage contract, and thus the rights of the girls were protected.

"Here resided the infirmarian, the Sister in charge of the sick both in the convent and in the hospital. . . . The instructions 'For Her Who Has Charge of the Pharmacy,' still extant in the Ursulines' archives, are interesting. She was required to 'transport herself to the door when she hears the bell to admit the doctor and other health officers, and she shall accompany them . . . to hear the directions, which will be inscribed in a book . . . and carefully preserved with the names of each for whom he has prescribed. . . . She shall be extremely solicitous to instruct herself thoroughly in everything that concerns her task, such as making syrups, etc. . . . and to know the herbs and their properties, the kinds of good drugs, the quantity to be used, and similar tasks. . . . She will have a cabinet . . . to contain everything pertaining to her position, keep it well stocked always with everything that can be made in the monastery so that there be obtained from the apothecary the least amount required.'

"The handling of the material in her pharmacy was also directed: 'She will keep all her vials in rows on the shelves, well closed and marked with a tag; all drugs packed and closed in boxes, the herbs in little bundles to be hanging, and the (medicinal) flowers in paper bags. She will be exact about giving no drug whatever without having weighed it well, and pass out nothing no matter how small except what the doctor has prescribed.' Such were some of the directives for Louisiana's first woman druggist." [7]

The next few years were among the most notable in the annals of the Ursuline story. When Louisiana was ceded from France to Spain and back again to France, this was not without causing some natural anxiety as to the convent's rights and privileges; and this anxiety was increased by the sale of the entire Louisiana Territory to the United States in 1803. Eventually the nuns' concern reached such a pitch that, after some correspondence with the Secretary of State—James Madison—they addressed a letter directly to the President of the United States himself—Thomas Jefferson. To this letter, Jefferson very graciously replied.

"Washington, May 15, 1804

"To the Soeur Therese de St. Xavier Farjon Superior; and the Nuns of the Order of St. Ursula at New Orleans.

"I have received, holy sisters, the letter . . . wherein you express anxiety for the property vested in your institution by the former governments of Louisiana. The principles of the

Constitution and government of the United States are a sure guarantee that it will be preserved to you sacred and inviolate, and that your institution will be permitted to govern itself according to its own voluntary rules, without any interference from the civil authority.

"Whatever diversity of shade may appear in the religious opinions of our fellow citizens, the charitable objects of your institution cannot be indifferent to any; and its furtherance of the wholesome purposes of society, by training up its younger members in the way they should go, cannot fail to ensure it the patronage of the government it is under. Be assured that it will meet with all the protection which my office can give it.

"I salute you, holy sisters, with friendship and respect,

"TH. JEFFERSON"

After that, correspondence flowed among the Ursulines of New Orleans and the President of the United States—James Madison; the Governor of Louisiana—William C. C. Claiborne; and various other dignitaries, all with satisfactory results. Then a letter addressed to His Holiness, Pius VII, by Mother St. Michel of Montpellier brought about even more significant consequences. She had received an appeal from her cousin, Sister St. Andrew Madier; she was greatly needed in Louisiana. Personally, she would have been quite willing to respond; but her services were so valued where she was that the Bishop declined to permit her departure; only the Pope, he said, could give such authorization.

Nothing daunted, Mother St. Michel addressed herself to His Holiness, with whom it was very difficult to communicate directly because of the strict custody in which he was kept by Napoleon Bonaparte. But eventually her letter reached Pius and she had made it sufficiently urgent to move him: following an inspiration to invoke the Holy Mother of God under the title of Our Lady of Prompt Succor, she promised to propagate this devotion in Louisiana provided she had a favorable reply. The answer came, not from the Pope himself, but from Cardinal di Pietro, giving the required permission. The Bishop relented and Mother St. Michel, accompanied by seven companions and, of course, taking with her the statue of her special patroness, embarked for Louisiana.

Her arrival marked the beginning of a cult which has prospered and increased through the years. The statue of Our Lady of Prompt Succor was the first to be officially crowned in the United States and to this day only one other has been accorded such an honor by virtue of a Papal indult.

"To relate all that Our Lady of Prompt Succor has since done for the Ursulines and her other clients would take us far beyond the limits of this sketch," the Rev. Henry Semple, S.J., sagely observes in his authoritative work, *The Ursulines in New Orleans*, which has furnished us with so much valuable material; and the same is certainly true as far as the present brief record is concerned. But at least the most historic occasion when Our Lady of Prompt Succor was invoked—the Battle of New Orleans—should be duly recognized, as its commemoration is one of special local significance to this day. "While Jackson and his men were valiantly fighting at Chalmette, the Very Rev. L. Wm. DuBourg, V.G., was saying Mass for their success in the Convent Chapel, wherein were assembled many devout clients of Our Lady of Prompt Succor, whose statue had . . . been removed . . . to the main altar, in order to animate the confidence of all present in her powerful intercession with her Divine Son, who was about to be mystically immolated on that altar. At the solemn moment of the Communion, a courier entered the chapel, crying out, 'Victory is ours!' Immediately after Mass, the Te Deum was sung, and ever since . . . a Mass of Thanksgiving has been annually offered up in the Ursuline Chapel, in fulfillment of the vow made on that occasion by the saintly Superioress Mother Mary Olivier de Vezin, in the name of the community."

General Jackson, who had requested the nuns to pray for victory, came to the convent and thanked them after the battle was won. He also asked Father DuBourg to hold a religious service of thanks to Almighty God.

On New Year's Day, 1821, the Ursulines decided to build another convent on a plantation recently purchased in the

suburbs. The principal cause for this decision was the opening
of streets through the convent enclosure; it was feared that
these would be an obstacle to the strict observance of cloister
rules and, eventually, the second convent was replaced by the
present plant, which includes a college as well as a school and
cloister and is one of the outstanding educational institutions
of the Deep South.

After the Ursulines left the convent dedicated in 1734, it
became the residence of the Bishop and, when the diocese was
raised in rank, the residence of the Archbishop and was used
for this purpose for many years. It was during this period that
a porter's lodge was added where visitors could be received
and announced before being ushered into the main building.
Outstanding among these was Mother Cabrini, who became
St. Frances Xavier, the first American citizen to be canonized.

The historic building is now the rectory of St. Mary's Italian
Church, served by the Oblate Fathers; and its present pastor,
Father Liberto, has taken an active part in preserving its best
traditions, and proudly points out the stained-glass window
in the present church commemorating the Battle of New Orleans. Largely through the efforts of the Patio Planters, co-
operating with the Society of Louisiana Landmarks, the
convent grounds in front of the building have been landscaped
and restored as a beautiful herb garden. Plans are now under
discussion for the restoration of the convent itself.

The fact that Beauregard House, where I spend my winters,
is located directly across the street from this venerable establishment has made the accomplishments of the Ursulines seem
very real and very close to me. Indeed, this house, which I
have been privileged to help restore and which was for a time
the home of the world's most famous chess player, Paul
Morphy, and of the great Creole general, Pierre Gustave
Toutant Beauregard, was built on land purchased from the
Ursulines. I like to feel that they would have been glad to
welcome me as their neighbor.

Part IV

ONWARD CHRISTIAN SOLDIERS

12

Francis Asbury, the Man
Without a Home

FRANCIS Asbury has been designated "the Bishop who, more than any other man, was responsible for the organization and early growth of Methodism in the United States." [1]

It is interesting to note that, whereas the early Spanish Catholic missionaries—Lull, Ignatius, Xavier and Solano—all came from great families, the first English Protestant missionaries—Carey, Morrison and Taylor—were all men of humble background. Francis' father, Joseph Asbury, was a gardener on a great estate and had a limited education; but his mother, Elizabeth, liked to read and encouraged her son to read. Much of this reading had a religious slant, for she was deeply devout; the stories she told her small son were nearly all Bible stories and by the time Francis was six or seven years old, he had begun to read the Bible for himself.

His first experience with formal education was not a happy one. His schoolmaster apparently belonged to the brutal type made memorable by Dickens; and when the boy was only thirteen, he decided that he would rather be an artisan than a scholar and apprenticed himself to a blacksmith by the name of Foxall, who not only treated him kindly during working hours, but made a companion of him. Part of this companionship took the form of attendance at the Methodist chapel at West Bromwich. Foxall was a Class Leader and, though Francis' parents belonged to the established Church of England and he had hitherto always worshipped with them, when he was asked if he would read sermons in his master's chapel, he willingly consented to do so. Three years later, at the age of seventeen, he began to preach as a layman. When he was twenty-one, he decided that he wanted to make preaching as a Methodist his lifework.

"The name Methodist had been bestowed in the early 18th century on a club at Oxford University. The club, with a membership of about a dozen students, met regularly to study the Bible. Because the members tried to lead orderly lives, attended church regularly and refused to waste their time, their fellow students derisively called them 'Methodists.' Two brothers, John and Charles Wesley, became the leaders of the group. Later, the Methodists started a school for beggar children in Oxford; and the Wesley brothers visited prisons where they preached to the debtors and thieves, and carried food to them as well. Feeling an acute sympathy for the poor, often neglected by other English churches, John Wesley, now ordained, rode about the countryside on horseback, preaching to the people.

"Letters came to John Wesley from America, asking for traveling preachers to work in the colonies. Wesley never considered that he had left the Church of England; circuit riding was his way of doing missionary work for his church. Methodist preachers began to go to the American colonies, and were welcomed. The preachers rode out on circuits as they did in England. There were never enough of them to go around. Young men found the work appealing, and many volunteered for it. Now a leader was needed to direct their work. At a conference in London in August, 1771, Wesley had an appeal to make.

" 'Our brethren in America call aloud for help,' said Wesley in his stirring voice. 'Who will go?'

"Young Francis Asbury sprang to his feet. 'I will go!' he cried." [2]

When Francis Asbury decided that he wished to become one of the Wesleys' active followers, no formal training had been required of him. At first, he had been a local preacher, riding about the English countryside as they did, and after reaching America he followed the same pattern. "The Methodist circuit riders in America were called the 'shock troops of the Lord on the frontier.' Shock troops are those especially fitted by training and discipline to lead the way for the others. The early 'shock troops of the Lord' led lonely lives; they had no homes, no families, nothing but their work. In their saddlebags they carried Bibles and hymnals, and a change of clothing. The hymnals were especially useful in their work. Many a lonely frontier congregation was cheered by singing the hymns that had been composed by Charles Wesley as he rode his circuit back home in England.

"A circuit rider never knew where he would spend the night. If he was lucky he would sleep under a roof. A barn would serve, or a schoolhouse; or he would find shelter in a settler's noisy cabin, teeming with children. Perhaps he might have to sleep on the ground beside a campfire. There were few roads, and the colonists were sometimes widely scattered.

"When Francis Asbury first saw the shores of America, he wrote in his journal, 'My very heart melted within me to think from whence I came, and where I was going, and what I was going about.' He rented no house, hired no lodgings; he simply set out on the road. He was from the first a circuit rider, a man whose home was in the saddle, traveling through rough frontier country sometimes thirty miles a day, perhaps 5000 miles in a year. Forty-five years after he began his work in America, he was still a circuit rider, although he was a bishop of the Methodist Church.

"Asbury's journal described his adventures and held up a mirror to reflect the way of life in the colonies through which he rode. He was never idle. He loved his work. There were drawbacks, of course; lack of privacy was one of the greatest. Usually he had not enough rest or sleep, not enough time to read. But always he carried books in his saddlebags and read them when he could, thinking about their contents as he jogged along on horseback. He even managed to study Hebrew so that he could better understand the Old Testament. From meeting to meeting he rode, preaching at as many as twenty or thirty meetings on one circuit.

"Asbury's earliest years in America were those preceding the American Revolution. He had time to get his work started before the colonists broke away from the mother country, and the Methodist Societies from the parent organization in England.

"His first circuit, in 1772, had Baltimore as its center. He rode 200 miles every three weeks, covering twenty-four meetings.

"On July 14, 1773, the first American Methodist Conference was held in St. George's Church, Philadelphia, where Asbury had preached his first sermon in the New World. Ten preachers came to this conference in 1773, and it was there that the Methodist Church in America had its beginning, though the official birthday has always been celebrated as the Christmas Conference of 1784.

"In November, 1784, a young Methodist preacher, Freeborn Garrettson, 'rode off like an arrow' with instructions from some of his fellow ministers to 'Gather all the preachers together at Baltimore on Christmas Eve.' He had 1200 miles to ride through the wilderness from North Carolina to New England, and it took six weeks to carry his message. But on Christmas Eve, sixty-three out of about eighty American Methodist preachers assembled in Lovely Lane Meeting House in Baltimore. John Wesley had ordained Dr. Thomas Coke in England and sent him to serve as superintendent of the Methodist Societies in America; Francis Asbury was to serve as associate superintendent. Asbury was then forty years old.

"The Christmas Conference lasted for nine days, during which time the assemblage formally welded the various Methodist Societies into one church. Instead of ordaining Asbury as his assistant superintendent, Coke ordained him as a deacon, then, the next day, as an elder, and on the third day consecrated him as a bishop. This did not please John Wesley, but the members of the Christmas Conference approved; from the first, Asbury was regarded by his fellow Methodists in America as their leader.

"Bishop Asbury continued his circuit riding. On his annual journeys he visited practically every state in the Union of those

days. He has been romantically compared to 'The Man Without a Country'; he was called 'The Man Without a Home.'
Once on the prairies of Ohio a stranger said to him, 'Where
are you from?' 'From Boston, New York, Philadelphia, Baltimore, or almost any place you please,' was Asbury's answer.
When, after many years, he preached in Washington, D.C.,
he found that nearly everyone in the community had come
to hear 'this man that rambles through the United States.'
'I am always on the wing,' he remarked once; then, apolo-
getically, he added, 'But it is for God. . . .' The only rest he
had was the short time during the American Revolution when
he had to go into hiding.

" 'The Man Without a Home' had a thousand homes throughout the land. He was an honored guest in mansions and in
pioneer cabins. Occasionally he stopped at a wretched tavern
where he might be overcharged, or even turned away. His
'allowance' as an itinerant preacher was scarcely enough to
provide him with clothes. None of the hardships mattered.
To him, souls were the only important things and his job was
to bring souls to God. He was always on the alert for a chance
to preach. When he stopped to take shelter from the rain he
talked and prayed with the woman who allowed him to sit
beside the fire in her poor cabin. He was not a remarkable
preacher; some of his listeners said that he prayed better than
he preached. But he was earnest, simple and direct, speaking
always straight from his heart.

"For forty-five years, until he had to be carried and placed
in a chair to preach his last sermon, he went about his work,
organizing scattered little groups of worshippers into the
American Methodist Church. As part of his duties as bishop,
he assigned the preachers to their pulpits. If they objected to
their assignments, he always said, 'Try it, and then if you don't
like it, complain; but try it first.'

"He constantly visited their stations, supervising their work
and conducting meetings. At the annual conferences he studied
his preachers, and tried to send them to places which would
benefit their health. At a session of the Western Conference
in 1806, noticing that some of the preachers appeared to be

needy, he is said to have given away first his coat, then his shirt and finally his watch.

"Because of the strenuous life he led, Bishop Asbury grew old before his time. When he was thirty-nine, someone referred to him as 'venerable.' When he was fifty-four, doctors advised him to stop preaching. He asked to resign his office at the General Conference the next year, but the request filled his hearers with such obvious dismay that he decided to keep going. After a time, his health improved a little, and once more he took up his labors.

"His devoted friends tried to spare him and protect him from unnecessary exertion. He had to give up horseback riding finally, and Spark, his last horse, was sold. Spark 'whickered after' him as he was led away by his new owner. That last bewildered whinny nearly broke the bishop's heart. He had loved all his horses—the faithful beasts that had carried him so many miles; perhaps he loved Spark the best of all. Never again would the bishop jog contentedly along the wilderness trails, raising his voice in a good, lively Wesley hymn: 'Love Divine, All Love Excelling,' or 'Jesus, Lover of My Soul.'

"Bishop Asbury now traveled in a light-four-wheeled carriage. Rheumatism bothered him more and more; at times he could not walk without crutches, could not bear shoes on his feet. Sometimes he had to be lifted from or into his carriage. But he continued to be seen at conferences, bright-eyed, silver-haired, alert. The last conference he attended was in Tennessee. He was unable to go home to rest after it was over. He had no home. He kept on going.

"On March 24, 1816, he preached a sermon in Richmond, Virginia. He then set out again, but the weather was so bad that he stopped to rest at the home of an old friend, George Arnold, about twenty miles from Fredericksburg. One week later, at four o'clock in the afternoon of Sunday, March 31st, he died.

"Francis Asbury was called the Prophet of the Long Road, and he did, indeed, ride a long road. He had even outridden John Wesley, who covered over 200,000 miles during his career. Bishop Asbury rode 275,000 miles over the trails of the American wilderness." [3]

Authorities differ as to the value of Francis Asbury's journal, which he began to keep on the day he sailed for America. Dorothy Heiderstadt considers it "an indispensable source book of American social history for the first forty years of the independence of the new nation." Wade Crawford Barclay, on the contrary, states, "Not infrequently, his journal is vague and inexact in dating important events, and certain of its dates have been proven to be incorrect." In the latter connection, however, it should be noted that the journal was written hastily and under very difficult circumstances and a slight error or confusion in regard to a date would not materially damage the general description and approximate time of an event. Neither would it affect the spiritual impact.

"Whither am I going? To the New World. What to do? To gain honour? No, if I know my own heart. [He begins, by saying.] To get money? No: I am going to live to God, and to bring others so to do. The people God owns in England, are the Methodists. The doctrines they preach, and the discipline they enforce, are, I believe, the purest of any people now in the world. The Lord has greatly blessed these doctrines and this discipline in the three kingdoms: they must therefore be pleasing to him. If God does not acknowledge me in America, I will soon return to England. I know my views are upright now; may they never be otherwise!" [4]

"The people [in the South] in general eat only two meals a day [he observes after one of his long journeys] the first about nine in the morning, and the second about four or five in the afternoon. They eat flesh at both meals. Our people in general drink coffee with the first meal, and water with the second. The people of the world drink either coffee or cyder with the first meal, and grog or cyder with the second. Their animal food is almost entirely pig-meat with sometimes shad-fish. I have hardly eat anything these ten weeks of the flesh kind, except swine's flesh and shad-fish. They have a great variety of fruit-pies, peach, apple, pear, and cranbury, and puddings very often. I esteem it one great blessing, that I prefer the Indian corn to the wheat. Besides, they do not in general manage their wheat properly in the South, so that the wheat-bread is but very indifferent." [5]

His general summing up of his mission shows him faithful to his first ideals. "I have nothing to seek but the glory of God; nothing to fear but his displeasure. I am determined that no man shall bias me with soft words and fair speeches: nor will I ever fear (the Lord helping me) the face of man, or know any man after the flesh, if I beg my bread from door to door; but whomsoever I please or displease, I will be faithful to God, to the people, and to my own soul." [6]

13

The Judsons, Protestant Pioneers to Burma

One hot day in the summer of 1806, a group of five earnest young students at Williams College foregathered in a grove where they were in the habit of holding prayer meetings. A sudden thunderstorm forced them to seek shelter in the nearest place that offered this, which happened to be a haystack. As a result of this famous "haystack meeting," now commemorated by an appropriate monument, North America's first missionary society was founded by Congregationalists four years later and given the title of The American Board of Commissioners for Foreign Missions. Two years later, the first representatives of this board were sent to Ceylon and India.[1] The most significant results of the haystack meeting, however, were those achieved in Burma by Adoniram Judson and his wife, née Ann (Nancy)

Hasseltine, and in Hawaii by Hiram Bingham, his wife Sybil Moseley and their twelve associates.

The latter movement has become the more famous of the two and countless books, both fiction and nonfiction, have been written about it. But the former was even more spectacular and adventurous and so far it has not received the widespread recognition that it deserves, although "Judson's record as a pioneer missionary in Asia has been the source of much inspiration to the cause of Protestant missions." [2] However, Gordon Langley Hall, in *Golden Boats from Burma*,[3] has made a valuable contribution toward overcoming the lack of information about this phase of the missionary movement, and I feel greatly privileged in being permitted to draw freely on his material.

Adoniram Judson, the son of a Congregational minister, was born in Malden, Massachusetts, in 1788 and was graduated with high honors from both Brown University and the Andover Theological School. At the age of twenty-two he went with three companions to Bradford, for the purpose of requesting elders of the church, who were meeting there, to send them as missionaries to the Far East. And, though the daring adventure he desired to undertake at first sounded "wild and romantic" to the "solemn-faced ministers" there assembled, his speech was a "resounding success." The impression which he made upon a young lady, at whose father's house he was entertained and with whom he immediately fell in love, was equally favorable. To be sure, when his prompt proposal of marriage reached her by letter, she replied noncommittally that her parents would have to give their consent; but she ceased to evade the issue when a second letter came, this time addressed to her father, though its contents might have caused a less intrepid girl to hesitate.

"I have now to ask," Adoniram Judson wrote to Deacon Hasseltine, "whether you can consent to part with your daughter early next spring, to see her no more in this world; whether you can consent to her departure and her subjection to the hardships and sufferings of a missionary life; whether you can consent to her exposure to the dangers of the ocean; to the fatal influence of the southern climate of India; to every kind of want and distress; to degradation, insult, persecution, and perhaps a violent death."

Fortunately, the distracted father did not realize how accurate a prophecy this was. Nor was he faced with an immediate separation from his favorite daughter. When Adoniram began his impulsive wooing, he was on the point of leaving for England, to seek the cooperation of the London Missionary Society. It took him some time to complete his assignment, so it was not until the following February that he and Ann were married and immediately sailed for India one bitterly cold day on the brig *Caravan,* Augustine Heard, Master.

During their long and perilous voyage, a matter of conscience arose to trouble Adoniram: while reading his Greek Testament, he became convinced that there was no Biblical authority for infant baptism. Since this was the established practice for Congregationalists and he had been sent out under their auspices, with Congregational money—a princely annual salary of $666.66!—the decision he was forced to make was a hard one. How could he tell his sponsors that he had become a Baptist by conviction? And yet, how could he, with complete honesty, do anything else? To his everlasting credit, let it be said that he chose the hard way and was eventually transferred to the American Baptist Foreign Missionary Society.

Upon their arrival in India, the Judsons were kindly received by William Carey, generally regarded as the founder of modern Protestant missions. This remarkable man had been apprenticed as a boy to a cobbler and his early education was rudimentary. However, he was a natural student and somehow he mastered Hebrew, Greek and Latin so thoroughly that he not only qualified as a minister, but laid the groundwork for familiarity with strange tongues that eventually enabled him to have Bibles printed, in forty different languages and dialects, on his own press. A village church was his first pastorage; however, he soon found that his greatest concern was not with his own immediate flock; he was troubled by the realization that he was not following the command of Jesus to the effect that His apostles and those who followed in their footsteps should carry the gospel to all parts of the world. His next step was active participation in the foundation of the London Missionary Society, and his departure for India followed close upon it. At Serampore he built a church, a school and a printing press and it was there that Adoniram and his bride were his grateful guests.

Though William Carey received the Judsons kindly, he warned them that he considered their Burma project impractical, in the light of his own son's experience in that country; moreover, the Indian civil authorities were anything but hospitable. They ordered the new missionaries to depart immediately and threatened them with drastic measures if they did not obey. Vainly they protested that they did not propose to remain in India anyhow, but—despite Carey's warnings—to leave for Burma as soon as they could transship. Their protests did not help them, because there was no immediate prospect of available transportation and they were obliged to spend most of their time in precarious hiding. But they remained undaunted and at last they succeeded in surreptitiously boarding *La Belle Creole,* a ship bound for the Isle of France, and from there, without too much trouble, they were able to get passage to Madras and thence to Burma. The first lap of their journey on the *Countess of Harcourt* was reasonably comfortable; but unfortunately the police authorities continued to harass them; so instead of awaiting more suitable transportation, they accepted passage on the *Georgiana,* a crazy old vessel, decrepit, smelly and dirty, which could offer them nothing better than a canvas shelter on the open deck. A few days out in rough water, Ann began to feel very sick and, with only Adoniram in attendance, she gave birth to her first child which was stillborn.

While Ann rested beneath the tentlike shelter, heartsick over the loss of her baby, Adoniram impatiently paced the ship's deck watching for the first glimpse of their promised land. His active mind was already filled with a new project. The Bible had never been translated into Burmese and he, Adoniram Judson, had appointed himself to do it.

After three weeks at sea, the creaking *Georgiana* finally

found the entrance to the Rangoon River, a mouth of the great Irrawaddy, and, running toward the prow, he feasted his eyes for the first time on the golden spire of the Shwe-Dagon Pagoda, most famed of all Burma's many temples. His heart leapt for joy. This was something Ann must share. Hurrying back, he lifted her wasted body into his arms, carrying her onto the open deck so that she might see for herself.

When it was time to go ashore the next morning, an arm-chair was found for Ann, who was still too weak to walk. Four Burmese men wearing nothing but loincloths knotted up in front slipped the bamboo poles through the chair and gently lifted it on their strong shoulders and hurried off to the custom-house. The law required that a tenth of every cargo be set aside for the King, and so the baggage of any traveler was thoroughly inspected. Adoniram was stripped to the skin and his clothing searched and Ann fared almost as badly; but noth-ing was found concealed, even among her many petticoats, so only a very small bribe could be demanded. Then the Judsons were allowed to dress and proceed to the mission home of Felix Carey, William's son, and his Burmese-born wife, a woman of Portuguese descent who gave the weary travelers a very warm welcome.

Their first requisite was to master the difficult language and it took some time to find a teacher who was willing to instruct Ann as well as Adoniram; but actually she learned Burmese much more quickly than her husband. Nearly five months passed before Adoniram believed he had a sufficient grasp of the language to warrant a formal call on Mya-day-men, the viceroy who had absolute power over the city of Rangoon. The missionary's reception was a very cool one and Ann, greatly incensed, decided she would take matters into her own hands and pay a visit to the vicereine. This proved to be a complete success. When the audience was over, the vicereine took Ann's hand in her own and announced, rather surprisingly, "You are like a sister to me."

Ann's mornings passed quickly as she dealt with household problems; Adoniram's were devoted to his studies with his Burmese teacher. Besides working on his translation of the

Bible, he was compiling a grammar and the material for a dictionary. Moreover, they were making friends. The Burmese would pay evening calls, bringing little gifts.

Six months after the Judsons' arrival in Rangoon, Felix Carey accepted an important government post at the court of King Bodawpaya in the Golden City of Ava. A few miles from Rangoon a sudden storm arose, overturning their boat. He had the dreadful experience of seeing his wife, small son and new baby drown before his eyes and the terrible shock, from which he was unable to recover either mentally or physically, ended his missionary career.

When the Judsons had been in Burma a little over two years, Ann gave birth to a son, with Adoniram again in the dual role of doctor and nurse. The ecstatic parents named him Roger Williams for the founder of the Rhode Island Colony and, this time, everything went well. Ann's health seemed to be better than it had been in a long while and for six months the baby throve. Then, for no apparent reason, he began to run a temperature. Added to Ann's fears for Roger were her anxieties over Adoniram: his constant studying had overtaxed his strength and his eyesight was badly impaired; he was convinced that the mission was doomed and he was in utter despair. Two months dragged by and though Roger showed no signs of actual improvement, he did seem to be holding his own. Then he was seized with a terrible paroxysm of coughing and two nights later he was dead.

Completely overwhelmed by their grief at the loss of their second child, the Judsons clung to each other in misery; they wanted to see no one; they tried to avert their eyes from the tiny new grave in the corner of the garden. A week had passed in this fashion when they were roused from their lethargy by a great noise in the mission house compound. Everywhere they looked there seemed to be people. At last they recognized the vicereine. She had been told of the little white child's death only that day and was very affected by the news. Smiting her breast in the Burmese expression of grief, she cried in a loud voice, "Why did you not send me word, that I might have come to his funeral?"

The parents were deeply touched, Ann explaining that in their sudden and great sorrow the thought had not occurred to them. A few days later they received a further communication from the vicereine. She had thought long over their troubles, coming to the conclusion that they both needed a change of scene. In memory of the little white child she was arranging a procession of elephants. A conveyance would be sent to fetch them at the appropriate time. In due course, a large elephant arrived with a beautifully draped howdah (seat) strapped to its back, and the huge beast with the Judsons seated on it joined the rest of the parade. They had never seen such a procession. The vicereine, dressed in a brilliant gown of white and red silk, rode ahead of the Judsons' elephant. Her beast was a little larger than theirs and the howdah in which she sat was covered with gilt that glittered in the bright morning sunshine. The procession was led into the jungle by a guard of thirty red-capped men carrying either spears or guns. Behind the Judsons' elephant were three or four more bearing the viceroy's son and important government officials. Following on foot were some three hundred brightly attired men and women.

The journey lay through cool, thick jungle, so overgrown in places with bamboo strands and coarse elephant grass that the elephants themselves were needed to clear a passageway through. Huge teak trees, sometimes towering one hundred and twenty feet above the ground, cast their long shadows on brilliant orchids, strange wild fruits and hanging vines. Butterflies and moths of every conceivable color darted in search of the sunlight over the heads of the intruders.

At last the vicereine signaled for the procession to halt under a spreading banyan tree. Mats were unrolled so that the guests of honor might sit with their regal hostess, who did all in her power to make them happy. With her own hands she twisted garlands of blossoms for her American friends. Then, gathering fruit, she herself pared it as a mark of condescension and devotion.

It was already dark before the elephant set them down in front of the mission house. Tired out, their hearts full of gratitude, Adoniram and Ann went indoors to spend their most relaxed night since the death of their little one.

Soon thereafter Ann started a school for thirty little girls. More often than not the native pupils were accompanied by their mothers and Ann could not resist what seemed to her a heaven-sent opportunity to talk to them about Christianity. In her spare moments, she was preparing a Burmese catechism for her younger students; next she decided to translate the Book of Jonah for the benefit of her "older" pupils. With the exception of her footwear, she now dressed like a Burmese woman. Somehow she could never get used to open sandals. By New England standards of the early eighteen hundreds her mode of attire would appear to be somewhat immodest, perhaps even daring, yet it suited her tall, well-developed figure very well. From the waist up she wore a blouselike garment of black lace or yellow gauze known as an *aingyi,* while her *longyi* or skirt made of brilliant flowered silk was gathered in folds at the breast. Adoniram voiced no objections, but refused to follow his wife's lead and clung to his funereal black suits.

During the month of October, 1816, George H. Hough, a new missionary, and his wife Phebe arrived from America with their two children *and a printing press.* Hough was to print whatever the Judsons had written or translated into Burmese. Adoniram was delighted, for he was sure that once the King in Ava heard of the wondrous new press he would want to see it work for him. A few requests for the newly printed books came in; the vicereine discussed religion with Ann and actually allowed her daughter to read the catechism; more pupils applied for admission to the school; Adoniram's health took a turn for the better and he began work on his Burmese dictionary. There was only one drawback—they had not made a single conversion. However, in a general way, everything seemed to be going as well with the mission as could be expected. Then suddenly, one critical situation followed another in swift succession. Hitherto Burma had been blessedly free from cholera, despite its prevalence in India; now during the hottest season of the year, Rangoon was stricken. Next came a new cause for alarm. There had been frequent rumors of war ever since the Burmese king had plundered his own rebellious borderland, thus causing the inhabitants to flee into British territory. From time to time he had crossed the border in an effort to force the refugees back into Burma, and there had been some skirmishes with British outposts, resulting in damage to life and property. The British, who had their hands full in India, had not hastened to deal with the Burmese intruders. Now it looked as if they were about to retaliate.

To Hough, thoroughly disheartened by the lack of converts and terrified lest he should catch cholera, the threat of war was the final straw; he declined to remain at his post. As soon as passage could be secured, he and his family would be on their way to Calcutta. However, they were still at the mission house in mid-September when, most unexpectedly, two missionaries, James Colman and Edward M. Wheelock, arrived from America. Though only in their early twenties, both were married and had brought their wives with them. Unfortunately, neither young man was in good health and Wheelock was practically bedridden; his wife Eliza had visualized herself as the heroine of a glamorous existence in Burma; instead she found she was not only expected to nurse an ailing husband, but to perform the same humdrum household tasks that had bored her so in New England. She made no attempt to hide her resentment of Ann and the efficient way in which she managed the mission house. However, not even Ann could stretch space originally intended to house two families to accommodate four. Therefore, it was with mixed emotions of relief and regret that the Judsons finally watched the Houghs sail for India early in November of 1818.

Ann and Adoniram were equally adept at concealing their disappointment: she, because she could not overcome Eliza's antagonism and he, because the poor health of the new missionaries prevented them from being of more assistance. Then, spurred on by Ann, Adoniram decided to build a zayat. This was a small building where Buddhist lay preachers could give instructions. The Judsons' was the first Christian zayat ever built in Burma. It cost two hundred dollars and it was almost thirty feet long and twenty feet wide. The thatched bamboo porch in front had steps leading up to it. Inside, the walls were covered with whitewashed boards, while the windows were glassless openings.

On Sunday, April 4, 1819, they held their first service. Adoniram, sitting on the porch of his new *zayat,* invited the Burmese to enter.

"Ho! Everyone that thirsteth for knowledge," he shouted over and over. The result was a first congregation of fifteen grown-ups and a large number of curious children, the latter naked except for their colorful bracelets, necklaces and trinkets.

Before long, there was a daily increase in visitors to the *zayat,* but Adoniram and Ann were particularly encouraged by the repeated visits of one Maung Nau, the young, hard-working employe of a timber merchant. Then, after six years of praying for a convert, the Judsons watched with joy in their hearts as Maung Nau suddenly stood up before a congregation of thirty people and loudly confessed his belief in Jesus. A few weeks later, while Ann and a curious crowd of men, women and children looked on, Adoniram baptized his first convert in a pond near the *zayat.*

News of the death of King Bodawpaya at Ava threw the country into a state of fear and unrest, for such a passing could mean civil war. Early one morning, Adoniram joined his abnormally quiet Burmese neighbors as they waited by the river for the coming of the sacred messengers from the golden city and listened as they proclaimed the death of the King and the ascendancy of his grandson, Bagyidaw, to the throne.

Despite the feeling of uneasiness prevalent in Rangoon, Ann and Adoniram saw no reason to change their mode of existence. However, the reports of Adoniram's *zayat* and the increased attendance at the mission services was extremely displeasing to the Buddhist priests, and the Judsons were subjected to a fanatical attack. They realized that, without protection from such indignities or any official sanction to teach, the mission was doomed. If the King granted permission for the Judsons to expound Christianity, no one would dare to persecute them.

Adoniram would appeal to their old friend Mya-day-men, who now occupied the position of Wungyi, or prime minister, in Ava, to act as their intermediary. While Adoniram busied himself with preparations for the trip to Ava, Ann tried to cope with the recalcitrant Eliza and her sick husband. Eliza had finally convinced him that his very life depended on their "escaping" to Bengal and thirteen days out of Rangoon, Wheelock, in a state of pain-crazed madness, jumped overboard and was never seen again. As for Eliza, she continued on to Calcutta, where she lost little time in remarrying. But Colman's health had improved and Adoniram decided it would be wise to take the younger man with him to Ava. Though they knew King Bagyidaw could not read English, they concluded that a Bible, written in that language, would be the most appropriate offering for him; since he was known as "the Golden One," the missionaries, at great expense, had all six volumes covered with gold leaf. They departed on a river boat for Ava, arriving on January 25, 1820.

Adoniram's first task was to get in touch with Mya-day-men, who greeted his friend with real feeling; and as for his wife, she could hardly contain her emotion as she inquired after "Mrs. Yoodthan," as she called Ann. Mya-day-men immediately agreed to help them to obtain their greatly desired audience. That same evening they learned the King would see them the next day.

Maung Yo, a respected official, came to escort the missionaries. They were given places of honor in front of the many dignitaries who thronged the reception room of Maung Zah, a member of the King's privy council, and were seated in the order of their importance. After greeting the missionaries in a friendly manner, Maung Zah asked to see their petition and, before he finished reading it, a messenger suddenly appeared who announced that the Golden One was approaching. Maung Zah hurried the missionaries from the room, and they followed him through a maze of passages that terminated in a brilliant audience hall, each section of which was covered with gold, including the pillars surrounding the umbrellalike dome. With folded hands, Adoniram and Colman knelt, feeling both eager and afraid at the awesome prospect of seeing the Burmese king.

The Golden Presence had marched unattended into the room. He was just over five feet tall and very bowlegged. His face was not unpleasant but was spoiled somewhat by a curious slanted forehead. His *engyee* or jacket was made of white muslin, while his *patso* was of the scarlet only royalty might wear. His knotted, turbanlike headdress enclosed his long black hair. He could not fail to notice the Americans, for they were the only men in the room who were not prostrate before him.

"Who are these?" he demanded.

"The teachers, Great King," Adoniram replied in excellent Burmese.

"What, you speak Burmese?" The King was agreeably surprised to hear his own language spoken by a foreign teacher. "Are you teachers of religion?" he asked.

"Yes," Adoniram replied.

The King asked a few minor questions and then was silent. Maung Zah, who all this time had been lying flat on the floor awaiting his cue, slowly lifted his face and proceeded to read the all-important petition in which the missionaries requested permission to preach their religion and also asked exemption from molestation for those who were guided by their preaching.

The King held out his hand for the petition and Maung Zah crawled forward to present it. Then the Golden Eyes carefully read it through, while Adoniram handed Maung Zah a copy of his tract specially abridged for the occasion. As the Golden Eyes turned to the tract Adoniram silently prayed.

Bagyidaw began to read, "There is one Being who exists eternally; who is exempt from sickness, old age, and death; who is, and was, and will be, without beginning and without end. Besides this, the true God, there is no other God—"

The Golden Eyes flashed with anger; with contempt the Golden Hands threw the offending tract on the floor. Maung Yo coaxingly opened a gold-covered volume of the Bible to show the King but there was no response.

Maung Zah then spoke for the Golden Lips. "Why do you ask for such permission? Have not the Portuguese, the English, the Moslems, and people of all other religions, full liberty to practice and worship according to their own customs? In regard to the objects of your petition, His Majesty gives no order. In regard to your sacred books, His Majesty has no use for them. Take them away."

Then the Golden Feet walked away, leaving two dejected missionaries behind them.

On his return to Rangoon, Adoniram called in his second and third converts and reported the unsuccessful outcome of his trip, warning them that troublous times lay ahead; they might even be put to death because they had embraced the religion of Jesus. To the Judsons' great surprise, the converts showed not the slightest indication of wavering and soon there were two more converts, one a woman. This female convert planned to open a school for boys so that they would not have to depend on Buddhist priests for their education. Many Burmese, inspired by the first converts, now came to the mission seeking information and again things looked brighter. Then both Judsons were stricken with fever and, though Adoniram gradually recovered, it was evident that Ann must leave Rangoon. She went home and it was more than two years before she was able to return from the United States, where her recovery became complete.

Meanwhile, a Dr. Jonathan Price, accompanied by his wife and baby, arrived in the city. The Baptist Board had financed his medical studies so, though Price was not a missionary, Adoniram had no choice but to share his quarters with the new arrivals. The doctor quickly established a successful practice and news of his magical powers soon found their way to the Golden Ears, who ordered him to make an official visit to Ava. Adoniram, though reluctant to interrupt his translation of the Bible into Burmese, accompanied him so that he might act as interpreter.

At their first audience, the King completely ignored the missionary; but Maung Zah remembered him and, after greeting him cordially, suggested it might be a good idea for him to prolong his stay in Ava.

When they were again summoned to the Golden Presence,

the King deigned to notice Adoniram. "And you, in black," he demanded, "what about you? Are you a medical man, too?"

"Not a medical man," replied Adoniram, "but a teacher of religion, Your Majesty."

"Have any embraced your religion?" The question so surprised Adoniram that his heart seemed to give an extra beat.

"Not here in Ava," he replied, but such an evasive answer did not satisfy the curious king.

"Are there any in Rangoon?" he asked.

"There are a few."

There was deep silence. None of the Burmese present in the audience stirred from their prostrate positions. Then the Golden Lips moved to discuss cosmography and astrology! Adoniram breathed with relief, for the King now knew that some of his own subjects had become Christians, yet had not lost his temper.

It seemed they would be detained in Ava for some time because the King wished to know more of Price and his magical powers. This provided Adoniram with an opportunity to cultivate a number of friendships close to the royal court. Through his contact with the King's eldest half brother, he obtained permission to build a *kyoung*—a residence for holy people— and in two short days the neat house of bamboo and teak was completed. A disciple would live there while Adoniram was absent in Rangoon. In January of 1823, Adoniram left Ava to collect his household goods and chattels.

His joy at being reunited with Ann was clouded only by the fact that the long-rumored war with the English now seemed imminent. The British were not at all eager for war, but there had been a number of incidents which they could not afford to ignore. The Burmese had opened fire on British civilians sailing on the Naaf River; they had also attacked a British outpost on the isle of Shahpuri. Finally they kidnapped two British naval officers whom they had invited to discuss the border troubles.

Six weeks after leaving Rangoon, the Judsons landed at Ava and Ann immediately began plans for opening another school. But as soon as he heard of their arrival, Dr. Price hastened to greet them with the unpleasant news that foreigners were no longer welcome at court—even his medical prowess had lost its magic. Price thought it wisest for the Judsons to stay with him on the other side of the river. Soon afterward the news that a British fleet had captured Rangoon reached them, and the Judsons found themselves in real difficulty. They had become friendly with a young Englishman, Henry Gouger, who had made a fortune trading with the Burmese. It was his financial accounts that implicated the missionaries, for the Burmese found that he had paid sums of money at various times to Adoniram and Price. They failed to understand that Gouger was only cashing their checks, which he later sent to his own Calcutta bank for reimbursement. The Burmese could not envisage anybody being so stupid as to give away good silver for "useless" pieces of paper. It was perfectly clear; the Americans were spies in the pay of the British.

One evening, the Judsons were about to sit down for dinner when they heard a terrible commotion outside. Suddenly the door was broken down and in rushed more than a dozen Burmese led by two fearsome-looking characters—one flourishing a black book and the other bearing the dreaded tattooed spot on either cheek. Ann had seen Spotted Faces, as they were called, before. Everyone knew how these "children of the prison" were cut off from all contact with law-abiding citizens, so that they were forced even to marry others of their kind. When their own prison terms were completed, they were appointed executioners, torturers and jailors. The Spotted Face tied Adoniram's hands behind his back and dragged him off to prison. Though the house was guarded, a Burmese convert, Maung Ing, managed to slip out for news of Adoniram. He returned to relate that the teacher was still alive although his legs were held fast by three pairs of fetters locked to a long pole. After many appeals to the King's sister, Ann was successful in securing permission to have Adoniram transferred from the vermin-infested main cell to an open shed; and one afternoon when she brought him food, she told him they were going to have another child.

It was born the following January—a tiny, sad-looking little girl, to whom her mother gave a very long name: Maria Elizabeth Butterworth. As soon as Ann was strong enough to walk to the prison Adoniram hobbled to the gate to see his new daughter, and even the Spotted Faces assembled to look at the child.

In May, while ministering to Adoniram, Ann was suddenly ordered to go to the Governor's house. To her great relief, she found he merely wanted to question her about the inside of a European pocket watch. When he finally dismissed her, she quickly crossed the road to the prison gates, but before she reached them one of her servants intercepted her with the news that the white prisoners had been taken away. Rushing back to the Governor, Ann demanded to know if it was true. He admitted that it was—his object in sending for her had been only to spare her the pain of parting from Adoniram. "The prisoners are to be sent to Amarapura," he told her. "Why, I know not. I will send a man immediately to see what is to be done with them."

The next morning Ann set out by river for Amarapura and learned the prison was located in the village of Oung-pan-la, which she reached just before nightfall. Adoniram gave one look at her and sobbed, "Why have you come? I hoped you would not follow. You cannot live here." Then he collapsed.

Gradually, Ann managed to piece together details of the death march. The men had been roped together in pairs with a Spotted Face in charge of each two men, driving them forward like horses. Every step had been sheer agony.

Ann's immediate task was to find a place to stay. The chief jailer, seeing her distress, allowed her to use a storehouse. Morning came and with it food, for a friend of Dr. Price arrived with rice and curry which Ann shared with the prisoners. She was allowed to visit her husband and found him a little better, but then another disaster occurred: the village was stricken with smallpox. Ann herself had been vaccinated and had some idea of what to do. She inoculated Maria and the jailer's children. The baby caught the smallpox, but the jailer's children were hardly affected. Ann's fame swept through the village and soon she was asked to inoculate almost every child in the place. Fortunately for her none of them died. However, just as Maria was recovering, Ann herself came down with a bad attack of dysentery and was so ill that she was totally unable to do anything for herself. Her faithful Bengalese servant, Koo-chil, completely forgetting his caste, cared for her, looked after the child, searched for food and fed Adoniram. Owing to her sickness, there was no supply of natural milk to feed Maria. The jailer's wife, moved with compassion, persuaded her husband to allow Adoniram, still wearing his fetters, to hobble around the village with Maria in his arms begging a little milk from the nursing mothers. They responded with loving kindness and little Maria lived.

The war was coming to an end. Sir Archibald Campbell, the British commander, had even offered the King of Burma a treaty but the Burmese were still suspicious. Adoniram and his fellow prisoners were hustled into carts one day and taken to Amarapura. Here they were placed in separate rooms where each in turn was required to translate Sir Archibald's peace terms into Burmese. In this way, by comparing the individual efforts, the Burmese knew they could tell if the prisoners were translating the truth. Toward the end of October, 1825, Sir Archibald was informed by the Burmese that they had never heard of relinquishing territories or paying indemnities. It was clear to him that they were only trying to gain time.

Adoniram was needed as a translator, so he was released from prison at last. He was taken to Ava, but Ann was left to her own resources and, accompanied by Koo-chil, she went by boat. Next morning she called on her old friend the Governor to have him explain Adoniram's position. It seemed he was to be sent to Maloun where the Burmese forces were encamped. The kindly Governor arranged for Adoniram to call on Ann before his departure. She quickly packed food, mattress, blanket and pillow; but the most exciting parting gift was the news that the precious translation of the New Testament was safe. Ann had secreted it in a hard pillow which she brought to him at the prison; when he had been transferred, a Spotted Face had confiscated it. However, he had decided the hard "interior" wasn't worth keeping and had thrown it away, luckily to be found by Maung Ing when he went to the prison in search of a keepsake of his beloved "Yoodthan."

At Maloun, Adoniram met with the Burmese and British officials who held daily talks on board a vessel moored in the river. The British demanded a crore of rupees (approximately a million British pounds sterling), together with four territories. The Burmese were to be allowed fifteen days of armistice to take the treaty to the Golden Presence. After hearing nothing at the end of this period, the British advanced on Maloun, where the only item of importance they found in the Burmese camp was their own treaty; nobody had had the courage to lay it in the Golden Hands!

On the last day of the year Adoniram finally obtained his release. He rushed to the mission house where his joy turned to horror at what confronted him—inside the door sat a Burmese woman nursing a thin and dirty baby. He did not even recognize it as his own little Maria and hurried into the bedroom. Stretched over the foot of the bed lay what looked to be the lifeless body of his wife. Two weeks after he had left for Maloun, Ann had fallen victim to cerebral meningitis; but the crisis passed and she recovered.

The King had at least heard of the treaty of Maloun and, although the British had agreed, on payment of the indemnity, to leave all Burma with the exception of the coastal provinces to her own people, he and his court could not believe they would keep their promise, concluding that the intention was first to impoverish the Burmese and then to march on the capital. Ava was the scene of frantic activity as efforts were made to ensure its impregnability. The mission house was leveled as cannons were erected. To the Burmese plea for better terms, the British replied that the first installment on the indemnity must be paid in twelve days. They also demanded that all foreign prisoners must be allowed to leave the country. This was too much for the Golden Ears. The other foreign prisoners he would gladly let go—they had been nothing but a nuisance anyway—but the teacher Yoodthan, his remarkable wife and their child, he was unwilling to release, for at last he had come to realize how valuable the services of the Judsons might be.

"They are not English," he cried, "they are my people. They shall not go."

As a matter of fact, Adoniram did not particularly want to leave Burma. The war had nothing to do with him. Had he not come to Burma to found a Christian mission? To offend the Burmese government might well destroy the work he had already begun. So it was decided that Ann should go to Amherst, which the British had chosen to be the capital of the provinces now under their control, as it seemed the most likely place for her to regain her health. Adoniram would accompany her part way, as he had been persuaded by the British governor general to act as adviser and translator in Ava during the negotiation of a commercial treaty between the East India Company and the Burmese government.

As they boarded their river boat, the Judsons watched the piles of gold and silver bars that were begrudgingly being loaded into the waiting ships. For the last time Ann glanced back at the Golden City with its palaces and pagodas. With Adoniram by her side she felt at peace as the golden boats from Burma slipped into the moonlit night.

On their way, the Judsons were invited to stay at the British camp, where Ann's appearance caused a tremendous sensation. The British treated her like visiting royalty and her greatest triumph came at the state dinner given by Sir Archibald for the Burmese commissioners with whom he had been negotiating what history knows as the Treaty of Yandabo. Flags and banners turned the camp into a wonderland. Hangings of gold, red and yellow bunting welcomed the rather uneasy guests. A long dinner table had been set up; even a regimental band was provided. Sir Archibald, wearing a splendid uniform, himself led the grand procession. As it reached the Judson tent, the British commander entered alone and reappeared shortly afterward with Mrs. Judson on his arm. Poised and smiling, Ann accompanied him in to dinner where she was given the place of honor at his right hand.

Amherst was situated on a pleasant peninsula in the Salween River. The British provided Ann with a temporary home there where she immediately began to supervise the construction of a new mission house and school. Unfortunately, the hardships she had sustained had so weakened her that another bout of fever contracted from the baby proved fatal. On October 26, 1826, at the age of thirty-six, she died. Little Maria later joined her mother in death.

She had crossed wide oceans to reach this strange, exciting land of Burma. The years had been hard, yet she would not have exchanged her life with Adoniram for any other. Never once, from the day she linked her destiny with his, had she lost faith in her Christian convictions. Through every tribulation and hardship they rose up to succor her.

Epilogue

In 1963 Burma celebrated the one hundred and fiftieth anniversary of the arrival of the Judsons; Adoniram's Burmese translation of the Bible is still in use; and the whole Burmese Christian community now exceeds six hundred thousand. More than two hundred thousand of these Christians are members of the two thousand Baptist churches. Here is the answer to the question: Was the Judsons' mission worthwhile? These Christians support their own churches and ministers, and there are many Christian schools. While American Foreign Missions have given assistance with leadership training and Christian literature, the Christians of Burma have been notable for their self-support and self-direction of their churches, and for their own mission work.

Among the statues forming part of the lacelike reredos at Riverside Church in New York City is a delicately carved figure of Ann. Its choice is, perhaps, as significant as the figure of Junípero Serra in Statuary Hall at the Capitol.

14

China—A Record Span, Including
Matteo Ricci, the Leading Jesuit
Pioneer after Xavier

There is no country, as far as I know, where the span of time covered by missions is as extended as it is in China. According to tradition, as we have already noted, St. Thomas went there in the first century; and though this tradition does not rest firmly on indisputable fact, it represents more than a probability. As early as the beginning of the sixth century, some disciples of Nestorious, a Syrian patriarch of Constantinople who denied the hypostatic union in Jesus, established themselves there and began the first permanent and active workers for Christianity. The spread of Catholic missions beyond this sect began early in the fourteenth century when the great John DiMonte Corvino was sent to Tartary by Pope Nicholas IV and became the first Archbishop of Peking. He was favorably received by the Mongols, who began by treating him with tolerance and ended by treating him with respect, affection and veneration; but his successor, Nicholas de Bentra, though twenty-six laborers were sent to assist him, was not able to save the hierarchy Corvino had established and the missionary movement lost impetus and strength.

More than two hundred years were to pass before it showed definite signs of revival, though it never ceased entirely. Then Francis Xavier dreamed of going there. Though this was temporarily defeated by his untimely death, it came true through his followers. Slowly the realization had come that culture, even though it was unchristian culture, must be recognized as such or no progress would be made among the peoples where it was indigenous. This realization had first come in India. Now it came in China. "Here the missionaries faced not only a high culture, but a unified political entity living an all but completely self-contained existence behind a wall of isolationism. China was more than a state. She was a world unto herself, and a closed world. She saw herself as synonymous with civilization. Outside her borders nothing existed but barbarism. China could be tolerant of that other barbarian world, but only upon condition that she have as little contact with it as possible. The aggressive fever of expansionism which had fired the imagination of the pushing Western world had no counterpart in late Ming China. The spirit of high adventure, lust for empire, for power, prestige, wealth, and zeal for the spread of Christianity, had dotted the seas with Spanish and Portuguese sails. Europeans were landing on every shore, pushing on from conquest to conquest, eager, curious, acquisitive. China was a stranger to this spirit. . . .

"This was the China which St. Francis Xavier had vainly tried to enter. This was the challenge faced by the missionaries who followed him. The task of introducing and finding a sympathetic hearing for the unheard-of and revolutionary doctrines of Christianity seemed hopeless. If Europeanism proved wanting in India, it would prove totally inept in China.

"Toward the end of the sixteenth century a realization of the errors of Europeanism began to appear among a few missionaries. They were chiefly Jesuits, members of the newly founded religious order known as the Society of Jesus. They developed methods of apostolate which represented a sharp break with the dominant spirit of the age. These methods aroused criticism and have been the subject of debate ever since.

"Much of the criticism stemmed from the fact that few understood at the time or have understood since what the Jesuits were attempting to do. They were accused of being innovators, of compromising the faith. Actually they were attempting to restore the genuine ideal of Christianity as the leaven of the world; to renew the authentic character of the world mission of Christianity; to revive methods of cultural adaptation which had played a prominent part in the earlier centuries of Christian expansion.

"The spirit of the Society of Jesus was admirably suited to the development of these methods of apostolate. The order was young, having been canonically established by Pope Paul III on September 27, 1540. Religious orders, like individuals, generally manifest in the days of their youth a flexibility which is wanting to their more advanced age. With age comes caution: a partiality for the well-worn paths of the tried and true; a reluctance to recognize that in a world which never stands still the tried and true often becomes outmoded and false; an unwillingness to embark upon new adventures.

"St. Ignatius of Loyola, founder of the Jesuit order, was not afraid to break new trails. His Constitutions imposed no narrowly defined limitations upon the methods of apostolate proper to his followers. He decided against the adoption of a distinctive habit for members of the Society. One of the first rules of the order required its members to learn the language of the country in which they resided. This seems an obvious thing to do. Yet this first principle of cultural adaptation had been generally ignored. It was the common practice in missionary countries to teach the faith through interpreters. Some members of older orders looked askance upon his innovations and were not easily reconciled. There is evidence that some of the hostility to the methods later employed in China was not unrelated to this attitude. . . .

"The methods employed during the twenty-five years that followed the death of Francis Xavier showed no advance upon the narrow Europeanism characteristic of the age. The missionaries who attempted to penetrate China made no effort to overcome their ignorance of Chinese language and customs. An exception can be made for the Augustinian de Rada who in 1575 took back to Manila one hundred volumes of Chinese works on a variety of subjects and, reporting his experiences and observations, gave to Europe the first authentic picture of China and her institutions. For the others, the religion, history, philosophy, literature and even language of China held no interest.

"It was an Italian Jesuit, Alessandro Valignano, who gave an entirely new direction to the enterprise." [1]

I

"A doctor of civil law and with some years experience in the court of Pope Paul IV, he [Valignano] brought to the Society of Jesus, which he entered in 1566 at the age of twenty-eight, rare intellectual and spiritual gifts. In 1573 the general of the Society appointed him superior, with the title of visitor, of all the Jesuit missions in the East Indies, a geographical expression which included Japan and China." [2]

Valignano reached Macao in October of 1577 and spent nine months there. He developed a high esteem for the Chinese and an insight into the causes of previous failures. He realized that "instead of attempting to graft itself as a foreign substance upon the resistant and unfriendly body of Chinese culture, Christianity was to revert to its original character of leaven. Entering quietly into the body of Chinese culture it must endeavor to transform it from within. . . .

"He wasted no time in implementing the new policy which he was fully conscious of introducing. The Jesuits at Macao were not equal to the task. They were too deeply imbued with the spirit of Europeanism. . . . Valignano asked the Jesuit provincial at Goa to send him the Italian Bernardino de Ferrariis. He was not available. In his stead the provincial sent Michele Ruggieri, also an Italian.

"Ruggieri arrived in Macao in July, 1579, only to learn that Valignano had sailed for Japan two weeks before. He had, however, left orders for Ruggieri to learn 'to read, write, and speak' Chinese. It was the first step toward the cultural penetration of China.

"In November, 1580, Ruggieri for the first time visited Canton with the Portuguese merchants who were permitted to make two trading visits a year, one in the spring, the other in the fall. En route he persuaded his companions to observe the formalities of Chinese etiquette to which they ordinarily paid little attention. So pleased were the Chinese officials by the improvement in Portuguese manners that they insisted upon Ruggieri's presence at all public audiences. . . . Thus quite simply, as signs of benevolence multiplied, the doors which for so many years had remained firmly closed in the face of frontal attacks, began to open to the gentle pressure of sympathetic understanding.

"If Chinese officialdom appreciated Ruggieri's efforts, his fellow Jesuits in Macao did not. From the beginning he suffered from their lack of comprehension and sympathy. They told him he was wasting his time. Ironically they said that the Chinese was not living who would be converted at the sound of his voice. The Jesuit superior persisted in interfering with his Chinese studies by applying him to ministerial tasks in Macao. Even the energetic intervention of Valignano from Japan failed to end petty obstructionism. . . .

"Three years later, six months after his own arrival in Macao, Matteo Ricci described Ruggieri's years in Macao as a kind of martyrdom at the hands of the Jesuits there." But in late 1582 Ruggieri was granted approval for a small piece of land on which to build a house and church in Chaoching, and he took with him the young Jesuit priest, Matteo Ricci. They "arrived in Chaoching on September 10, 1583. There they established on the property given them by the viceroy the first Christian establishment in the interior of China. . . . Through whatever valleys of misfortune she may have passed since and however prostrate she may be at this moment, the Catholic Church has never ceased since that day to live in China. Valignano had been justified and the carping critics of Ruggieri put to shame." [3] As for Ricci, he has become known as "the leading pioneer after Xavier."

"Born in the very year that Xavier died, apparently frustrated, Ricci, a Jesuit and well educated in mathematics and astronomy, arrived in Macao in 1582. By his knowledge of geography, mathematics, and astronomy, he won the somewhat grudging respect of a number of Chinese scholars and officials.

He set himself to the diligent study of Chinese and the Confucian classics and became expert in them. He believed that Christianity could so be presented to the scholars and the masses as to win them without requiring them to make a complete break with Confucianism. For translating the word God he employed terms which he found in the Confucian classics, *Shang Ti* and especially *T'ien,* thus seeking to present Christianity as something not entirely new and to say, as Paul had long before said at Athens: 'Whom ye ignorantly worship, him declare I unto you.' He believed that the ceremonies in honor of ancestors which constituted an integral part of family life and those celebrated in the Confucian temples did not possess a religious significance in the sense that would make participation in them compromising for Christians. Thus a Chinese might become a Christian while still remaining a loyal member of his family, an official, and a Confucian scholar. Thanks to his friendship with scholars and officials, Ricci succeeded in establishing a residence for himself and his fellow-Jesuits in the capital, Peking. Before his death he had seen the conversion of a number of important persons, including an imperial prince." [4]

Fortunately, to his talents as a mathematician, an astronomer, geographer, and linguist, Ricci added those of a commentator. He kept a journal and entered into an extended correspondence which embraced both the mission field and the home front. We are therefore enabled to inform ourselves from the most reliable source regarding many aspects of his life.

"In 1595, 'as an exercise in Chinese letters,' Ricci composed a small treatise on Friendship (*Chiao-yu lun*). It was a subject bound to interest Chinese scholars, never tired of discussing the 'five human relations' which formed a central feature of Confucian moral doctrine. It was the first of a series of works which were to spread his fame into every corner of the empire. Ricci had established a genuinely warm friendship with the two princes of the imperial family resident in Nanchang. To one of them, Prince Chien-an, he dedicated his essay on friendship. Its success astonished even Ricci. Many scholars desired to make copies of it. One of them had it printed and published. Before long, references to it began to appear in other books. Three years later, writing from Nanking, Ricci could report:

"This *Amicitia* has won more credit for me and for Europe than anything else we have done; because the other things give us the reputation of possessing ingenuity in the construction of mechanical artefacts and instruments; but this treatise has established our reputation as scholars of talent and virtue; and thus it is read and received with great applause and already has been published in two different places. . . .

"Peking was the mecca which every year drew thousands of scholars, both those already holding office and those who, through the crucible of the examination system, were preparing for official careers. Ricci left a description of this feature of life in Peking and its effect upon his work:

"In some years, besides the imperial audiences, doctoral examinations, both civil and military, are held. In other years, there are examinations for the civil and military licentiate. Other years bachelors are selected for certain offices. And then one month every year is appointed for officials from the provinces to visit Peking to congratulate the emperor on his birthday; another month is set aside for appointments to certain offices, another month for appointments to other offices, etc. Among the thousands who thus flock here from the provinces, there are many who either already know the Fathers in Peking or in other residences, or who have heard of us and our teachings, or have seen the books which we have published. As a result, we have to spend the entire day in the reception hall receiving visitors. Although the fatigue is great, we try always to welcome cordially all who come, thus rendering them benevolent. To all we speak of the things pertaining to our holy faith. . . .[5]

"The mission inaugurated in Peking by Ricci had a long but chequered history. Soon after his death the Jesuits were given charge of a revision of the Chinese calendar and of the bureau of astronomy which was closely connected with it. They thus had official position and status. From time to time they faced persecution, largely instigated by those who accused them of plotting for the overthrow of the dynasty or by jealous rivals for their position in the astronomical bureau. Yet the change of dynasty from the Ming brought by the Manchu conquest in the middle of the seventeenth century did not displace them. Under the greatest of the Manchu rulers, best known under the designation K'ang Hsi, who reigned from 1661 to 1722, and who was therefore a contemporary of Louis XIV of France and Peter the Great of Russia, they long enjoyed imperial favor. In 1692 what was in effect an edict of toleration was issued.

"Reinforcements came. Some of these were to the Jesuits, among them a contingent from France, men who by their scholarly attainments won the friendship of K'ang Hsi, for that Emperor had an eager and inquiring mind. Other orders and societies also established themselves in China. They included Dominicans, Franciscans, and Augustinians from Spain by way of the Philippines, Italian Franciscans sent by the Propaganda, and members of the Paris Society of Foreign Missions. By the beginning of the eighteenth century Christianity was making marked progress." [6]

But shortly thereafter "misfortunes began to beset the course of Christianity. They arose from a number of causes. The Portuguese insistence upon extending the *padroado* over all China proved a handicap. The waning of Spain and Portugal reduced the support of missions from those lands. More serious was a prolonged and bitter division among the missionaries known as the rites controversy. It centered about the methods which had been adopted by Ricci. Even some of the Jesuits were not at first convinced that these were not compromising the faith. Members of other missionary bodies, especially Dominicans and the Society of Foreign Missions of Paris, perhaps not uncontaminated by jealousy of the Jesuits, were emphatic that to follow the course pursued by Ricci would denature Christianity. They appealed to Rome. The struggle lasted for almost a century, from the first appeal to Rome, in 1643, to the final Papal bull, in 1742." [7]

In 1773 the Pope dissolved the Society of Jesus. They were expelled first from Portuguese domains, both in Europe and overseas, and then France, Spain and Naples took similar action. It was not until 1814 that "the Pope authorized their full legal existence throughout the world. However, the lapse, lasting as it did for a generation or more and in a period when the Roman Catholic Church was suffering from an accumulation of other reverses, brought severe losses, from some of which there was no recovery. The extensive missions which the Jesuits had initiated in Asia, the Americas, and Africa were entrusted to other orders, in China to the Lazarists, in parts of India to the Society of Foreign Missions of Paris, and in much of the Americas to the Franciscans. Yet in the transition there was inevitable loss of headway. . . .

"In the year 1815 the outlook for Christianity in the Chinese Empire seemed very bleak. That realm, the most populous of any on the globe, was all but hermetically sealed against the foreigner. The Portuguese retained a slight toe-hold at Macao, near Canton. The Russians were permitted a tenuous semi-political, semi-ecclesiastical mission in Peking. Western merchants were allowed a strictly limited commerce through one port, Canton, and in that port were confined to a narrow strip of land, the 'Thirteen Factories,' along the river. Diplomatic and even consular relations on terms of equality were not permitted, nor was travel within the empire possible for foreigners. A few Roman Catholic communities continued, the fruits of heroic missions of earlier, less adverse days. Roman Catholics may have totaled 200,000, and were widely scattered. They were served surreptitiously by a few Chinese and still fewer foreign priests. In Canton the sole Protestant missionary, Robert Morrison, maintained a precarious residence as a translator for the East India Company, devoting himself chiefly to the preparation of Christian literature. The one colleague sent him before 1815 was compelled to leave China and sought contacts with the Chinese through their overseas emigrants in the British-owned Malacca." [8]

II

Robert Morrison, the "sole" Protestant missionary to whom Latourette refers, was an Englishman, the son of a Scotch laborer, born in the little Northumberland town of Morpeth in 1782. When he was three years old the family moved to Newcastle-on-Tyne, where his father established himself as a last and boot-tree manufacturer. As a youngster, Robert was far from being a brilliant student but he rapidly showed improvement and by the time he was sixteen, when he "yielded himself to Christ," after a brief period of sowing wild oats, he studied strenuously to improve his mind, although working twelve to fourteen hours a day in his father's trade. In 1801 he began to prepare for the ministry and soon thereafter entered Hoxton Academy, London, a Congregational theological college afterward called Highbury College. Apparently his earlier lassitude in regard to learning had been completely overcome, for while at Hoxton Academy he "mastered the elements" of Latin, Greek and Hebrew and when the London Missionary Society sent him to Gosport for further training, he studied medicine, Chinese and astronomy in preparation for his hoped-for work in China.

In 1807 he sailed for Canton via New York, since the hostility toward missionaries, which was later to prove such a handicap to the Judsons' progress toward Burma, had made the western route seem preferable. But there was plenty of hostility in Canton. Morrison found that he not only could not preach openly, but that a Chinese who was caught helping him improve his knowledge of the language would be subject to the death penalty. Happily, he found a man who was willing to take the risk—a certain Abel Yon, a Chinese Roman Catholic from Peking. It is one of the few recorded instances that I have found where a Protestant missionary accepted and acknowledged help from a Catholic.

After spending a few years in Canton where his achievement

was marked chiefly by his progress in the language, Morrison moved to Macao for the improvement of his health and there married Miss Mary Morton, the daughter of a resident Irish physician, and accepted the position of official translator for the East India Company, with apparent forgetfulness on both sides of any previous strain. However, he continued to make missionary work his main interest and this took the dual form of extensive translating and extensive travel. A Chinese grammar was followed by a six-volume Chinese dictionary and the translation of the New Testament and eventually by the translation of the entire Bible, a work in which he was helped by an associate, the Rev. William Milne, who joined him in 1813. The field of his endeavors, other than literary, included Java, Penang and Malacca.

More than forty years elapsed before there was another noteworthy Protestant contribution to Chinese missions. Then, in 1846, the American Board Mission was established in Foochow and the following year the first two Methodist missionaries arrived there. One of these was a certain Judson D. Collins, a graduate of the University of Michigan, whose experience had hitherto been limited to that of a Local Preacher, but who was determined to give his life to missionary work in China. "When Bishop Janes, to whom he had written, replied that the Church had no mission in China and had not authorized the establishment of one, Judson D. Collins answered, 'Bishop, engage me a place before the mast, and my own strong arm will pull me to China, and support me while there.' Authorization quickly followed." [9]

The other young man chosen for the difficult post was Moses C. White, a native of Oneida County, New York, who had been graduated from Wesleyan University with high honors after distinguishing himself in his senior year as an exhorter, a class leader and a local preacher. Subsequently he had attended the Yale Theological Seminary, had been assigned to the St. John's Street Church in New Haven as Junior Preacher, and had then been transferred to the pastorate of the church at Milford, Connecticut, while continuing to carry on a full course of study at Yale. He was therefore much more thoroughly prepared for his work than Collins and he had a second advantage in the eyes of the Board: he was married. Quite as decisively as the Catholic Church believed celibacy was an advantage to its missionaries, the Protestants believed the same of matrimony.

"The possible location of the mission had been limited to the five free ports [Canton, Shanghai, Amoy, Foochow and Ningpo] and Hong Kong. Foochow had been chosen, largely on the recommendation of George Smith (later Bishop of Victoria) of the Church Missionary Society of England. . . . The missionaries sailed on April 15, aboard the *Heber,* from Boston. White was accompanied by Jane Isabel Atwater, whom he married on the eve of his departure. Four months and twenty days later—September 4—they arrived at the mouth of the Min River. It had been a long wearisome journey of 12,000 miles, southeastward across the Equator into the South Atlantic Ocean, around Cape Horn, northwestward again across the Equator to Canton, and finally along the China coast in a lorcha to the Min. Thence they proceeded up the river to Foochow, landing with their effects on September 7. They took up residence in a house which had just been engaged by the missionaries of the American Board. Within a week they had hired a Chinese teacher and had begun to study the language." [10]

By this time, the doctrine of "Europeanism" had been entirely discarded. Collins and White had been told in no uncertain terms, "it is expected that each member of the mission will strive to master the language at the earliest period, and will neither omit opportunity nor efforts for securing that important end. Preaching the Gospel of Christ, to few or many, as God may give you occasion, you will consider your one great task. As subordinate to this other things may require your attention, for example, healing the sick and the establishment of schools.[11] This brief paragraph, with the addition of a single item—distribution of literature—constituted the outline of the missionaries' program for the first decade. Language study alone consumed a good part of their time." [12]

Neither Collins nor White had qualified as a medical missionary, although White had taken a few incidental courses in medicine and "rumor soon spread through the streets and byways of Foochow that a foreign doctor had arrived and he found himself importuned to save the lives of men, women, and children whom native doctors had given up to die. Within a few weeks scarcely a day passed without one or more applying to him for medical aid. . . . In February, 1848, White opened a dispensary adjoining his house, where he received patients and gave out drugs. As specific authority had not been given for medical practice on so extensive a scale he sought Board approval for the new departure. On September 27, 1848, the Board decided

" 'That we approve of Bro. White's course in opening a dispensary for medical purposes in connection with the missions and that we would approve of his renting an additional room for similar purposes, if . . . it becomes desirable, nevertheless we recommend that all expenditures be made with great caution & economy.'

"At the same time an appropriation of $300. was made 'for the purchase of medicines for the present year,' and a committee authorized 'to purchase and forward medicines by the next vessel to the amt. of $200.00.' The Board recommended that in no case should a fee be charged 'for medical treatment,' but added that it could see no objection to the acceptance of such presents as might be offered, those of monetary value to be credited to the Missionary Society." [13] (It is interesting to note that after White's return to the United States, he settled as a physician in New Haven and became a teacher in the Yale Medical School! The amount of instruction and experience requisite for the practice of medicine have certainly changed a good deal in the last hundred years.)

The response to the news of the Collins-White arrival in Foochow and its first results were so immediate and enthusiastic that reinforcements were indicated. Robert S. Maclay, of the Baltimore Conference, and Henry Hickok and his wife, of the Genesee Conference, were promptly sent out to join the two young Methodist volunteers and Hickok was appointed Superintendent of the China Mission "and entrusted with broad powers of administration." [14] The pattern established in conformity with the direction of the Board was faithfully followed. The ultimate aim of the Mission—conversion of the Chinese to Christianity—was never forgotten or overlooked; but there was due recognition of the fourfold obligation to learn the language, heal the sick, establish schools and distribute literature before the great goal could be reached. The lasting success and the enormous expansion of the Foochow mission, in which women as well as men played a notable part, seems proof positive of the wisdom of the course it pursued.

"In 1914 the total [of Protestant missions] was said to be 5,462. The missionaries were from scores of societies and many denominations. In 1895 about two-thirds were from the British Isles, approximately one-third were from the United States, and between two and three percent were from the Continent of Europe. In 1914 about half were from the United States, about two-fifths from the British Isles, and nearly one-tenth from the Continent of Europe. The organization having the largest number of missionaries was the China Inland Mission. It was begun in 1865 by J. Hudson Taylor. [See "The Story of Medical Missions."] Conservative theologically after the Evangelical pattern, it accepted 'willing, skilful workers' regardless of their denominational affiliation. As its name indicates, it sought to reach the regions untouched by other Protestant missions. It promised no fixed salaries but distributed among its members what came in. It was adamantly opposed to going into debt and it never directly solicited gifts. It depended on prayer for recruits and funds, and such Biblical words as *Ebenezer* and *Jehovah Jireh*, carrying the assurance, 'hitherto hath the Lord helped us' and 'the Lord will provide,' were prominent. In 1914 it had over 1,000 missionaries on its rolls." [15]

III

"The body of Roman Catholic missionaries was progressively augmented. The staffs of orders and societies already present were greatly enlarged and new orders and congregations entered. They were almost entirely from the Continent of Europe. The French led, especially through the Society of Foreign Missions of Paris, but Germans, Italians, Spaniards, and some others were also represented. In 1914 the total foreign staff was not far from 2,500. Roman Catholic missionaries placed their chief emphasis upon winning converts and building the Church. In this they persisted in spite of chronic persecutions and a tragic loss of life through the Boxer madness. In 1912 the total number of Roman Catholics was reported to be 1,431,258, approximately a seven-fold increase in a hundred years. That the Church was taking root was seen in the growing numbers of Chinese who were entering the priesthood or becoming lay brothers or sisters, and the many organizations of Chinese Christians which were springing up. In addition to building the Church, the Roman Catholics had schools, although not as many in the middle and higher grades as Protestants, they engaged in famine relief, maintained many orphanages and homes for the aged, and in Inner Mongolia had Christian colonies on lands owned by the mission." [16]

"Since the year 1914, two global wars, the ruthless aggressions of Soviet Russia and Red China, and the relentless tension of the 'cold war' have mocked the deep yearning of mankind for universal peace. The counsel given by Pope Pius XI to the distressed, confused nations is still largely unheeded.

" 'Neither peace treaties, nor the most solemn pacts, nor international meetings or conferences, nor even the noblest and most disinterested efforts of any statesman will be enough, unless in the first place are recognized the rights of natural and Divine law,' warned the Vicar of Christ. . . .

"Catholics have suffered bitter persecution in Russia, Mexico, Nazi Germany, 'Loyalist' Spain, and the countries of the Communist bloc. The Communist advance has engulfed China, North Korea, and northern Vietnam, and threatens other mission fields hitherto bright with promise. In the words of the United States Hierarchy: 'Christianity faces its most serious crisis since the Church came out of the Catacombs.' This serious crisis can be met only by totally dedicated missioners, and it calls for a selflessly resolute adherence to a fundamental objective of the Catholic apostolate." [17]

Fortunately, there has been no lack of such missionaries. In 1911, the Catholic Foreign Missionary Society of America was founded by Father James Anthony Walsh and Father Thomas

Frederick Price, with the former as the first Superior-General. The Society quickly became known by the name of its headquarters—Maryknoll—which stands high above the Hudson about thirty miles from New York City.

"Maryknoll's first little mission band, four priests, went overseas to South China in the autumn of 1918. The superior of the band was Father Price, who became known among the Chinese as 'The Holy Priest.' Maryknoll's cofounder was the first member of the society to lay down his life in the mission field. He died in Hong Kong, on September 12, 1919, the feast of the Holy Name of Mary." [18]

So many others have supplemented the work done by the Maryknollers that it would be impossible to include sketches of them all, however brief. But seven, at least, must be given as typical of the widespread dedication and faithfulness "even unto death."

"Father Godfrey Holbein, from Baltimore, and Father Clement Seybold, from Dunkirk, New York, arrived in the Passionist mission field in Hunan Province, China, in the autumn of 1924. The American Passionists had been in China only three years. Their mission territory was a difficult one, poor and bandit-ridden. The newly ordained Father Godfrey and Father Clement set about mastering the local dialect with the enthusiasm of dedicated youth. The two young Americans became to their Chinese people spiritual fathers, teachers, doctors, and friends, tending the sick and the dying when a famine struck their barren countryside.

"They were constantly on the watch for bandits. In 1926, as Chiang Kai-shek began his victorious drive northward from Canton, communistic troops moved up into Hunan. Those Chinese Reds had been indoctrinated with a hatred of everything foreign, and their presence placed the Passionists in continual danger. . . .

"In the spring of 1929, Father Godfrey and Father Clement made their annual retreat at the central mission house. When the retreat was over, they started back to their Christians, accompanied by Father Walter Coveyou, from Petoskey, Michigan. Father Walter, who had been a star promoter for the

missions in the United States, had just arrived in Hunan
Province.

"The three young Passionists stopped overnight at the mission of a confrere, Father Anthony. Two days later, as they
were riding through mountainous country, lurking bandits
seized the three priests and marched them about five miles to
a lonely spot. After the outlaws had stripped the Fathers, they
shot them and threw their bodies into a deep pit. . . . Father
Godfrey, Father Clement, and Father Walter were the first
American priests to shed their blood as missioners in China.

"If someone were to ask you who the most apostolic Catholic
layman of the first half of the twentieth century was, you could
not be far wrong if you should answer: 'Mr. Joseph Lo . . .
of Shanghai. He was known as the St. Vincent de Paul of China.'
Mr. Lo belonged to a family that had been Catholic for three
centuries. He was essentially a man of prayer, and he had an
intense devotion to the Holy Sacrifice of the Mass. Every morning of his busy life, he served Mass and received Holy Communion. His great charitable enterprises had their beginning
in the work of Catholic Action which he directed in Shanghai.
The members of his Catholic Action Society intensified their
own spiritual lives, taught catechism in the outlying districts
of the city, visited prisons, aided the poor and the sick, and
raised funds to build churches and chapels. . . . With the aid
of his patron, St. Joseph, he founded St. Joseph's Hospice—
which developed to include a dispensary, a hospital, a refuge,
an orphanage, a school, and a workshop. He brought in, to staff
the hospice, the Sisters of Charity; and later, for the boys'
school, the Salesian Fathers.

"Funds were never lacking for the hospice. Mr. Lo, who
liked to call himself 'The Coolie of St. Joseph,' had made his
heavenly patron the treasurer of his institution. So evident was
the selflessness of the Christian founder's charity, that the hospice was supported by non-Christian Chinese as well as by
Catholics. In the closing years of Mr. Lo's life, St. Joseph's
Hospice had a population of about two thousand outcasts.

"St. Joseph's Hospice was not the only institution to which

Mr. Lo gave his time and his resources. He assumed responsibility for the Sacred Heart Hospital in Shanghai; aided the Home for the Aged, conducted by the Little Sisters of the Poor; and founded in the suburbs a hospital for the insane, the first institute of its kind in the whole of China. . . . Between August, 1937, and the date of his own death [in December of that year] Joseph Lo personally baptized two thousand wounded Chinese soldiers.

"Father Vincent Lebbe, a young Vincentian missioner from Belgium, began his work in China in 1901. . . . Father Lebbe was not satisfied with preaching to the Christians; he also reached out with burning charity to the pagan multitudes. He converted entire villages. In the large city of Tientsin, he inaugurated conference halls, where the Faith was preached to thousands of non-Christians. Mass conversions followed. Father Lebbe founded Catholic Action and a Catholic press in his beloved China. . . .

"In the year 1920, the great Belgian missioner left the land and the people he had served so ardently, and he did not know when or how he would return to them. During the following years, Father Lebbe worked among Chinese students in France and in Belgium, winning some three hundred future leaders for the Church in China. On October 28, 1926, Father Lebbe had the immense happiness of witnessing, at St. Peter's in Rome, the consecration of six Chinese bishops by the Holy Father himself.

"Soon afterward, one of the newly consecrated Chinese prelates asked that Father Lebbe return with him to China. The Belgian apostle thus became the first European missioner to work under a Chinese bishop. Before leaving Europe, Father Lebbe founded in Belgium a society of priests whose special vocation is to place themselves under the orders of indigenous bishops in mission lands.

"On his return to China, Father Lebbe became a naturalized citizen of the country, in order to be wholly one with his adopted people. In 1928, he opened a monastery for Chinese monks; and in the following year, he founded a similar community of Chinese nuns. Father Lebbe's religious were to be 'Trappists in their monastery, and missioners outside of it.'

"When Japan attacked China, Father Lebbe's monks served as volunteer stretcher-bearers. Father Lebbe himself organized hospital work and carried on an apostolate among the soldiers. Several of the Chinese monks were put to death by Communists. In 1940, the founder himself was taken prisoner by the Chinese Reds, and he fell mortally ill of the hardships then endured. Generalissimo Chiang Kai-shek sent his private airplane to fly Father Lebbe to Chungking. There the missionary abbot's life ended, on June 24, 1940.

"When Father Lei Ming Yuan [his Chinese name] died, Chiang Kai-shek decreed a day of national mourning; and he said of the apostle, 'His memory is immortal.' Never, since the time of the seventeenth-century Matteo Ricci and his Jesuit successors, had the highest civil authorities of China manifested such esteem for a Catholic priest.

"In December, 1936, when the Chinese Communists made Yenan in northern Shensi Province their headquarters, Spanish Franciscan missioners had developed in that ancient city a flourishing Christian community of some ten thousand Catholics. The eighteen-year-old Louis Liang was one of their most promising seminarians. At the end of a few months, Mao Tsetung drove the Franciscans out of Yenan. Louis Liang escaped to neighboring Shansi Province, where he was ordained to the priesthood in 1940.

"After his ordination, the young Chinese priest made brilliant studies at the University of Peking; and his Franciscan bishop counted on him for important educational work. But Father Liang thought more and more frequently of the shepherdless Catholics at the Communist headquarters. In 1945, he obtained permission to return to Yenan and almost certain death.

"The Communists agreed to allow I ther Liang to stay in Yenan, where he found that terror and persecutions had thinned out the Catholic community to a small group of heroic faithful. From the first, the Reds surrounded the Chinese priest with spies; and in 1947, they haled him four times before a people's court. During these so-called trials, Father Liang was suspended from a beam and cruelly beaten. The Communists would no doubt have proceeded to his execution; but just then they were obliged to flee before the Nationalist troops approaching in force from the south. In the course of their flight, the Reds abandoned their priestly prisoner in a village hut. Because of the tortures Father Liang had suffered, he was a very sick man. A Nationalist soldier found the priest and cared for him. But the Nationalists' victory was not permanent; and when the Communists returned to the village, a spy told them that the sick priest had been helped by a Nationalist soldier.

" 'So you were a running dog of the Nationalists all the while!' the Reds triumphantly stated to Father Liang. They killed the helpless priest on April 15, 1947. They had seen that no amount of 'brain-washing' would ever obliterate this twenty-nine-year-old apostle's belief in God and in eternal life.

"When the Communists took Shanghai, in May, 1949, the Sorbonne-educated Chinese Jesuit, Father Beda Chang, was rector of St. Ignatius College at Zikawei and professor of Chinese literature at Aurora University. The Reds forced their distinguished opponent out of St. Ignatius College; and in August, 1951, they placed him under arrest. Father Chang was then a man forty-six years of age, in flourishing health. In the course of the succeeding months, the Communists announced that Father Chang had 'joined' the schismatic Church sponsored by the Reds; but no one gave the slightest attention to this crude lie. On November 11, Father Chang's brother was summoned to the place of the priest's imprisonment. There he found the Chinese Jesuit's blackened, wasted, and naked corpse lying on the prison floor. The Catholic priest had died suddenly of a 'brain tumor,' the jailors said.

"The Reds forbade a solemn funeral procession for their victim; but to their amazed anger, thousands of Christians thronged to all of the city's Catholic churches the following morning as Requiem Masses were sung throughout Shanghai. Two hundred priests in Shanghai that day privately celebrated the Martyr's Mass in red vestments for the soul of their heroic confrere." [19]

15

The Story of Medical Missions

There is widespread impression that medical missions represent a comparatively recent development in the work of Christian envoys. Nothing could be further from the truth. Indeed, David Livingstone—himself among the greatest modern exponents of healing—is quoted as saying, "God had only one Son, and He was a medical missionary." And Herbert Welch, a bishop of the Methodist Episcopal Church, who reminds us of this statement, gives emphasis to it by adding, in *Men of the Outposts*, "The school and the hospital, instead of being annexes to the church, have often been the vestibule through which the needy multitudes have entered the church. Jesus sometimes healed or fed before He preached. Meeting men on the plane of their immediate and pressing necessities, He was able to carry them with Him to the plane of spiritual lack and supply. His ministry of love to their bodily needs persuaded them of His sincere interest in their welfare and opened their hearts to His message of a Father's love."

Remembering this, thousands of His disciples have followed the same pattern, in as far as they have been able. St. Luke was a physician, as well as an evangelist. From the earliest Christian times, every monastery has had its Brother Infirmarian, every convent its Sister Infirmarian. With the beginning of the missionary movement, priests with a certain amount of medical knowledge supplemented the work of the doctors who, likewise, nearly always went along. In the New World, Spanish law provided for a physician, as well as a teacher and a priest, at every Indian "Reduction" of four hundred and fifty families, besides those whose work kept them in urban centers. In an emergency, teacher, doctor and priest were one and the same person. But normally there was really a trinity of missionaries with correlated duties. (And, possibly, this is a fitting occasion to dwell for a moment on the term "Reduction," for not an uncommon, though seriously unenlightened, criticism of Spanish colonial government is that they "reduced" the Indians, a charge made by persons who believed this means the aborigines were slaughtered, when it actually means that they were shepherded!)

As we have seen, Francisco Solano, the "Wonder Worker of the New World," had been Director of Hospitals in Montoro during an epidemic of the plague which occurred before he left Andalucía, and had shown almost superhuman efficiency as well as superhuman dedication in his terrible task; and the Ursuline nuns—the first educators of women on the North American continent—correlated nursing with their teaching, both in Quebec and in New Orleans.

Provisions for medical missions in the Orient were, from the beginning, similar to those in the Americas and, with the inauguration of Protestant missions in the nineteenth century, another equally worthy and efficient pattern began to take shape. Bishop Welch gives us many reminders of this. Take Korea as a striking example. "The first Protestant missionary to Korea, Dr. Horace N. Allen, found his way to favor through medical practice. And when the war between Japan and China was being fought partly on Korean soil, and an epidemic of typhus fever broke out in the camps, it was the brave and sacrificial service of Christian doctors and nurses which convinced observers that their religion was more than a foreign theory, it was a vital fact. Ten years of preaching and teaching had not won their confidence; they were still suspicious of the motives and intentions of these intruders from the West. But actions spoke louder than words; now they 'believed for the very works' sake.' " [1]

I

So it has been elsewhere. Peter Parker was said to have "opened China to the gospel at the point of a lancet." J. G. Kerr, of Canton; W. R. Lambuth, of Soochow, Peking, and all the world, graduate both in theology and in medicine; J. K. McKenzie, of Hankow and Tientsin; J. C. Hepburn, early comer in Japan; and others around the globe have proved through toil and triumph the wisdom of the Master's method.

Among these, James Hudson Taylor, founder of the China Inland Mission, should certainly be given a place of pre-eminence. At the time of his "call" most of the missionary work in China was in the treaty ports and emphasis had not yet been placed on their medical aspects. "After deciding to devote his life to China, he concluded that medical and surgical knowledge would be wise preparation for work there in connection with the teaching of the gospel. He therefore studied medicine at Hull and later at the London Hospital. At the same time, he visited and alleviated the sufferings of the poorest families. In anticipation of meeting with famine in China, he practiced the greatest economy. His daily bill of fare was generally a two-penny (four-cent) loaf of brown bread with water and a few apples. He walked daily eight or nine miles to the hospital.

"In 1853, Taylor was sent to China by the Chinese Evangelization Society. In Shanghai, he began to study the Chinese language and ministered daily to the suffering. He was informed that to go inland would mean certain death, but he adopted the native costume and made short trips inland. Finally, he and a Presbyterian missionary, Rev. William Burns, ventured on long inland trips at the risk of their lives.

"In 1860, Mr. Taylor's failing health caused him to return to England. There he organized the China Inland Mission, to train workers for inland missions; and in 1866, he sailed again for China, but this time with sixteen volunteer coworkers, all without any guaranteed salary. From Shanghai, they went to various inland points at the risk of their lives. Later more helpers arrived. By the close of 1885, there were two hundred twenty-five missionaries and fifty-nine churches, with a membership of one thousand six hundred fifty-five native Christians. During the next decade, training homes were established and books and tracts were prepared. The work grew rapidly, and when Mr. Taylor died in Changsha in 1905, the mission had two hundred five stations and eight hundred forty-nine missions." [2]

"There is something both convincing and uplifting in the sight of men and women devoting themselves to the laborious, often offensive, and sometimes perilous tasks of medicine and surgery on behalf of those with whom they have no personal connection," Bishop Welch observes. "Years ago I visited in Harbin the great hospital of the Plague Prevention Service maintained at that time in Manchuria by the Chinese government. At its head was Dr. Wu Lien-teh, now chief of the Quarantine Service of China. He was a graduate of Cambridge University, a student of bacteriology and kindred branches in continental Europe, and had studied under Metchnikoff, who had devoted his Nobel Prize money to continuing the work of Pasteur, while he himself went on living in his modest two-room apartment. When I asked Dr. Wu why he had gone to Manchuria to fight the plague, he answered airily, 'Oh, they needed a bacteriologist just when I was free, and so I came.' Now, I knew the deadly nature of the plague against which he was set—not the bubonic, but the pneumonic plague, with its hundred percent mortality. One whiff of the tainted air—and in three or four days death was certain. I knew that one of his Chinese colleagues, whose spectacles had for an instant displaced his mask while he was in an infected house, had died shortly before. And so I pressed my question. 'Well,' he then answered more soberly, 'I thought if I could possess the same spirit as my old teacher, it would be well. I would rather discover the germ of pneumonic plague, than to be a millionaire!' And I could not forbear saying to him, 'I think you must be one of the friends of Jesus.' This brilliant scholar, perhaps the highest authority on plague, devoting himself to the saving of lives and homes, seemed to recall the saying of our Lord, 'Greater love hath no man than this, that he lay down his life for his friends.' If there is any greater, it must be that of the man who lays down his life for strangers." *

II

What is true of China is similarly true of Africa. We have come to think of David Livingstone as a famous explorer rather than as a famous missionary, but, as a matter of fact, he was outstanding in the latter capacity; and Bishop Welch is especially helpful and enlightening in tracing the career of this great man.

"Livingstone was born near Glasgow, March 19, 1813, in humble circumstances. The boy showed no extraordinary promise, and at ten, as was common in those days, he was compelled to leave school to work in the near-by cotton-mill, that he might add to the family's slim exchequer. Long hours were the rule —6 A.M. to 8 P.M., with brief intervals for meals—but the lad, when deprived of a teacher, developed such determination to learn that he bought a Latin grammar out of his first week's wages, devoured books as he tended the loom, and then, after his weary workday, went to night-school for a couple of hours before returning home, to go on with his reading until his mother blew out the candle! His special interest was in the fields of travel and science, and his book learning was reinforced by observation of the rocks, plants, and animals which he could spy on Saturday afternoon rambles.

"His studies were so successfully mastered that at twenty-three he was prepared for college and, while he continued summer work in the mill, he began to attend the winter sessions of the University of Glasgow. Medicine and divinity were the lines he pursued. At the age of twenty-five he stopped his studies, went to London, and offered himself to the London Missionary Society, which, while supported also by other churches, was the chief organ for foreign work of the Congregational churches, such as the Livingstones attended. Those in charge hesitated for some time about accepting this new recruit. The stocky, quiet, steady man did not greatly impress them as a likely missionary. He was tested as a preacher, but entirely forgot his sermon, and after the announcement of his text to the little country congregation, had to flee from the pulpit and from the church! He was given another trial, however, and was at last listed among the approved candidates.

"Livingstone had heard that a medical missionary could sometimes find entry where a clergyman was barred; and this argument, coupled with his natural taste for scientific pursuits, led him to complete his medical course in Glasgow. Then he was ready for assignment to a field. His reading had given him some knowledge of China and his thoughts had turned to that country, still young in Protestant occupation, as his first choice. The London Missionary Society had had Robert Morrison there as the leader of a long succession of gallant missionaries. But it had also had its heroes in India and Robert Moffat in Africa. The latter came back to England at this time on furlough and a lengthy interview with him, made thrilling by the tale of his work and then of the vast regions yet unvisited, induced young David to say, 'I will go to Africa.' The Society too agreed that he might fit best in that field, and the appointment was made.

"Livingstone soon became fascinated with the great continent to which he had been allocated. At that time only the fringes of most non-Christian lands had been occupied; the map of Africa, in particular, was practically still a blank except for the coasts. Here was a challenge for the bravest, the wisest, and the most adventurous.

"He landed at what is now Port Elizabeth just three hundred years after Francis Xavier had first gone to India. His first ten years have been called his period of apprenticeship; during which he went as far as Lake Ngami, which he was the first white man to see; spent two years in wandering alone among the native tribes, learning their language and their ways; and gained some reputation as a doctor. In 1844 he married Mary, the daughter of his counselor, Robert Moffat, and with her established three homes in quick succession. No sooner had they built and equipped one home, largely by the labor of their own hands, than circumstances forced a move; until it grew clear to the young husband that they were to have no settled abode. But to this he reconciled himself, for he had already become persuaded that the white man's part was to pioneer, to open up new territory which must be left to the natives to develop.

" 'Without haste, but without rest,' like Goethe, he pressed on in response to 'the call of the wild,' sometimes with his wife and the small children who had come to the home; across trackless deserts, almost perishing from weariness and thirst, and tormented by the inefficiency, the ingratitude, or the enmity of native chiefs and people. He heard stories of a fertile and well-populated land still beyond, and did succeed in making contact with the friendly Makololo people of the Zambezi region.

"This period was brought to an end by the necessity for the return of the family to England for the education of the children and because of the mother's impaired health. At Cape Town, Livingstone bade them farewell, promising to rejoin them in two years, and little thinking that it would be five years before he looked on their faces again. The outcome of his efforts up to this time was encouraging. He had won the confidence and affection of some native friends to such an extent that, while the people, though they trusted him and were willing to live and work under his direction, still failed generally to accept the religion which animated him; yet some did believe, and among them the head of the tribe with which he associated most closely. 'How is it,' this chief asked Livingstone, 'that you have not come sooner to tell us these things? Our fathers have passed into the darkness without knowing whither they were going.' As Livingstone was preaching the gospel, he was practicing medicine too, and, in addition, did not forget to make and record frequent observations on climate, topography, and the animal and plant life of these new areas. His task in Africa was well begun.

"The second period of work included the first 'great journey.' This took him still farther north, then off to the west for the fearful trip to the Portuguese settlement of Loanda on the Atlantic Coast; then east twenty-five hundred miles of indescribable hardship clear across the continent to the mouth of

the Zambezi on the shore of the Indian Ocean. On this tour
he averaged two hundred miles per month, an almost incredible distance when the country and the conditions of travel are
taken into account. It was now that he looked for the first time
upon the awe-inspiring spectacle of the great Victoria Falls,
by which the Zambezi enters its fearsome canyon. His search
for the truth concerning the river system of the great continent
was not yet successful; nor was his effort to find a suitable
location for a missionary station in this bewildering country.
But at least he had opened up much new territory, gained
invaluable knowledge, and was preparing the way for travelers
and missionaries who might come after him.

"The worth of his achievements was at once recognized
when he returned to England in 1856. To his own amazement,
this modest man found himself hailed as hero overnight. He
was lionized by press and by people. He was summoned to
interviews with royalty. He received the gold medal of the
Royal Geographical Society and was made one of its honorary
Fellows. The freedom of the cities of Glasgow, Edinburgh, and
London was presented to him. Degrees from Oxford and Cambridge came to him unsought. France and other foreign countries, through their learned societies, added their plaudits. The
man who had been sent out sixteen years before with doubts
and misgivings was now acclaimed one of the greatest of explorers and messengers of the gospel. His book, entitled *Missionary Travels*, written at this time, leaped into immediate
popularity. And when, at the end of fifteen months, and after
a farewell banquet attended by a host of notables, Livingstone
set sail for Africa again, it was with the consciousness that the
interest, the good wishes, and the prayers of great numbers
were behind him.

"He did not, however, return as a missionary of the London
Society. Some of the supporters of the Society had questioned
whether they should sponsor a work which reached so far beyond the usual missionary activities; and sensitive to these
implied criticisms and likewise desirous of a larger liberty of
action, Livingstone resigned. But the Government now gave
him the title of British Consul for East Africa and the Interior,

and leader of an official expedition to explore more thoroughly the Zambezi region. Fortunately, also, his book had achieved such financial success that he was henceforth independent. Yet, though technically no longer a 'missionary,' he never ceased to regard his evangelistic purpose as superior. He refused to yield to suggestions that he should now devote his whole attention to scientific discovery. Above even that, which appealed so strongly to his orderly and inquiring mind, was the determination to do his part in making Africa Christian. 'The end of the geographical feat is the beginning of the missionary enterprise,' he insisted. Proud as he was of his blue Consul's cap with its band of gold braid, which gave him a certain standing and brought him needed help, he continued to look upon himself as an ambassador of Christ.

"In that spirit he went on his second 'great journey,' from 1858 to 1864, which was the least satisfactory in its outcome of all. His wife, who had returned to Africa with him, leaving the older children in England, died in 1862, and left him desolate indeed. But with the other members of the expedition, he went on, fighting the slave trade, helping the missionaries, and digging into the still unsolved problem of the mysterious lakes and rivers which refused to give up the secret of their connection to this tireless investigator.

"In 1864-5 he enjoyed another furlough in England, repeating in milder form his earlier triumphs; and then with new endorsements from the Government and the Royal Geographical Society, he sailed once more for Africa and his final seven years of service and sufferings. He had two well-defined purposes in mind—the suppression of the slave trade and the discovery of the sources of the Nile. He searched about Lakes Nyasa and Tanganyika, but it was left for others to come to the great Nyanza Lakes and the final solution of the problem which had allured and mocked him. Livingstone journeyed around Lake Mweru, which Dan Crasford later made famous, and Lake Bangweolo (a lake larger than all Wales), near which he finally died. His plans were thwarted by natives or slave-hunters. He had long illnesses. So completely out of touch was he with the homeland that for more than two years no tidings of him reached England. He was reported dead, and even when that rumor was disproved, his whereabouts and welfare were unknown, until in the fall of 1871 he was found at Ujiji by Henry M. Stanley, the Americanized Welshman who had been dispatched by the *New York Herald* to discover and help him." [4]

Rather inexplicably, at least to this editor, Bishop Welch gives us no detailed account of this famous meeting; however, Alan Moorehead, in *The White Nile*, more than makes up for this lack.

" 'When my spirits were at their lowest ebb," Moorehead quotes Livingstone as saying, " 'the Good Samaritan was close at hand, for one morning Susi [Livingstone's faithful native servant] came running at the top of his speed and gasped out, "An Englishman! I see him!" and off he darted to meet him. The American flag at the head of the caravan told of the na- tionality of the stranger. Bales of goods, baths of tin, huge kettles, cooking pots, tents, etc., made me think, "This must be a luxurious traveler, not one at his wits' end like me." ' " Stanley's famous description is more lively:

" 'Selim said to me, "I see the Doctor, sir. Oh, what an old man! He has got a white beard!" And I—what would I not have given for a bit of friendly wilderness, where, unseen, I might vent my joy in some mad freak, such as idiotically biting my hand, turning a somersault, or slashing at trees, in order to allay those exciting feelings that were well-nigh un- controllable. My heart beats fast, but I must not let my face betray my emotions, lest it shall detract from the dignity of a white man appearing under such extraordinary circumstances.

" 'So I did that which I thought was most dignified. I pushed back the crowds, and, passing from the rear, walked down a living avenue of people, until I came in front of the semicircle of Arabs, before which stood "the white man with the gray beard." As I advanced slowly toward him I noticed he was pale, looked wearied, had gray whiskers and moustache, wore a bluish cap with a faded gold band around it, had on a red-sleeved waistcoat, and a pair of gray tweed trousers. I would have run to him, only I was a coward in the presence of such a mob—

would have embraced him, but that I did not know how he would receive me. So I did what moral cowardice and false pride suggested was the best thing—walked deliberately up to him, took off my hat, and said, "Dr. Livingstone, I presume?"

" ' "Yes," he said, with a kind smile, lifting his cap slightly.

" 'I replaced my hat on my head, and he replaced his cap, and we both grasped hands, and then I said aloud: "I thank God, Doctor, I have been permitted to see you."

" 'He answered, "I feel thankful that I am here to welcome you." '

"This then is the story of an incident which has been more frequently recalled than any other single event in African exploration. And yet a strange air of unreality remains. One is bound to wonder why it should have taken so long for help to arrive. . . .

"In the twentieth century, of course, radio and aircraft have entirely altered the nature of exploration, and it requires a slight effort to remember that only fifty years ago it was nothing unusual for a ship or a traveler to be lost sight of for many months; but even so it is strange that Livingstone's silence was received with so much complacency. Long before—actually in 1869—his [Stanley's] employer James Gordon Bennett of the *New York Herald* had summoned him to an interview and had said: 'I want you to attend the opening of the Suez Canal and then proceed up the Nile. Send us detailed descriptions of everything likely to interest American tourists. Then go to Jerusalem, Constantinople, the Crimea, the Caspian Sea, through Persia as far as India. After that you can start looking round for Livingstone. If he is dead bring back every possible proof of his death.'

"Stanley, the most assiduous foreign correspondent who ever lived, had accomplished this program in fourteen months. He was full of surprises. He was a man whose real name was not Stanley at all, but Rowlands, a Welshman who was an American, a soldier who was a sailor, and now a journalist who was leading a successful expedition into the center of Africa. In all the world no two men could have differed so much from one another as Livingstone and Stanley, nor could there have been two men who, for the moment, were so beholden to one another. Livingstone needed medicine, supplies and news of the outside world, and his younger visitor had them all. Stanley needed fame—the 'kudos' of having found this celebrated man, and in fact he received a great deal more. His brief companionship with Livingstone was, 'the supreme experience of his life. He had come close to moral greatness, and he was startled, captivated, subjected by it.' " [5]

"Four happy months were passed by the two men together" —to resume Bishop Welch's narrative—"and the good food, needed medicines, fresh clothing, news of the outside world, and congenial companionship did much to restore to Livingstone good spirits and good health. Stanley said that he seemed to drop ten years of his age while they were together. But the indomitable explorer refused to go back with Stanley to England, and when Stanley left him in March, 1872, looking back at the 'old man in gray clothes,' both knew it was a final parting.

"Livingstone continued his travels in the lake region, although at the last he had, because of sheer weakness, to be carried in a litter, 'all but dead from fever, semi-starvation, and dysentery.' In April of 1873 he was in a little hut built for him by his native 'boys,' who affectionately cared for him so far as their limited knowledge and ability make possible. Several of them were with him on that last night in early May when, toward midnight, he was seen to be kneeling at his bedside, his face in his hands, his head resting on the pillow. When he was discovered at dawn in the same position, they saw that the end had come and their grief knew no bounds. They buried this soldier's heart where he had fallen on the field of his battle, and then carried his emaciated body a thousand miles to deliver it into British hands. A year later it was laid in its last resting-place in the Abbey which has become a shrine of reverence for those who have served nobly their country and their kind." [6]

The funeral services, conducted with impressive ceremony, were attended by persons of every rank from the highest to the lowest, united in their veneration for one of the greatest men of his period; and *Punch* published a poem which voiced the tribute of thousands who could not, themselves, express it:

Open the Abbey doors and bear him in
    To sleep with kings and statesmen, chief and sage;
The missionary come of weaver-kin,
    But great by work that brooks no lower wage.

He needs no epitaph to guard his name
    Which men shall prize while worthy work is known;
He lived and died for good—be that his fame:
    Let marble crumble; this is Living-stone.

III

For many reasons, the story of Albert Schweitzer seems a natural sequel to the story of David Livingstone. It is not only the "essentiality of Africa" to both which binds them together. It is "kindness, gentleness and compassion," the conference of blessing, the conviction that, when it came to a question of what should or should not be done, "of course he had to go."

"Dr. Schweitzer, son of a Lutheran minister, was born January 14, 1875, in Kayserberg, Alsace, which was then part of Germany. He spent most of his early years at Guensbach, near Strasbourg, and embarked on a scholastic career that included organ lessons and theological instruction, and which took him to Munster, Mulhouse, Paris and Strasbourg. He held doctor's degrees in medicine, philosophy and theology. . . . At the age of thirty, Dr. Schweitzer decided he had lived long enough for science and art and would henceforth devote himself 'to the direct service of humanity.' He decided to become a physician and go to Africa.

"For the next six years, he studied medicine at the University of Strasbourg, served a period of internship, and gave a series of lectures and concerts to raise money. Then he packed his bags and set out for Africa with his wife, the former Helene Bresslau, whom he had married in 1912. Dr. Schweitzer undertook his voyage as an agent of the Paris Missionary Society, which at first was reluctant to send him because of his unorthodox theological ideas. Dr. Schweitzer had to promise to be *'muet comme une carpe'* (as silent as a carp). The society relented and the physician-missionary was soon preaching as well as practicing.

"His first operating room at Lambaréné was a windowless henhouse, his first clinic an open courtyard. Patients were savages, who came to him with malaria, leprosy, sleeping sickness, dysentery, elephantiasis, tropical ulcers and strangulated hernia. They watched suspiciously as he performed his first operations, but soon they were spreading his fame as the white magician who could kill (anesthetize) a man, take away his pain, and bring him back to life. As the only doctor in a large area, he had patients who came from hundreds of miles away, on foot or in canoes.

"His work was interrupted by World War I, when overzealous French officials interned him as a German. He spent the years of his internment in France, writing a book on the mysticism of St. Paul. When Alsace-Lorraine reverted to France he became a French citizen. For six years after the war, Dr. Schweitzer remained in Europe, giving lectures and concerts, studying obstetrics, dentistry and tropical hygiene, and writing the first two volumes of *Philosophy of Civilization*. By 1924 he had enough money to return to Lambaréné. He found what he expected— his hospital fallen in ruins. Dr. Schweitzer immediately set to work building a new hospital with the help of the natives, now won over to *'le grand docteur.'* This time he also had a staff of a dozen European doctors and nurses working with him.

"Except for periodic visits to Europe and one to America, Dr. Schweitzer remained at Lambaréné for the rest of his life, building, healing and conducting simple religious services. . . .

"Dr. Schweitzer was certainly the most famous physician of modern times. Perhaps his fame even eclipsed that of Hippocrates. He was also a missionary, theologian, philosopher, author and musician. His work in all these fields was memorable. For example, his books on Jesus, Goethe and Bach contain rich insights and are still respected. He was one of the world's greatest organists until he went to Lambaréné in the rain forest of West Africa to found his hospital, which, with its ramshackle tin roofs, became more famous than any gleaming medical center. . . .

"In 1952, he was awarded the Nobel Peace Prize. But he was too busy at his hospital to go to Olso to receive the $33,200 award until two years later. He used the money to improve the huts of the leper colony which he built not far from his hospital on the banks of the Ogowe River. In these two primitive institutions he treated over a million and a half sick people in his more than half-century in Africa.

"He was known at first only to scholars—musicologists, philosophers, historians. But his fame grew steadily until, on his only visit to the United States, in 1949, he was saluted as one of the great men of the century. In 1963, a Gallup Poll found that he was among the ten most admired persons in the world. . . .

"As he began his tenth decade of life, Dr. Schweitzer, a tall man with a walrus moustache, dressed in dirty cream-colored pants, white shirt with a black bow tie and a pith helmet, went about his tasks vigorously. He had given up surgery with advancing age but still supervised the hospital with a fierce, sharp eye. . . .

" 'The ethic of reverence for life is the ethic of love widened into universality,' he wrote. 'It is the ethic of Jesus now recognized as a necessity of thought. . . . Anyone who has accustomed himself to regard the life of any living creature as worthless is in danger of arriving also at the idea of worthless human lives, the idea which is playing so disastrous a part in the thought of our time.' . . .

"On his 90th birthday, Dr. Schweitzer told his fellow workers: 'I feel at home here and I belong to you until my dying breath.' . . .

"Before losing consciousness for the last time, Dr. Schweitzer put his personal affairs in order, and formally handed the hospital over to Dr. [Walter] Munz, who had actually been carrying out the duties of chief doctor and administrator since February, when Dr. Schweitzer's failing health made it advisable that he ease his workload. . . . He died September 4, 1965, at the jungle hospital where he had spent the last half century as a medical missionary. . . . He was buried . . . in a plain wooden coffin in a grave dug by a group of silent, barefoot Africans . . . in front of his jungle house. . . . A choir of leprous children sang a last farewell as the coffin was lowered. . . .

"Dr. Albert Schweitzer has been accurately described, because of his work for the sick in the African jungle, as a humanitarian. He has been, with equal accuracy, termed a humanist, because of the philosophy he distilled from his theological studies. But his impact upon his times has been above all that of a great human being. He was no 'Renaissance man' with the suggestion of dilettantism which that implies today. Rather, he accomplished as much in each of three disparate fields—scholarship, music and medicine—as would have served an ordinary man a full career. More, he wrapped his concrete achievements in an aura of respect for life—all life—and in a devotion to easing pain that made him, very literally, an inspiration to millions." [7]

IV

The story of medical missions continues on its triumphant way in many different directions; an excellent article in *Time* gives further aspects of these.

"Framed along with the medical diploma and the other parchments of professional achievement on the wall of Dr. Alan R. Crain's Washington, D.C., office hangs a reminder of a recent six-week vacation. It is no mounted marlin or spread of ten-point antlers—only another certificate. '*Nay chung-nhan,*' it begins, which is Vietnamese for 'This is to certify,' and goes on to let it be known with gold seal and red ribbon that Dr. Crain served this spring as a visiting orthopedic surgeon at the crowded, understaffed Cho-Ray Hospital in Saigon.

"WITHOUT PAY. Such a working vacation is hardly the relaxing change of scenery a doctor might order for a patient, but Dr. Crain and a small but dedicated number of U.S. physicians are choosing the prescription for themselves. Through a program coordinated by MEDICO, the CARE-affiliated international medical cooperation agency co-founded by the late Dr. Tom Dooley, the doctors volunteer to spend a month practicing their specialties in out-of-the-way places in Africa, Latin America and the Far East. They usually pay their own way and always work without pay. At local clinics and hospitals, they train native doctors in modern medical techniques and treat patients who crowd in from hundreds of miles away.

"Since 1959, when the first 'vacationer' went to Jordan for a month, at least 175 U.S. doctors have offered their services in a dozen countries. During a 40-day visit to Jordan, a surgeon examined 635 patients, performed 69 operations on almost every affliction known to orthopedics. In Hong Kong, three prominent eye surgeons performed a series of delicate corneal transplants. When Algeria gained its independence last July, fewer than 200 doctors were left to care for 11 million people, many suffering from epidemic diseases and war injuries. MEDICO rushed in emergency teams of doctors and nurses; now eight one-month doctors are on duty in Algiers. The volunteer system, says Dr. Peter D. Comanduras, co-founder and now chief of MEDICO, demonstrates that 'a great deal can be done with very little money in bringing the latest in medical science to underdeveloped countries.'

"WEARY BUT READY. On Dr. Crain's trip, except for a two-day excursion into neighboring Cambodia, he had no time for sightseeing. He was kept busy day after day at the hospital. There were two native orthopedic surgeons to train and a ward teeming with patients, many of them mangled victims of Viet Nam's guerrilla war. The cases, Dr. Crain says, were fairly routine—muscle and nerve operations, bone grafts and other reconstructive procedures. But not the conditions. Flypaper hung over the operating table, amoebic dysentery was rampant, and blood for transfusions was in short supply. The thousand-bed hospital was so crowded that sometimes two beds were pushed together to accommodate three or four patients. Americans in Saigon quipped that 'semiprivate at Cho-Ray means two in a bed.'

"Like many vacationers, the doctors return weary but enthusiastic. Several volunteers have made more than one trip. Dr. Crain says that it will take him four months to recover financially and to catch up on his case load back home, but he is all ready to pack his instruments and go again. 'They're setting up a program in Afghanistan,' he says. 'I'd like to go there.' " [8]

I hope very much that he will and that I may hear an account of his trip, as I did a vivid and inspiring account of his service in Saigon, from his own lips, over a pleasant dinner at the Salle de Bois in Washington. Though he is always a delightful host, I have never found Dr. Crain—a personal friend as well as a trusted physician—more engaging than when he described this "vacation" of his.

v

The spheres of usefulness developed by MEDICO and CARE are complemented by those of HOPE. This project is "the principal activity of the People-to-People Health Foundation, an independent, non-profit corporation formed by the American people for the purpose of carrying out a program of cooperation in the field of health between people in the United States and those people in newly developed nations of the world. The word 'HOPE' stands for Health Opportunity for People Everywhere.

"Project HOPE brings the skills and techniques developed by the American medical, dental and paramedical professions to the people of other nations in their own environments, adapted specifically to their needs and their way of life. The services of the Foundation are rendered by the people of the United States in a unique, challenging and heart-warming endeavor.

"HOPE began in the fall of 1958 when President Dwight Eisenhower asked a prominent Washington, D.C., heart specialist, Dr. William B. Walsh, to initiate a project aimed at international goodwill and understanding through personal contacts— a real people-to-people endeavor.

"The project which Dr. Walsh submitted was the plan for the world's first peacetime hospital ship, a reconverted 14,000-ton veteran of World War II and the Korean conflict. The *Consolation* was refitted and rechristened the S.S. *Hope,* a name that would soon become a symbol of friendship and mercy to distant lands where new therapies, new medical texts and equipment were not available, and where not infrequently there was only one doctor for every 250,000 persons." [9]

Hope sailed on her first voyage in 1960—to Indonesia. When she left there, the Indonesian *Times* stated, in commenting on the service she had rendered, "It will be a long time before this act of American generosity is forgotten. The East forgets many things, but never loses its reverence for a teacher."

In June of the following year, *Hope* served at Viet Nam, and Dr. Walsh himself has written so fully and graphically of her service at her first two posts in his recent book *A Ship Called Hope,* published by E. P. Dutton and Company, that any further comment by the present editor would be superfluous.

In 1962, *Hope* shifted operations to South America, anchoring off the northern Peruvian city of Trujillo. After she left there, one of her chaplains, Father John F. Magner made the following comment:

" 'Even to the most hardened Yankee-haters in Peru the sight of American doctors and nurses with the same sweat and dirt on their faces as the people of the Trujillo slums had vast impact. Believe me, we weren't popular when we arrived in Peru in May, 1962. But by the time we left ten months later, it was a very different story.' " [10]

From Peru, *Hope* moved on to Ecuador and I had my first glimpse of her when the *Santa Cecilia,* on which I sailed southbound to Callao, made a brief stopover at Guayaquil, where I went into town for dinner at the Hotel Humboldt. This is located on the Malecón which borders the river Guayas; and, as I feasted on the tiny oysters and succulent lobster which are among the most delicious specialties of the city, my eyes rested on a graceful white ship, lighted from stem to stern, which rode at anchor directly opposite my vantage point on the hotel's high terrace. This ship, my Ecuadorian host informed me, was *Hope*: and he went on to speak with gratitude and enthusiasm of the good work she was doing in his country. I had not previously known she was there and did not have time to visit her then; but I had been eager to do so ever since a letter from my friend Peter Grace had first outlined the important role which the Grace Line was playing in her venture. Before I went back to the *Santa Cecilia* that night, I had decided my itinerary on the way north, three months later, must allow for at least a week in

Guayaquil, so that I could personally acquaint myself with *Hope;* and, with this schedule in mind, I engaged passage on an Italian ship, the *Verde,* which would take me from Callao to Guayaquil, and on the fine new Grace liner, the *Santa Mariana,* which would be leaving the latter port for New York City some days later. I also communicated with our Consul General at Guayaquil, Mr. Alton W. Hemba, telling him I would greatly appreciate anything he might do to put me in touch with *Hope.*

It would be impossible to imagine more pleasant and effective cooperation than was given me by him and all the consular staff. On our arrival, my secretary, Marjorie Lillibridge, and I were met at the dock by Mr. Fred Shaffer, the Consul, and Mr. Anthony Chappel, the Cultural Attaché, not only with a car for ourselves, but with a truck for our baggage; and as we drove into the city from the fine new maritime port, where *Hope* is now anchored, we discussed a program which would enable me to make the most of my time. The Consul General and Mrs. Hemba invited Marjorie and myself to a buffet supper at their charming house, where several of the doctors and nurses, connected with *Hope,* were among our fellow guests; and Mrs. Hemba took us in her car to luncheon on the ship. These pleasant social events were combined with and followed by several conferences and tours of inspection and the sum total of my impressions has been most happily expressed in the *NMU Pilot,* the official publication of the National Maritime Union:

" 'HOPE is a very unusual project in every way. It is a living symbol of the desire of the American people to give a hand to others all over the world who do not have all the health opportunities that we have. It is a real expression of our spirit of brotherhood. . . . The prestige that the *Hope* is building for America is hard to fully appreciate without a firsthand look. The fine doctors, nurses and the efforts of the crew have brought a real hope to thousands of people and have let the Ecuadorians know what America really stands for.

" 'While I was aboard the ship, I had a chance to watch the Ecuadorians, many of them Indians who are proud descendants of civilization thousands of years old, come aboard. They came from the cities and they came from the mountains. Some had severe cases of beriberi, gangrene and other diseases that had almost completely destroyed their spirit.

" 'As they came aboard and were received by the medical personnel and the crew it was plain to see that they felt weak and beaten.

" 'When these people were given medical help, provided completely free, an amazing change came over them. Leaving the ship, their faces were bright and filled with the thanks they felt in their hearts. This sign of appreciation was a rich reward for the efforts made by the doctors and the crew.

" 'A special vote of thanks is certainly in order for the medical staff on the *Hope*. . . . They gave up valuable jobs in American hospitals to do this work and the U.S. owes them a debt of gratitude.' "

VII

Still another example of usefulness and dedication is shown in the story of a nun who flies the sick out of the desert, battling tropical storms and freak air currents as she does so. This is Sister "Mike" of Worcester, Massachusetts, who got permission from the Vatican to learn how to operate a plane and who today is believed to be Africa's only flying nun. Dennis Neeld gives a vivid account of her work in an Associated Press dispatch:

"The nun, her full name is Sister Michael Therese, flies in supplies and ferries out the sick from Lorugumu, site of a tiny Roman Catholic mission in Kenya's arid northern desert. . . . The mission consists of the living quarters of the [four] nuns, a schoolhouse-dispensary, and Sister Michael's hangar.

"Sister Michael, a Medical Missionary of Mary, took to the air with only 40 hours' flying time. She learned to fly at Bedford, Massachusetts, won her wings in 1963, and came out to Kenya a month later. Now she has logged 400 hours in an area where sudden tropical storms and freak air currents can make a pilot's life hazardous. . . . Sister Michael's red-and white-striped Piper Cub provides a splash of color against the tawny drabness of the desert. It is the first plane most of the local Turkana tribesmen ever have seen. . . . Besides being a pilot, Sister Michael is a qualified surgical technician and her skills are useful in the tiny four-bed dispensary at Lorugumu.

"The flying nun prefers these primitive conditions to those of civilization. 'There is nothing in your way when you are flying in the desert and the mountains are your guide,' she said. 'It's also so much easier to make the landing strip in this country. You don't have to worry about town planning permission and other red tape.' " [11]

VIII

I find great solace to a heavy heart in writing so happily about Dr. Crain, Ship *Hope* and Sister "Mike" because this brief account of medical missions cannot be brought to a close without some mention of what recently happened in the Congo, and that makes tragic reading. At least fifty white hostages were slaughtered by Congolese rebels while Belgian paratroopers—flown in by the United States Air Force—were endeavoring to rescue them. One of these white hostages was Dr. Paul Carlson. Both *Life* and *Time* have made him and his fellow victims the subjects of cover pictures and lead articles and I am privileged to quote from these magazines.

"Everywhere Dr. Carlson went, the Congolese called him *Monganga Paulo*—'my Dr. Paul.' He was a missionary doctor serving 100,000 people, and he did so with a genuine love of God and God's people. His patients responded to his warmth. And then he was caught up in a burst of wanton savagery that stunned the civilized world—and he paid for his work with his life. . . .

"Carlson grew up near Los Angeles, married a nurse and slaved through medical school to become a surgeon. In 1961 he visited the Congo and returned to tell his wife Lois, 'It does something to you to work out there.' He and Lois took their two children and a nurse to a hospital at a place called Wasolo —which means 'end of the world' in the native tongue—far up in the Ubangi country. Carlson put in 18-hour days treating every sort of illness, but his temper was always even and mild. He liked to joke and laugh, he talked constantly, and plainly he was happy. When rebels moved into the area, he sent his family and nurse out. He stayed just a little longer, planning to leave in time. But he didn't make it." [12]

"Periodically sentenced to death as an 'American spy,' periodically reprieved when things seemed to go well for the rebels, Dr. Paul Earle Carlson, 36, caught a slew of bullets through head and back as he tried to escape the slashing gunfire." [13]

Pages and pages have been and could still be devoted to the widespread atrocities connected with this slaughter. Instead of quoting from these horrors, I have chosen to present a portion of the last message that he sent to his church and members of his family in Los Angeles.

"Hello to all of you. Things here are relatively quiet despite all the turmoil and the big thing right now is the wedding of two of our Congolese. At least that's the way things are now. The table is all set and the kids are riding high, just waiting.

"Despite all the things we've been worrying about and you've been hearing, as far as we can tell we've been in the good will of the people in the area here.

"It is approximately two weeks now since Stanleyville fell to rebel forces. Last Sunday night [Congolese] church leaders met with us and discussed the whole thing. They asked us to stay, reminding us that, if necessity forced it, they would have boats so they could take us out by river. It's now over a week since that meeting and the army is regrouping. Some are between us and Stanleyville and we will have to see what comes next. We daily listen to the radio to see what we might expect.

"In the meantime, many other things have made life uncertain. Visas haven't come through for our missionaries so we don't know when classes will begin for Wayne and Lynn. Other changes are occurring. We hear all the United Nations doctors have been pulled out of our province. The reason—we really don't know. This leaves our four mission doctors as virtually the only medical care in the whole Ubangi province. In days like this we certainly have to leave the future in God's hands.

"Continue to uphold us in prayer. Pray that through the trials we face here we may be an effective witness for Christ and that through the trials being faced, we may see growth in the Congolese church.

"It is always very hard to know what to say to the Congolese because they do not realize what has gone on elsewhere in the world. They do not realize that in this century more people have died for Christ than died in the early centuries, which we think of as the days of martyrs." [14]

And so we seem to have gone the full cycle from the first to the twentieth century—stained with martyrs' blood!

16

Missionary Hymns

I began this book with a reference to my earliest experience in churchgoing at the New Old South in Boston and the announcement of missionary hymns that Dr. Gordon made at the end of his sermons on foreign missions. Because these early memories have had a distinct bearing on the general subject of this book and because the hymns themselves have a merit of their own, it seems to me appropriate to close the book with a more extended reference to them.

The missionary spirit began to stir among Protestants long before the actual work among pagans was under way; and this spirit revealed itself not only in sermons which have been lost to us, but in hymns that have come down to us. The earliest of these—at least, the earliest with which I am familiar—which begins

> "Jesus shall reign where'er the sun
> Does his successive journeys run . . ."

was written in 1719 by Isaac Watts, an English dissenting clergyman. He was first the assistant pastor and later the pastor of the Independent Chapel in Mark Lane, London. Because of ill health, he was forced to abandon his pastorate and lived in semiretirement with Sir Thomas Abney at Abney Park. There he wrote numerous theological and metaphysical works which were, however, of secondary importance to his hymns, of which he composed several hundred. These "embodied the stern doctrines of Calvinism but reflected also his belief that Christian truth could be expressed in the imagery of true poetry. The relatively few of his hymns which survive in present-day hymnals are among the finest examples of English metrical hymnody." [1]

Even more famous than the hymns written by Isaac Watts was the hymn beginning "All hail the power of Jesus' Name," written by Edward Perronet in 1779. In the first half of the nineteenth century, which saw the establishment of Protestant missions in Burma, Hawaii, India and China, missionary hymns began to multiply in number and by 1860, there were a large number of them. They were very widely sung, not only by the missionaries themselves but by their sponsors in the home churches; and Kipling lifted two lines from Heber's "Greenland's Icy Mountains," written in 1819, to use as the opening lines of his poem "The Heathen."

> ("The heathen in his blindness
> Bows down to wood and stone.")

ALL HAIL THE POWER OF JESUS' NAME
by Edward Perronet, 1779

All hail the power of Jesus' name!
Let angels prostrate fall;
Bring forth the royal diadem,
And crown him Lord of all.

Crown him ye martyrs of our God,
Who from his altar call;
Extol the stem of Jesus' rod,
And crown him Lord of all.

Let every kindred, every tribe,
On this terrestrial ball,
To him all majesty ascribe,
And crown him Lord of all.

O that, with yonder sacred throng,
We at his feet may fall;
We'll join the everlasting song,
And crown him Lord of all.[2]

FROM GREENLAND'S ICY MOUNTAINS
by R. Heber, 1819

From Greenland's icy mountains,
From India's coral strand,
Where Africa's sunny fountains
Roll down their golden sand;
From many an ancient river,
From many a palmy plain,
They call us to deliver
Their land from error's chain.

What though the spicy breezes
Blow soft o'er Ceylon's isle;
Though every prospect pleases,

And only man is vile;
In vain with lavish kindness
The gifts of God are strown;
The heathen in his blindness
Bows down to wood and stone.

Shall we whose souls are lighted
With wisdom from on high,
Shall we to men benighted
The lamp of life deny?
Salvation! oh, salvation!
The joyful sound proclaim,
Till earth's remotest nation
Has learned Messiah's name.

Waft, waft, ye winds, His story,
And you, ye waters roll,
Till, like a sea of glory,
It spreads from pole to pole;
Till o'er our ransomed nature
The Lamb of sinners slain,
Redeemer, King, Creator,
In bliss returns to reign.[8]

IN THE CROSS OF CHRIST I GLORY
by John Bowring, 1825

In the cross of Christ I glory,
Towering o'er the wrecks of time;
All the light of sacred story
Gathers round its head sublime.

When the woes of life o'er-take me,
Hopes deceive, and fears annoy,
Never shall the cross forsake me;
Lo! it glows with peace and joy.

When the sun of bliss is beaming,
Light and love upon my way,

From the cross the radiance streaming
Adds more lustre to the day.

Bane and blessing, pain and pleasure,
By the cross are sanctified;
Peace is there that knows no measure,
Joys that through all time abide.[4]

MY FAITH LOOKS UP TO THEE
By R. Palmer, 1830

My faith looks up to Thee,
Thou Lamb of Calvary,
Saviour divine!
Now hear me while I pray,
Take all my guilt away,
Oh, let me from this day
Be wholly Thine.

May Thy rich faith impart
Strength to my fainting heart,
My zeal inspire,
As Thou hast died for me,
Oh, may my love to Thee
Pure, warm, and changeless be,
A living fire.

While life's dark maze I tread,
And griefs around me spread,
Be Thou my guide;
Bid darkness turn to day,
Wipe sorrow's tears away,
Nor let me ever stray
From Thee aside.

When ends life's transient dream,
When death's cold sullen stream
Shall o'er me roll;
Blest Saviour, then, in love,

Fear and distrust remove;
Oh, bear me safe above,
A ransomed soul! [5]

THE MORNING LIGHT IS BREAKING
by F. S. Smith, 1832

The morning light is breaking;
The darkness disappears;
The sons of earth are waking
To penitential tears;
Each breeze that sweeps the ocean
Brings tidings from afar,
Of nations in commotion,
Prepared for Sion's war.

See heathen nations bending
Before the God we love,
And thousand hearts ascending
In gratitude above;
While sinners now confessing,
The gospel call obey,
And seek the Saviour's blessing,
A nation in a day.

Blest river of salvation!
Pursue thy onward way;
Flow thou to every nation,
Nor in thy richness stay:
Stay not till all the lowly
Triumphant reach their home;
Stay not till all the holy
Proclaim "The Lord is come!" [6]

LORD, A SAVIOUR'S LOVE DISPLAYING
by Ernest Hawkins, 1851

Lord, a Saviour's love displaying,
Show the heathen lands Thy way;

Thousands still like sheep are straying
In the dark and cloudy day.

Shades of death are gathering o'er them,
Lord, they perish from Thy sight!
Let Thine angel go before them;
Bring the Gentiles to Thy light.

Fetch them home from every nation,
From the islands of the sea;
By the word of Thy salvation
Call the wanderers back to Thee.

Thou their pasture hast provided,
Grant the blessing long foretold;
Let Thy sheep, divinely guided,
Find at last the one true fold.[7]

HARK! HARK, MY SOUL!
by F. W. Faber, 1854

Hark! hark, my soul! Angelic songs are swelling
O'er earth's green fields, and ocean's wave-beat shore;
How sweet the truth those blessed strains are telling
Of that new life when sin shall be no more.

Refrain

Angels of Jesus,
Angels of light,
Singing to welcome the pilgrims of the night!

Onward we go, for still we hear them singing,
"Come, weary souls, for Jesus bids you come,"
And through the dark, its echoes sweetly ringing,
The music of the gospel leads us home.

Refrain

Far, far away, like bells at evening pealing,
The voice of Jesus sounds o'er land and sea,

And laden souls by thousands meekly stealing,
King Shepherd, turn their weary steps to Thee.

Refrain

Rest comes at length: though life be long and dreary,
The day must dawn, and darksome night be past;
Faith's journeys end in welcome to the weary,
And heaven, the heart's true home, will come at last.

Refrain

Angels, sing on! your faithful watches keeping:
Sing us sweet fragments of the songs above;
Till morning's joy shall end the night of weeping,
And life's long shadows break in cloudless love.[8]

Refrain

ETERNAL FATHER! STRONG TO SAVE
by W. Whiting, 1860

Eternal Father! strong to save,
Whose arm doth bind the restless wave,
Who bid'st the mighty ocean deep
Its own appointed limits keep;
Oh, hear us when we cry to Thee
For those in peril on the sea!

O Saviour, whose almighty word
The winds and waves submissive heard,
Who walkedst on the foaming deep,
And gavest light, and life and peace;
Oh, hear us when we cry to Thee
For those in peril on the sea.

O Sacred Spirit, who didst brood
Upon the chaos darkened rude,
Who bad'st its angry tumult cease,
And gavest light, and life, and peace;

Oh, hear us when we cry to Thee
For those in peril on the sea.

O Trinity of love and power!
Our brethren shield in danger's hour;
From rock and tempest, fire and foe,
Protect them where-so-e'er they go,
Thus ever let there rise to Thee
Glad hymns of praise from land and sea.[9]

HASTEN THE TIME APPOINTED
Ascribed to Jane Borthwick, 1858

Hasten the time appointed,
By prophets long foretold,
When all shall dwell together,
One Shepherd and one Fold.
Let every idol perish,
To moles and bats be thrown,
And every prayer be offered
To God in Christ alone.

Let Jew and Gentile, meeting
From many a distant shore,
Around one altar kneeling,
One common Lord adore.
Let all that now divides us
Remove and pass away,
Like shadows of the morning
Before the blaze of day.

Let all that now unites us
More sweet and lasting prove,
A closer bond of union,
In a blest land of love.
Let war be learned no longer,
Let strife and tumult cease,

All earth His blessèd kingdom,
The Lord and Prince of Peace.

O long-expected dawning,
Come with thy cheering ray!
When shall the morning brighten,
The shadows flee away?
O sweet anticipation!
It cheers the watchers on,
To pray, and hope, and labor,
Till the dark night be gone.[10]

Bibliography

Barclay, Wade Crawford, *History of Methodist Missions, Part I, Early American Methodism* 1769-1844, *Vol. I, Missionary Motivation and Expansion.* (New York: The Board of Missions and Church Extension of The Methodist Church, 1949).

————, *History of Methodist Missions, Part II, The Methodist Episcopal Church,* 1845-1939 (in two volumes) *Vol. III, Widening Horizons—1845-1895.* (New York: The Board of Missions and Church Extension of The Methodist Church, 1957).

Baudier, Roger, Sr., K.S.G., *Through Portals of the Past.* Privately printed in New Orleans.

Benavides' Memorial of 1630. Translated by Peter P. Forrestal, C.S.C., with An Historical Introduction and Notes by Cyprian J. Lynch, O.F.M. (Washington, D.C.: Academy of American Franciscan History, 1954).

Bertrand, Louis and Sir Charles Petrie, *The History of Spain.* (London: Eyre & Spottiswoode (Publishers) Ltd., 1952).

The Bible Designed to Be Read as Living Literature. Edited by Ernest Sutherland Bates. (New York: Simon and Schuster, 1936).

Coke, Thomas, *Extracts of the Journal of the Late Rev. Thomas Coke.* (Dublin: R. Napper, 1816).

The Columbia Encyclopedia. Edited by William Bridgwater and Elizabeth J. Sherwood. (Morningside Heights, New York: Columbia University Press, 1950).

Daniel-Rops, Henri, *The Heroes of God.* Translated from the French by Lawrence G. Blochman. (New York: Hawthorn Books, Inc., 1959).

Delaney, John J. and James Edward Tobin, *Dictionary of Catholic Biography.* (Garden City, New York: Doubleday and Company, Inc., 1961).

Dennis, Amarie, *St. Francis Borgia.*

Domínguez, Fray Francisco Atanasio, *The Missions of New Mexico, 1776.* Translated and Annotated by Eleanor B. Adams and Fray Angelico Chavez. (Albuquerque: The University of New Mexico Press, 1956).

Donahue, William H., *Mary of Agreda and the Southwest United States.* (Washington, D.C.: Reprinted from Volume IX—January, 1953—Number 3, *The Americas*).

Dunne, George H., S.J., *Generation of Giants.* (Notre Dame, Indiana: University of Notre Dame Press, 1962).

Gallico, Paul, *The Steadfast Man.* (Garden City, New York: Doubleday and Company, Inc., 1958).

Geiger, Maynard J., O.F.M., *The Life and Times of Junípero Serra.* (Washington, D.C.: Academy of American Franciscan History, 1959).

Goad, Harold Elsdale, *Franciscan Italy.* (London: Methuen and Company, Ltd., 1926).

Goudge, Elizabeth, *My God and My All.* (New York: Coward-McCann, Inc., 1959).

Hall, Gordon Langley, *Golden Boats from Burma.* (Philadelphia: Macrae Smith Company, 1961).

Heiderstadt, Dorothy, *Ten Torchbearers.* (New York, Edinburgh, Toronto: Thomas Nelson and Sons).

The Holy Bible, Douay Version. (New York: Catholic Book Publishing Company, 1957).

HOPE News.

Horgan, Paul, *Rome Eternal.* (New York: Farrar, Straus & Cudahy).

The Hymnal, as Adopted by The General Convention of The Protestant Episcopal Church in the United States of America. (New York: Henry Frowde).

In Excelsis. (New York: The Century Company).

Jameson, Anna, *Sacred and Legendary Art.* (Boston and New York: Houghton Mifflin and Company, 1895).

Kent, Mark L., M.M., and Sister Mary Just of Maryknoll, *The Glory of Christ.* (Milwaukee: The Bruce Publishing Company, 1955).

Keyes, Frances Parkinson, *St. Anne: Grandmother of Our Saviour.* (New York: Julian Messner, Inc., 1955).

King, Grace, *New Orleans, The Place and the People.* (New York: The Macmillan Company, 1937).

Larsson, Raymond E. F., *Saints At Prayer.* (New York: Coward-McCann, Inc., 1942).

Latourette, Kenneth Scott, *A History of Christianity.* (New York: Harper and Brothers, 1953).

———, *Christianity in a Revolutionary Age.* (New York: Harper and Brothers, 1961).

Lawson, James Gilchrist, *Famous Missionaries.* (Grand Rapids, Michigan: Zondervan Publishing House, 1939).

Leckie, Robert, *These Are My Heroes.* (New York: Random House, 1964).

Life, December 4, 1964.

Louisiana: A Guide to the State. Compiled by Workers of the Writers' Program of the Works Project Administration in the State of Louisiana. (New York: Hastings House, 1941).

Maynard, Theodore, *Saints for Our Times.* (Garden City, New York: Image Books, Doubleday and Company, Inc., 1951).

Moorehead, Alan, *The White Nile*. (New York, Evanston and London: Harper and Row, Publishers, 1960).

Neeld, Dennis, Associated Press Dispatch Appearing in the March 21, 1966 *Times-Picayune*, New Orleans, Louisiana.

New York *Herald Tribune*, September 6 and 7, 1965.

New York Times, June 6, 1964.

Nigg, Walter, *Warriors of God*. Edited and translated from the German by Mary Ilford. (New York: Alfred A. Knopf, 1959).

Palma, Ricardo, *Tradiciones Peruanas Completas*. (Madrid: Aguilar, 1961).

Palóu's Life of Fray Junípero Serra. Translated and Annotated by Maynard J. Geiger, O.F.M., Ph.D. (Washington, D.C.: Academy of American Franciscan History, 1955).

People to People Health Foundation, Inc. (Grace Line publication, Grace Line, Inc., Agents).

The Pilgrim Hymnal. (Chicago-Boston: The Pilgrim Press).

Royer, Fanchón, *The Franciscans Came First*. (Paterson, New Jersey: St. Anthony Guild Press, 1951).

———, *St. Francis Solanus, Apostle to America*. (Paterson, New Jersey: St. Anthony Guild Press, 1955).

The Saints, A Concise Biographical Dictionary. Edited by John Coulson. (New York: Hawthorn Books, Inc., 1958).

Saponaro, Michele, *The Fishers of Men*. (New York: Hawthorn Books, Inc., 1962).

Saxon, Lyle, *Fabulous New Orleans*. (New York-London: D. Appleton-Century Company, Inc., 1941).

Scofield Reference Bible. Edited by the Reverend C. I. Scofield. (Oxford: The University Press).

Sherley-Price, Leo, *St. Francis of Assisi, His Life and Writings as Recorded by His Contemporaries*. (New York: Harper and Brothers).

Sticco, Maria, *The Peace of St. Francis*. Translated from the Italian by Salvator Attanasio. (New York: Hawthorn Books, Inc., 1962).

Time, June 14, 1963 and December 4, 1964.

Timmermans, Felix, *The Perfect Joy of St. Francis*. Translated from the Flemish by Raphael Brown. (New York: Farrar, Straus and Young, Inc., 1952).

A Treasury of Catholic Reading. Edited and selected by John Chapin. (New York: Farrar, Straus and Cudahy, 1957).

The Ursulines in New Orleans. Edited by Henry Churchill Semple, S.J. (New York: P. J. Kenedy and Sons, 1925).

Walker, Williston, *Great Men of the Christian Church*. (Chicago: The University of Chicago Press).

Walsh, Thomas, *The Catholic Anthology.* (New York: The Macmillan Company, 1928).

Welch, Herbert, *Men of the Outposts.* (New York, Cincinnati, Chicago: The Abingdon Press).

Writings of Junipero Serra. Edited by Antonine Tibesar, O.F.M. (Washington, D.C.: Academy of American Franciscan History, 1956).

Ziegler, Isabelle Gibson, *The Nine Days of Father Serra.* (Toronto: Longmans, Green and Company, 1951).

Notes and References

Introduction

1. St. Mark 16:15.
2. The Acts of the Apostles 2:1-4.
3. St. Mark 16:20.
4. St. Luke 10:1.
5. St. Luke 10:3-9.
6. Robert Leckie, *These Are My Heroes* (New York: Random House).

1. The Earliest Christian Envoys

1. Michele Saponaro, *The Fishers of Men* (New York: Hawthorn Books, Inc.).
2. According to reliable tradition, Joachim, the husband of Anne, had a brother, Jacob, much younger than himself. Jacob was the father of a numerous family and it is probable that he and Joachim had several sisters. The family chart, as presented by Émile Rey in his book, *L'Aïeule du Christ Sainte Anne de Jérusalem,* which has been officially approved by the Vatican and which is accepted unconditionally by the White Fathers in charge of St. Anne's Sanctuary at Jerusalem, gives the various relationships as follows:

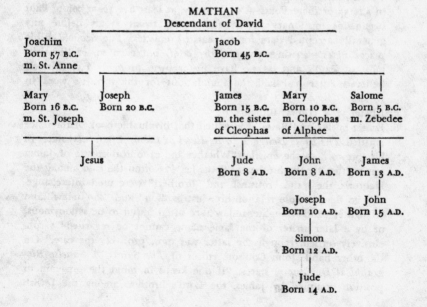

MATHAN
Descendant of David

Joachim Born 57 B.C. m. St. Anne		Jacob Born 45 B.C.		
Mary Born 16 B.C. m. St. Joseph	Joseph Born 20 B.C.	James Born 15 B.C. m. the sister of Cleophas	Mary Born 10 B.C. m. Cleophas of Alphee	Salome Born 5 B.C. m. Zebedee
Jesus		Jude Born 8 A.D.	John Born 8 A.D.	James Born 13 A.D.
			Joseph Born 10 A.D.	John Born 15 A.D.
			Simon Born 12 A.D.	
			Jude Born 14 A.D.	

3. Frances Parkinson Keyes, *St. Anne: Grandmother of Our Saviour* (New York: Julian Messner, Inc.).

4. Michele Saponaro, *The Fishers of Men.*

5. Herbert Welch, in *Men of the Outposts,* in introducing his biographical sketch of Francis Xavier, says: "Born in Spain, educated in France, he labored in Italy and was sent by Portugal to the East, where several nations felt his touch. India had already become to the Christian Church 'a land of high desire.' Tradition had it that Thomas, the doubting Apostle, had gone to India in 52 A.D., and after preaching there had met a martyr's death."

2. *The First Letter-Writing Missionaries*

1. As a first act of obedience to the Master, the company decided to reconstitute itself and elect a twelfth brother to replace the betrayer. They chose two: Joseph Barsabas, called the Just, and Matthias. They let Jesus decide between the two by casting lots, and the lot fell on Matthias. (From *The Fishers of Men* by Michele Saponaro.)

2. John Coulson, *The Saints, A Concise Biographical Dictionary* (New York: Hawthorn Books, Inc.).

3. John 14:12.

4. The Douay Bible presents Peter's two epistles as having been written in A.D. 35 or thereabouts—that is to say, at least five years before Paul began his missionary travels and nearly twenty years before any generally accepted date for his earliest epistles. The Scofield Bible places Peter's writings considerably later, but even so, earlier than most of Paul's and, as we have just shown, probably Paul himself believed Peter had laid the foundations for the former's work in Rome.

5. I Peter 1:1-9 (Douay Bible).

6. Ernest Sutherland Bates, who edited that invaluable book of reference entitled *The Bible Designed to Be Read as Living Literature,* states in his foreword to the epistle: "Whether the canonical epistle of James was written by the brother of Jesus [as was often the case among the Hebrews, the terms "cousins" and "brothers" were used interchangeably to denote close relationship, just as "son" and "son-in-law" and "daughter" and "daughter-in-law" are often found to be synonymous] or by a later writer of the same name cannot be regarded as conclusively settled, though the latter was most probably the case." On the other hand, John Coulson, editor of *The Saints, A Concise Biographical Dictionary,* states: "If one keeps in mind the pre-eminent position occupied by James, the Lord's brother, among the Jewish

converts at Jerusalem, he would appear the most likely author of the Epistle of James, a letter addressed primarily to the convert Jews of the Dispersion."

The Rev. C. I. Scofield, D.D., editor of the *Scofield Reference Bible,* in his foreword to the epistle, gives us another interesting sidelight on the question. "Tradition fixes the martyrdom of James in the year 62, but his Epistle shows no trace of the larger revelations concerning the church and the distinctive doctrines of grace made through the Apostle Paul, nor even of the discussions concerning the relation of Gentile converts to the law of Moses, which culminated in the first council (Acts 15), over which James presided. This presumes the very early date of James, which may confidently be set down as *'the first Epistle to Christians.'* By 'the twelve tribes scattered abroad' we are to understand, not Jews, but Christian Jews of the Dispersion. The church began with such (Acts 2.5-11), and James, who seems not to have left Jerusalem, would feel a particular pastoral responsibility for these scattered sheep. They still resorted to the synagogues, or called their own assemblies by that name (Jas. 2.2, where 'assembly' is 'synagogue' in the Gr.). It appears from Jas. 2.1-8 that they still held the synagogue courts for the trial of causes arising amongst themselves. The Epistle, then, is elementary in the extreme. To suppose that Jas. 2.14-26 is a polemic against Paul's doctrine of justification is absurd. Neither Galatians nor Romans was yet written." The Douay Bible does not even question the authorship of the epistle in question, though in this case we have a reversal of judgment regarding dates; Douay putting it later than Peter's, whereas Scofield puts it earlier.

7. James 1:1-12, 1:17-27. (King James Version of the Bible.)

3. *St. Paul, The First Famous Missionary*

1. John Coulson, *The Saints.*
2. Ibid.

4. *St. Patrick in Ireland*

1. Michele Saponaro, *The Fishers of Men* (New York: Hawthorn Books, Inc., 1962).
2. Ibid.
3. Paul Gallico, *The Steadfast Man* (Garden City, New York: Doubleday and Company, Inc., 1958).
4. Ibid.
5. Ibid.
6. Ibid.

7. John Coulson, *The Saints, A Concise Biographical Dictionary* (New York: Hawthorn Books, Inc., 1958).
8. Paul Gallico, *The Steadfast Man.*
9. Ibid.
10. The *Confession* and *The Letter to the Soldiers of Coroticus* are quoted in their entirety in *The Steadfast Man.*
11. Raymond E. F. Larsson, *Saints at Prayer* (New York: Coward-McCann, Inc., 1942).

5. *The Blessed Ramón Lull*

1. Henri Daniel-Rops, *The Heroes of God.* Translated from the French by Lawrence G. Blochman (New York: Hawthorn Books, Inc., 1959).
2. Ibid.
3. Ibid.
4. Mark L. Kent, M.M., and Sister Mary Just of Maryknoll, *The Glory of Christ* (Milwaukee: The Bruce Publishing Company).
5. Henri Daniel-Rops, *The Heroes of God.*
6. John J. Delaney and James Edward Tobin, *Dictionary of Catholic Biography* (Garden City, New York: Doubleday & Company, Inc., 1961).
7. Henri Daniel-Rops, *The Heroes of God.*

6. *Francis of Assisi, Dominic de Guzmán and Anthony of Padua*

1. James Gilchrist Lawson, *Famous Missionaries* (Grand Rapids, Michigan: Zondervan Publishing House).
2. This is in accordance with the Biblical injunction, Matthew 5:39 and Luke 6:29.
3. Leo Sherley-Price, *St. Francis of Assisi, His Life and Writings as Recorded by His Contemporaries* (New York: Harper & Brothers).
4. Matthew 5:11-12.
5. Leo Sherley-Price, *St. Francis of Assisi.*
6. Ibid.
7. Maria Sticco, *The Peace of St. Francis.* Translated from the Italian by Salvator Attanasio (New York: Hawthorn Books, Inc.).
8. Harold Elsdale Goad, *Franciscan Italy* (London: Methuen & Company, Ltd., 1926).
9. Elizabeth Goudge, *My God and My All* (New York: Coward-McCann, Inc., 1959).
10. Hilary Carpenter, *The Hounds of God,* as quoted in *A Treasury of*

Catholic Reading, edited and selected by John Chapin (New York: Farrar, Straus & Cudahy).

11. Harold Elsdale Goad, *Franciscan Italy.*
12. Felix Timmermans, *The Perfect Joy of St. Francis.* Translated from the Flemish by Raphael Brown. (New York: Farrar, Straus & Young, Inc., 1952).
13. Harold Elsdale Goad, *Franciscan Italy.*
14. Maria Sticco, *The Peace of St. Francis.*
15. Ibid.
16. Felix Timmermans, *The Perfect Joy of St. Francis.*
17. John Coulson, *The Saints.*
18. Harold Elsdale Goad, *Franciscan Italy.*
19. John Coulson, *The Saints.*
20. Elizabeth Morrow was the wife of Dwight Morrow, the eminent financier and Ambassador to Mexico; she was the mother of Anne Morrow Lindbergh, the author, and herself an author of note, as well as Trustee and Acting President of Smith College.

7. *Ignatius and Xavier*

1. The names of the others present at this meeting were Diego Laynez, Alfonso Salmerson, Simon Rodriguez and Nicholas Bobadilla.
2. They did not, at this time, take any other vows. Those were made later when the Society of Jesus was officially recognized by Pope Paul III.
3. They were even canonized at the same time, in 1622, by Pope Gregory XV, the same pope, incidentally, who canonized Teresa of Avila, Peter of Alcantar, Philip Neri and numerous others outstanding in the Calendar of Saints.
4. Walter Nigg, *Warriors of God,* the Great Religious Orders and Their Founders, edited and translated from the German by Mary Ilford (New York: Alfred A. Knopf).
5. Ibid.
6. Ibid.
7. This quotation is given as presented by Amarie Dennis in her excellent book, *St. Francis Borgia.* She gives as her source *Monumenta Ignatiana: Epistolae et Instructiones,* Vol. II, page 233.
8. In this connection, it is interesting to know that John Wesley was also a regular reader of Thomas à Kempis.
9. Walter Nigg, *Warriors of God.*
10. Diego Laynez, also spelled Lainez, was one of Ignatius' earliest disciples and his immediate successor as general of the Order. Laynez, in

turn, was followed by Francisco Borja, the nobleman to whom Ignatius sent his celebrated instructions regarding moderation of austerities, and is himself now enrolled in the Calendar of Saints as an outstanding missionary.

11. Walter Nigg, *Warriors of God.*

12. Williston Walker, *Great Man of the Christian Church.* (Chicago: The University of Chicago Press).

13. Walter Nigg, *Warriors of God.*

14. Raymond E. F. Larsson, *Saints at Prayer.*

15. Herbert Welch, Bishop of the Methodist Episcopal Church, *Men of the Outposts*—The Romance of the Modern Christian Movement. (New York: The Abingdon Press).

16. Thomas Walsh, *The Catholic Anthology.* (New York: The Macmillan Company).

17. Raymond E. F. Larsson, *Saints at Prayer.*

18. Theodore Maynard, *Saints for Our Times* (Garden City, New York: Image Books).

19. Henri Daniel-Rops, *Heroes of God* (New York: Hawthorn Books Inc.).

20. John Coulson, *The Saints.*

21. Paul was one of his leading disciples.

22. John Chapin, *A Treasury of Catholic Reading* (New York: Farrar, Straus & Cudahy).

23. Thomas Walsh, *The Catholic Anthology.*

24. John Chapin, *A Treasury of Catholic Reading.*

25. John Coulson, *The Saints.*

26. In this connection, it is interesting to note that, a few years later (1927), Pope Pius XI, the successor of Pius X, proclaimed Ste. Thérèse of Lisieux co-Patron with St. Francis Xavier of Missions and Missionaries. This was only two years after her canonization and nearly twenty years before she was proclaimed co-Patron, with Joan of Arc, of France. Though this gentle little saint had hardly ever left Normandy, except for her one remarkable journey to Rome, her most ardent longing, once she realized that of becoming a Carmelite, had been to go to Hanoi, Indo-China as a missionary; and the Prioress of Carmel in Lisieux, Marie de Gonzague, consented to this arrangement when an appeal for volunteers came in. But Thérèse was already ill and, before she could start off, it was evident that her illness was a mortal one; henceforth, it was only through her prayers that she could help the missionary cause. That these were sufficiently powerful to earn her recognition as a co-Patron with Francis Xavier, who

had given years of actual *work* to the missionary field, may be taken as another proof positive of the efficacy of prayer.

8. *Francis Solano, "Wonder Worker of the New World"*

1. Fanchón Royer, *St. Francis Solanus, Apostle to America.* (Paterson, New Jersey: St. Anthony Guild Press, 1955).
2. Ibid.
3. Ibid.
4. Ibid. The passage referred to is Luke 10:2.
5. There seems to be some confusion as to the exact date. According to Fanchón Royer (who quotes extensively from Angel Hiral, O.F.M., Spanish translator of the 1906 Paris edition of *S. Francisco Solano, Apóstol de la América del Sud,* and Francisco Cabré, O.F.M., *Semblanza de San Francisco Solano, Apóstol de la Argentina y el Perú*), "both Hiral and Cabré state that this took place 'probably in the year 1579, when Francisco was twenty-seven years of age.'" But as she herself points out, "This is a contradiction of known facts. If he was ordained at the age of twenty-seven, the year would have been 1576."
6. Fanchón Royer, *St. Francis Solanus.*
7. Ibid.
8. Ibid.
9. Ibid.
10. Ibid.
11. There were two sets of laws, one for Spaniards and one for Indians. The nomad Indians were encouraged to gather together in groups to form villages which were known as reductions, with approximately four hundred and fifty families to a priest. They were also supplied with doctors and teachers.
12. Centering in present-day Mexico, New Spain incorporated Central America from the Panama border north through Texas, New Mexico, Arizona and the Californias, as well as eastward through Florida.
13. Perú, first called New Castile, then included the southern sections of modern Colombia, Venezuela and British Guiana following a straight line south to a point below Buenos Aires on the east and thence west in a direct line to the Pacific Ocean. Thus all of Ecuador, Perú, Bolivia and large sections of Brazil, Argentina, Chile, Paraguay and Uruguay belonged to New Castile.
14. The arrival in June of 1524 of the first full Franciscan mission to the American mainland had been preceded by Pedro de Gante and his companions, Juan de Tecto and Juan de Ayora, in 1523.
15. St. Francis had prohibited his followers from riding horses.

16. Fanchón Royer, *St. Francis Solanus.*
17. Fanchón Royer identifies this island as Santo Domingo, but other authorities disagree with her, as Santo Domingo was not on the route usually taken by the Spanish ships at this time; and the eminent cartographer Luis Ugarte, who traces the route that was usually taken, leaves this small island without a name.
18. Fanchón Royer, *St. Francis Solanus.*
19. Ibid.
20. Ibid.
21. Cuzco is two hundred and fifty miles inland and has an altitude of 11,207 feet.
22. These towns were Londrés, Cañete, and Córdoba del Calchaquí.
23. Whatever the district boundary lines during the sixteenth century, Cochangasta was built close to the site of the present city of La Rioja, capital of the province of the same name; for during our own time, Fray Bernardino Gómez' undertaking to restore the ruins of the original Cochangasta chapel, to erect an elementary school "for the children of this diminished populace" as well as a shrine dedicated to St. Francis Solanus was forwarded when the municipality of La Rioja passed an ordinance (during 1930) to rename an old avenue with "the Puerta de la Quebrada" (the Doorway to the Ravine) *San Francisco Solano.*
24. Fanchón Royer, *St. Francis Solanus.*
25. Argentina, Bolivia, Paraguay and Uruguay.
26. Fanchón Royer, *St. Francis Solanus.*
27. Ibid.
28. A medieval, pear-shaped instrument resembling a violin but having only three strings.
29. Although Cabré gives Trujillo as the scene of this charming episode, other authorities place it in Lima, and the picture in question is still preserved in a small side chapel at San Francisco.
30. Fanchón Royer, *St. Francis Solanus.*
31. Ibid.
32. Ibid.
33. Fanchón Royer gives a different version of this episode. "From a cause now unknown, there had existed between the Augustinians and the Franciscans of Lima a disaffection of some two years' standing. Regardless of this open breach, a member of the former community had attempted to visit Fray Francisco a day or so before his death, a consolation that was refused him. The dying friar was also saddened by the prohibition, but in order to lift his friend's spirits, had sent

word that the latter must not be distressed, because within four days the Augustinian would most certainly be able to see him, and what was even better, from that point on, the coldness between their Orders would disappear. Now, spontaneously, the Augustinians arrived at the Franciscan house in a body to honor him who had, from his earliest youth, possessed the genius to pacify quarrels on any level; moreover, the visitors were received as cordially as though they had been invited. This did, indeed, mark the end of a most regrettable disagreement between two bodies of men who had dedicated their lives to spreading the love of Christ and who should surely have been above any such *desgracia*." The present editor finds both versions equally delightful.

9. The Franciscans of New Mexico and Their Mystic Helpmeet, María de Agreda

1. *The New York Times*. June 6, 1964.
2. The material quoted is a condensation of excerpts from Peter P. Forrestal's translation of *Benavides' Memorial of 1630*.
3. Ibid.
4. Ibid.
5. The Mother Luisa to whom the Indians referred lived in Mexico; she belonged to the same Order as María de Agreda and therefore would have worn the same habit. Though she was the object of widespread veneration and the missionaries did have her portrait, Benevides and his companions were quite ready to believe that it was not she who had inspired the thirst for Christianity among the Jumanos; but the mysterious lady whom Marcilla and Zúñiga had urged the missionaries to identify.
6. The material quoted is a condensation of excerpts from "Mary of Agreda and the Southwest United States" by William H. Donahue.
7. Peter P. Forrestal, op. cit.
8. The material quoted is a condensation of excerpts from *The Missions of New Mexico, 1776* by Fray Francisco Atanasio Domínguez. Translated and Annotated by Eleanor B. Adams and Fray Angelico Chavez.
9. This and the quotations from Domínguez which follow are from *The Missions of New Mexico, 1776*.

10. Junípero Serra, Founder and Colonizer

1. Maynard J. Geiger, O.F.M., Ph.D., *The Life and Times of Junípero Serra* (Washington, D.C.: Academy of American Franciscan History).
2. Ibid.

3. The cathedral was commenced shortly after the Spanish conquest of the island in 1229.

4. Maynard J. Geiger, *The Life and Times of Junípero Serra.*

5. Fanchón Royer, *The Franciscans Came First* (Paterson: St. Anthony Guild Press).

6. Cf. Geiger, op. cit., p. 263.

7. When a former student of Serra's, Antonio Noguera, heard of his teacher's departure, he wrote on the initial pages of the Compendium Scoticum which he had copied through the three years of Serra's teaching the following: "May their souls rest in peace for I will never see them again. Written by me, Francesch Noguera, sub-deacon, a pupil of philosophy of the first and fellow-student of the other. I was a friend of both. April 13, 1749."

8. Palóu does not give the name of the guardian. This item of information was kindly supplied to this writer by Fray Ignacio Omaechevarría of the Archivo Ibero-Americano, Madrid.

9. Geiger, op. cit., p. 13.

10. Ibid., p. 263.

11. Verger left Palma on June 5 while Crespí and Vicens sailed on September 4. The latter two consequently did not meet Serra and Palóu at Cádiz before sailing.

12. The italics are mine. I think this is extremely interesting and important.

13. This royal patronage was bestowed upon the Spanish sovereigns by Pope Julius II in 1508 in the bull, *Universalis ecclesiae.* For all practical intents and purposes the king of Spain became the vicar of the pope in administrative ecclesiastical affairs in the Indies.

14. Again, the italics are mine. I think this is a very important point.

15. Geiger, op. cit.

16. The original of this letter was discovered shortly before 1913 in Palma but is now in the Capuchin Convent in Barcelona. Reprinted from Geiger.

17. Fanchón Royer, *The Franciscans Came First.*

18. Geiger, op. cit.

19. Ibid.

20. Ibid.

21. Our Lady of Guadalupe.

22. Royer, op. cit.

23. Geiger, op. cit., p. 21.

24. A painting of Sahagún likewise hangs in the friary of San Fernando.

25. Geiger, op. cit., p. 21.

26. Ibid., p. 22.
27. Geiger, op. cit.
28. Royer, op. cit.
29. Again the italics are mine, because I feel the point made to be one of great importance.
30. Henri Daniel-Rops, *The Heroes of God.*
31. Who was named Carlos Francisco de Croix.
32. Royer, op. cit.
33. Henri Daniel-Rops, *Heroes of God.*
34. Royer, op. cit.
35. "His Excellency the Viceroy, Marqués de Croix, had completed his term of office, and His Excellency, Bailio Fray Don Antonio María Bucareli y Ursúa, had begun his period as Viceroy. [Dé Croix handed over the reins of government to Bucareli on September 22, 1771, at San Cristóbal. Bucareli arrived in Mexico City on September 23.] At the same time, the Visitor General, Don Joseph de Gálvez, had already returned to the Court and was appointed to the Supreme Council of the Indies, of which he was a counselor. Today he is Counselor of State, President of the Council of the Indies and Secretary of State and of the Universal Office of the Indies. [Gálvez was still alive when Palóu was writing this life at San Francisco, California, but the year it was published in Mexico City he died at Aranjuez, Spain—June 17, 1787.]

"Because of these changes and the time necessary for the new viceroy to become acquainted with the business of his vast government, the proposed establishment of five missions between Velicatá and San Diego was suspended. . . . A new factor entered when the Reverend Dominican Fathers of the Province of Santo Domingo in Mexico City desired to participate in these spiritual conquests. To this end they obtained a royal cedula in which His Majesty ordered that one or two missions bordering on heathen territory be given them. In view of this, His Excellency the Viceroy told them to take up the matter with the Father Guardian of the College of San Fernando, who at that time was Reverend Father Lector Fray Rafael Verger, today Bishop of the New Kingdom of Leon. (In 1784-1785, at the time of writing.) The Provincial of the Reverend Dominican Fathers also did the same. (Fray Juan Pedro de Iriarte, O.P.) When our superior learned of their claim based on the new cedula they had obtained from His Majesty, and knowing that Old California was not divisible territory since it is a tongue of land between two oceans, he saw that with two religious orders in the same territory the only result would be serious confusion. Father Verger replied to the Reverend Father Provincial of the Dominicans that the two orders could not be together in the same territory; and that if His Paternity so desired, he would cede to him all the missioi s formerly administered by the Reverend Jesuit Fathers, together with the newly founded Mission San Fernando. Moreover, they would also have open to them this frontier of about one hundred leagues, populated by pagans along the coast, including everything up to the Port of San Diego. In this territory there were orders to build five missions. His Paternity could take charge of their founding. That prelate agreed to all this, so the contract signed by him and by our guardian was presented to His Excellency the Viceroy, who graciously signed it at a meeting of the Junta de Guerra y Real Hacienda on April 30, 1772. On the same day the decree to this effect was signed. This was carried out in the month of May in the following year, 1773, when the Reverend Dominican Fathers arrived in Lower California and I handed those missions over to them. As a result, our college was free of that burden and had greater opportunity to give its attention to these conquests of Monterey, or New California. Nine of us missionaries of Old California then went up to New California, while the rest returned to San Fernando College." (*Palóu's Life of Fray Junípero Serra*, translated and annotated by Maynard J. Geiger, O.F.M., Ph.D. Washington, D.C.: Academy of American Franciscan History.)

36. Royer, op. cit.
37. Ibid.
38. *Dictionary of Catholic Biography*, page 1050, gives the number as twenty-one, and Fanchón Royer, in *The Franciscans Came First*, as nine. Palóu estimates the number as ten, and Geiger, in his edition of Palóu's biography, appends the following note: "Father Serra actually founded only nine other missions, all in Upper California. In saying 'the other ten,' Palóu evidently includes Santa Barbara. Founded as a presidio April 21, 1782 (with Father Serra present), it was in the mind of the president actually Mission Santa Barbara. The official registers of baptisms, marriages and deaths, which he inscribed at the time, call the foundation 'Misión y Real Presidio de Santa Bárbara.' It is in this sense that Palóu speaks of the 'other ten.' For further details on this matter, cf. *infra*, chapter 52." So the correct number would seem to be either nine or ten, whichever way we prefer to reckon it. Palóu lists the foundation of the missions in the following chronological order:

1. San Fernando, Velicatá—1769
2. San Diego—1769
3. San Carlos, Monterey—1770; moved to Carmel—1771
4. San Antonio—1771
5. San Gabriel—1771
6. San Luis Obispo—1772
7. San Juan Capistrano—1776
8. San Francisco—1776
9. Santa Clara—1777
10. San Buenaventura—1782

39. Geiger, *The Life and Times of Junípero Serra.*
40. Royer, op. cit.

11. *The Ursulines of New Orleans, Pioneer Educators of Girls*

1. I have followed the translations of these as they are given in *The Ursulines in New Orleans*, edited by Henry Churchill Semple, S.J., but have greatly abbreviated the letters to avoid repetition; and, unless otherwise indicated, all quotations are from this same book.
2. The "great prodigy" to which Magdalene Hachard refers is bilocation, defined by Webster as "the state or power of being in two places at the same time." Several saints, besides Francis Xavier, are credited with this power and, as has been seen in *The Franciscans of New Mexico and Their Mystic Helpmeet, María de Ágreda,* so is Sor María, Abbess of the Conceptionist Convent in Ágreda, Spain.
3. The "little barrels" to which Magdalene Hachard refers were probably the ditty boxes used by sailors to hold sewing equipment and other necessities. Norman sailors were very proud of their ditty boxes, which were generally hand painted in a design which always included apples or apple blossoms, to emphasize one of Normandy's chief products. In the eighteenth and nineteenth centuries, these became increasingly elaborate and were used by pupils at boarding schools as well as by sailors. They are now a collector's item.
4. *Louisiana: A Guide to the State.* Compiled by Workers of the Writers' Program of the Works Project Administration in the State of Louisiana (New York: Hastings House, 1941).
5. Grace King, *New Orleans, The Place and the People* (New York: The Macmillan Company, 1937).
6. Lyle Saxon, *Fabulous New Orleans* (New York–London: D. Appleton-Century Company, Inc., 1941).
7. Roger Baudier, Sr., K.S.G., *Through Portals of the Past.*

12. *Francis Asbury, the Man Without a Home*

1. Kenneth Scott Latourette, *Christianity in a Revolutionary Age* (New York: Harper & Brothers, 1961).
2. My text is a condensation of *Ten Torchbearers* by Dorothy Heiderstadt (New York, Edinburgh, Toronto: Thomas Nelson & Sons).
3. Ibid.
4. My text is a condensation of Francis Asbury's *Journal*, as quoted in *History of Methodist Missions, Part I, Early American Methodism 1769-1844*, Vol. I, *Missionary Motivation and Expansion* by Wade Crawford Barclay (New York: The Board of Missions and Church Extension of The Methodist Church, 1949).
5. Thomas Coke, *Extracts of the Journal of the Late Rev. Thomas Coke* (Dublin: R. Napper, 1816).
6. Francis Asbury's *Journal*.

13. *The Judsons, Protestant Pioneers to Burma*

1. James Gilchrist Lawson, *Famous Missionaries* (Grand Rapids, Michigan: Zondervan Publishing House).
2. *The Columbia Encyclopedia,* edited by William Bridgwater and Elizabeth J. Sherwood (Morningside Heights, New York: Columbia University Press, 1950).
3. Gordon Langley Hall, *Golden Boats from Burma* (Philadelphia: Macrae Smith Company, 1961).

14. *China—A Record Span*

1. George H. Dunne, S.J., *Generation of Giants* (Notre Dame, Indiana: University of Notre Dame Press, 1962).
2. Ibid.
3. Ibid.
4. Kenneth Scott Latourette, *A History of Christianity* (New York: Harper & Brothers, 1953).
5. Dunne, op. cit. The quotations are from *Fonti Ricciane*, ed. Pasquale M. d'Elia, S.J. (Roma: Libreria dello Stato, 1942-1949), II, 353 f.
6. Latourette, op. cit.
7. Ibid.
8. Ibid.
9. Wade Crawford Barclay, *History of Methodist Missions*, Vol. III (New York: The Board of Missions of The Methodist Church, 1957).
10. *Twenty-eighth Ann. Rep., M.S.* (1846-47), pp. 41 f., 45; *ibid., 29th* (1847-48), pp. 40 ff., 44; S. L. Baldwin: "Some Problems Solved by

Methodism in China," *Gospel in All Lands,* February, 1889, p. 56; *Missionary Advocate,* II (1846), 3 (June), 27; *Minutes, B.M.,* IV, 476 f.; ibid., V, 12; J. M. Reid and J. T. Gracey, *Missions and Missionary Society of the Methodist Episcopal Church,* I, 416; I. W. Wiley, *China and Japan* . . . , p. 196.

11. "Founding and Early History of Our Chinese Mission, at Foochow, 1847-1853," pp. 21 f. in "Manuscripts by Moses C. White . . . Relating to the Founding of Methodist Missions in Foochow, China."

12. Barclay, op. cit.

13. *Minutes, B.M.,* V, 100; *Missionary Advocate,* VII (1851), 10 (January), 73; "Founding and Early History . . . ," p. 33, in White MSS. Collection. Quoted by Barclay.

14. Barclay, op. cit.

15. Latourette, op. cit.

16. Ibid.

17. Mark L. Kent, M.M., and Sister Mary Just of Maryknoll, *The Glory of Christ* (Milwaukee: The Bruce Publishing Company, 1955).

18. Ibid.

19. Ibid.

15. *The Story of Medical Missions*

1. Herbert Welch, Bishop of the Methodist Episcopal Church, *Men of the Outposts* (New York, Cincinnati, Chicago: The Abingdon Press).

2. James Gilchrist Lawson, *Famous Missionaries* (Grand Rapids, Michigan: Zondervan Publishing House, 1939).

3. Welch, op. cit.

4. Ibid.

5. Alan Moorehead, *The White Nile* (New York, Evanston and London: Harper & Row, Publishers, 1960).

6. Welch, op. cit.

7. New York *Herald Tribune,* September 6 and 7, 1965.

8. *Time,* June 14, 1963. Courtesy *Time;* copyright Time, Inc., 1963.

9. Grace Line publication, *People to People Health Foundation, Inc.,* Grace Line, Inc., Agents.

10. *HOPE News.*

11. Associated Press dispatch by Dennis Neeld appearing in New Orleans *Times-Picayune,* March 21, 1966.

12. *Life,* December 4, 1964. Courtesy *Life* Magazine; copyright Time, Inc., 1964. All rights reserved.

13. *Time,* December 4, 1964. Courtesy *Time;* copyright Time, Inc., 1964.

14. Ibid.

16. Missionary Hymns

1. *The Columbia Encyclopedia,* Edited by William Bridgwater and Elizabeth J. Sherwood.
2. *The Pilgrim Hymnal* (Chicago–Boston: The Pilgrim Press).
3. *In Excelsis* (New York: The Century Company).
4. *The Pilgrim Hymnal.*
5. *In Excelsis.*
6. *The Hymnal, As Adopted by the General Convention of the Protestant Episcopal Church in the United States of America* (New York: Henry Frowde).
7. Ibid.
8. *In Excelsis.*
9. Ibid.
10. *The Hymnal.*

Index